Celebrity Feuds!

BY THE SAME AUTHOR:

The Films of Jane Fonda

Conversations With My Elders

Hispanic Hollywood

Leading Ladies

The Lavender Screen

Hollywood Babble On

Hollywood Lesbians

Bette Davis Speaks

Hollywood Gays

Sing Out!

Hollywood & Whine

CELEBRITY FEUDS!

The Cattiest Rows, Spats, and Tiffs Ever Recorded

BOZE HADLEIGH

Taylor Publishing
Dallas, Texas

Designed by David Timmons

Published by Taylor Publishing Company
1550 West Mockingbird Lane
Dallas, Texas 75235
www.taylorpub.com

Library of Congress Cataloging-in-Publication Data:
Hadleigh, Boze.
    Celebrity feuds! / by Boze Hadleigh.
        p.   cm.
    Includes bibliographical references.
    ISBN 0-87833-244-8
    1. Motion picture actors and actresses—United States Anecdotes. 2. Celebrity—United States
Anecdotes. I. Title.
PN1994.9.H24   1999
791.43'028'092273—dc21   99-36748
                                                                                        CIP

10 9   8   7   6   5   4   3
Printed in the United States of America

All photos are from the author's private collection, except for the following:

p. 7, 13 Archive Photos; p. 15 Paramount Television/Archive Photos; p. 18 Archive Photos; p. 27
Darlene Hammond/Archive Photos; p. 31 Popperfoto/Archive Photos; p. 32 Frank Edwards/Archive
Photos; p. 40 Frank Diggs/Archive Photos; p. 69 Sonia Moskowitz/Archive Photos; p. 81, 85, 97,
107, 109 Archive Photos; p. 113 Frank Edwards/Fotos International/Archive Photos; p. 145
Reuters/Jeff Christensen/Archive Photos; p. 147 Reuters/Fred Prouser/Archive Photos; p. 150 Archive
Photos; p. 168 Bernard Gotfryd/Archive Photos; p. 177, 179 Archive Photos

ACKNOWLEDGMENTS

For ongoing assistance, thank you to Ronald M. Boze and Linda Fresia. Thanks to those who chose to speak with me for this project—feuds are not a subject many care to discuss, even those not directly involved in them. Thanks too to my editor, Camille N. Cline, as well as Fred Francis, Jim Green, and Sarah A. Tollett. For photographic assistance, Peter Bateman. Finally, and not least, Samson DeBrier, Louix Escobar-Matute, Bill Everson, Martin Greif, Cliff Harrington, Jim Kepner, Consuelo Montiel, Toshi Nishihara, James Pitula, Bob Randall, Paul Rosenfield, Leonardo Rossi, Bob Thompson, Angela Thorne-Bardry, Tony Verdugo, Wayne Warga, and Anthony Zanghi.

To Ronnie and Linda,
who don't know from feuds

CONTENTS

INTRODUCTION

"Choose your enemies wisely."—Walt Disney

". . . a feud would be counterproductive."—Barbra Streisand

"Feuds are good publicity but bad on the nerves."—John Wayne

"I relish a good fight with a worthy opponent!"—Bette Davis

"A feud is OK if you have nothing worse to do. "—George Michael

"Who's feuding who?"—Madonna

To feud or not to feud? Most celebrities don't, though it's more permissible than ever. Today's public is generally willing to hear more, forgive more, and even expects more. Celebrity misbehavior, particularly in Hollywood, Washington, D.C., and the sports world, has become a news staple. Role models are not always what they were—or seemed to be. Squabbles, fights, and outright feuding, which were once carried out in private and only reached the public via rumor, are now wide open in many cases.

Surprisingly, this is the first book on the subject. Some years ago, I looked up celebrity feuds at the Beverly Hills public library. The computer screen instead referred me to Kentucky, Tennessee, and Texas, and of course the Hatfields and McCoys. There was also a book about "writers' wars," about efforts to found the Screen Writers Guild in the face of stiff studio opposition.

The most engrossing parts of some biographies are the feuds between the protagonist and his or her cherished enemies. For, to feud with somebody, a VIP must in a way *care* about the other person. The opposite of love is not hate, but indifference. Pure contempt is often expressed by ignoring someone. Feuds are obsessions—they require nurturing, sustenance, and repetition. Feuds, like other growing entities, require time and feeding.

Feuds are quite consuming for those involved. For the spectator or reader, they're like an accident that makes one wince but holds one's eye—more so when they involve the rich and famous. The thing about Hollywood feuds—nearly all the feuds in this book feature "show people," from the business that there's no business like—is that they're usually well matched: A clash of the titans, a duel of the divas. It's not a superstar actress vs. her wardrobe mistress or a movie producer vs. his accountant, it's star vs. star, and the passions run hot.

As Englishman Quentin Crisp once said, "Being loved can never be a patch on being murdered. That's when someone really gives their all for you."

The dictionary defines a feud as a sustained quarrel. Sometimes the parties involved sustain it due to an exhibitionistic streak or a craving for publicity—neither unusual among celebrities. A feud can make two people more colorful and interesting, especially if they're related, like, say, superstar Julia Roberts and brother Eric, or former superstars Olivia de Havilland and sister Joan Fontaine, both in their eighties and still on the outs.

Some feuds do outlive their heat or their participants' youth. Writers Norman Mailer and Gore Vidal made it up eventually. Vidal and far-right William F. Buckley did not. Nor did Vidal and fellow gay writer Truman Capote—logical allies sometimes make vicious rivals. But then, feuds can involve mates—like Sonny & Cher or long-term lovers Clint Eastwood and Sondra Locke—or seekers after the same socio-economic dream—such as Diana Ross & the Supremes—or even parents and children—see how abominably the diva Maria Callas treated her mother or comedienne Martha Raye her daughter.

Many of the most heated feuds follow love (platonic or not) or lust. For instance, costars Sean Young and James Woods, who each claim not to have had the affair that most others say they did. Lurid stories of their post-affair or post-friendship doings cast each in a rather scary light, but had a more negative impact on Young's image and professional standing. In most feuds between a man and a woman, the woman still gets more blame.

Sometimes a feud just collapses from time or neglect. A forty-four-year estrangement following filming of *On the Waterfront* (1954) was ended when costar Rod Steiger chanced to meet Marlon Brando in a Montréal restaurant and simply declared, "I can't remember why we're not speaking."

★ ★ ★

How does a feud begin? Let us count the ways. They are as individual as the celebrities involved. But the seed of most feuds is jealousy. Or resentment. Example: Joan Crawford, who was older than Bette Davis and arrived in Hollywood first, resented her rival's talent and then her acclaim. Bette was jealous of Joan's beauty and youthfulness—especially after Crawford began looking younger than she.

Familiarity, or proximity, often breeds contempt. Davis and Crawford were both actors—feuds usually occur within a profession—both worked for a time at Warner Bros., and both made a film that was their big comeback. But both were pros and each put the Work and Image first. Hours after Joan Crawford died in 1977, Bette went to a party. After making her entrance, she went up to friend Burt Reynolds—who also figures in this book—and informed him, "Well, the bitch died today."

Reynolds immediately introduced the gentleman of the press next to him, whereupon Davis immediately added, "But she was *always* on time." *That* was a feud.

Usually it takes two to feud. Not always. One semi-legendary feud was the one between the kings of horror, Bela Lugosi and Boris Karloff. Semi because, although Lugosi came to hate Karloff's guts—as noted in the film *Ed Wood*—Boris, an English gentleman through and through, refused to publicly share his feelings about the Hungarian. Nor did he feel any need, for Bela was the jealous one and Boris the one with the bigger, more prestigious career. Ironically, Lugosi had enabled Karloff's stardom by haughtily declining the monster role in *Frankenstein*.

Some perceived feuds were merely frustration, particularly between stars who had to keep working together. Like Nelson Eddy and Jeanette MacDonald, who understandably longed to shine solo. Or Ginger Rogers and Fred Astaire. There was competition between them, and eventually separation, but no feud. Ginger was initially the bigger star, and won an Oscar, which Fred never did. He retired from the screen, then returned, and over the decades became far more esteemed than she did. Rogers finally huffed, "When we danced together, we both had to be perfect—and *I* had to be perfect dancing backwards!"

Some feuds become largely forgotten with time, like Milton Berle vs. Jackie Gleason, who used to brazenly steal Berle's material. Or Bob Hope's with Berle. Feuds between teams are less easily forgotten, since each time the performer appears, it's with his other half. Like Abbott & Costello, who due to space limitations are unfortunately not included here. Of course, not all feuds are evenly balanced—Costello disliked Abbott more than vice versa, for the resentment was mostly on the side of the shorter, funnier man whose name always came second.

Several of those involved in feuds refuse to admit it. Especially divas with big egos (redundant!) who prefer to be thought "ladies." Mae West never admitted to her vituperative catfight with Jayne Mansfield, and Bette Davis at times feigned to barely remember who Joan Crawford was. Of course, a potential feud can be nipped in the bud if one individual refuses to take it any further. Hugh Grant costarred in the film *Restoration* with drug-plagued Robert Downey Jr., who let the world know he disliked the British actor. Grant told the press he had nothing much to say about Downey, except that his crude remarks reflected on him and not his target.

Some VIPs have rationalized their non-responses, like Turgenev, who wrote to a friend about fellow Russian author Dostoevsky's ongoing slurs against him: "It would be out-and-out slander if Dostoevsky were not a madman, which I do not doubt in the slightest." He later added, "I treated him as I would a sick man." Few could resist such repeated provocation. However, lawsuits probably weren't that effective in czarist Russia.

A heated verbal exchange may contain the kernel of a notable feud. For instance, after Elton John reworked his Marilyn Monroe tribute song "Candle in the Wind" as a record-breaking tribute to Princess Diana, Rolling Stone Keith Richards jealously dismissed him with, "He writes songs for dead blondes." Elton, who soon after became Sir Elton, at once replied, "I am glad I have given up drugs and alcohol. It would be awful to look like Richards. He's pathetic, poor thing. It's like a monkey with arthritis trying to go on stage and look young."

Besides having the stomach for a feud, one needs the clout. An actress from TV's *Fresh Prince* claimed that after she objected to star Will Smith's sexism, she was worked out of the sitcom. Later interviewed in *TV Guide*, she insisted that though Smith has a problem relating to non-passive women, she didn't wish to pursue the issue. Again, a feud can be costly to a non-diva actress, or to anybody not on the same power level. Feuds create formal, not casual, enemies, and most feuds are for life—often outlasting more positive relationships.

There are two things to be said for feuds: the extra publicity and having an enemy who's out in the open. Superagent Sue Mengers once said that in Hollywood a celebrity has to be more attentive to possible enemies, since friends always declare themselves (including those who are genuine), but enemies almost never do.

Celebrity Feuds! is divided into three sections. The first is "Costar Wars," mostly featuring celebs who worked together repeatedly, as on TV—Sonny vs. Cher, Laverne vs. Shirley, Batman vs. Robin, and the cast of *I Love Lucy*, which had a few behind-the-camera secrets 1950s viewers weren't allowed to know about.

Some chapters could go into more than one category. The mythic Bette Davis vs. Joan Crawford hellcat-fight concludes the third section, "Deadly Rivals," but could fit into "Costar Wars," except that Bette and Joan didn't repeat their *What Ever Happened to Baby Jane?* success. Besides, they had long been rivals. James Woods and Sean Young, who worked together once in a minor movie that led to a major feud, were not rivals before meeting and so are found in "Costar Wars." Most chapters contain related sidebars, e.g., Woods vs. Young includes other antagonistic costars: Barbra Streisand and several men she worked with, and Bette Midler's leading man *and* her director on the film aptly titled *Jinxed.*

The second section, the emotional core of the book, is "Family Feuds!"—possibly the most riveting category. Where it might be fun or vicariously satisfying to read what X said about Madonna or Y about Michael Jackson, one is often shocked when a feud erupts out of the heart of a family. How could he say that about his own mother? How could she act that way with her brother? How could she do that to her own daughter? His own son? As with ordinary feuds, the seeds are jealousy and resentment, but even more deep-seated and ongoing. For, while one can divorce a spouse or break up with one's comedy partner or singing group, one can't really divorce one's relatives. Plus, with family, the rivalry often begins at birth. Or with birth order.

With some parents it's a control issue that boils down to "Do what I want, or I won't like you." This book includes men who turned against their daughters (or for that matter, wives or girlfriends) who didn't stay in "their place." Actress Geraldine Chaplin said, "My mother was disowned by her father [playwright Eugene O'Neill] because she married my father [Charlie Chaplin]. He had a reputation for seducing very young women . . . girls. She and her father never became reconciled, so I never met my grandfather, and I wish I had." Yet the marriage of Charlie and Oona lasted, apparently happily, for decades.

Control also enters the scene with some firstborns. ". . . so many firstborns are doctors, lawyers, engineers—they sit on school boards, on city councils, and in the United States Congress in numbers far greater than their percentage of the population as a whole would dictate," according to author Dr. Kevin Leman (see Bibliography). Lana Wood's memoirs reveal the extent to which her life was dominated by big sister Natalie Wood, not only as a sibling but as another actress. More often than not, same-sex siblings who enter the same field experience professional and personal friction, be they advice columnists like "Dear Abby" and "Ask Ann Landers" or thespians. The elder, who almost invariably gets there first, has the advantage. From then on, the talented (but often not *as* talented) younger one is compared to Big Sister, as with Lana Wood or the sisters of Barbra Streisand, Liza Minnelli, Dolly Parton, and Joan Collins (even though Jackie gave up acting for writing—which Joan later took up).

Younger brothers also fight for separate identity, as with Warren Beatty vis-à-vis Shirley MacLaine, or Cecil B. DeMille and mogul Jack L. Warner, who both resented their successful elder brothers, at that time deemed the heads of their families. Warner particularly detested eldest brother Harry, later admitting, "I hated the idea of anyone being over me or trying to tell me what to do." On the other hand, Jack didn't get along with his own son, nor with dozens of Hollywood personalities.

Too often, childhood resentments and patterns carry into the adult years. Joan Crawford was an abused child who then abused at least two of her adopted children. She envied her brother, the apple of her mother's eye, and eventually cut him out of her life too. Joan Fontaine chafed under the dictates of firstborn Olivia de Havilland and later experienced cool relationships with her two daughters, one of them adopted. As a teen, Eric Roberts became estranged from his mother, and later from sister Julia as well. By most accounts, Michael Jackson grew estranged from his father, brothers, sisters—everyone except perhaps his mother. Proving that the ties that bind aren't necessarily familial ones, but those of one's own choosing. As one showcase comedian put it, "If these people weren't your relatives, would you ever socialize with them?"

★ ★ ★

Finally, can one ever win a feud? The closest one usually comes is outliving the other guy. Like Bette Davis with Crawford or Gore Vidal with Capote. The remaining celeb can keep saying nasty things about the undear departed without fear of contradiction, reprisal, or lawsuit. Living longer means achieving more professionally; it also means that your version of events and personalities, if repeated often enough, becomes more familiar and may be accepted as fact.

Individuals who conquer others win a temporary victory; those who conquer themselves are truly strong. As the Buddha said, "Hate begets hate . . . . Only by *love* is hate ended."

Costar

Wars

LUCY & RICKY & FRED & ETHEL:
I Love Lucy

The four characters of *I Love Lucy*, monetary squabbles aside, were one big, happy family. So we remember them, and so we like to think of the actors who played them. After all, the two stars, Lucille Ball and Desi Arnaz, were a real-life unit—longtime marrieds, parents of Lucie and Desi Jr., and they were also Desilu, at the time a corporate giant of the small screen. Of course, Lucy and Desi eventually split up, and in time the public learned that all had not been a bed of roses, chiefly due to his alcoholism and skirt-chasing (Desi often boarded his mistresses on his yacht, the *Balboa*). Finally, Lucy publicly called him "a loser."

The proliferating book biographies have revealed that the marriage had been on the rocks *before I Love Lucy*, that the pioneering sitcom was undertaken as a last-ditch effort to save the Ball-Arnaz union, basically by keeping the traveling band leader on home turf where his older wife could keep an eye on him. The bios also disclosed what was more common knowledge, at least in Hollywood, where William Frawley had been an ongoing and outspoken presence in movies since his screen bow in 1915: that "Fred" and "Ethel" hated each other. True enough, the fictional Mertzes seemed one of those older married couples who could take or leave one another, uniting only when doing battle with their tenants.

Passion was never a part of the picture for Fred and Ethel. It was, however, for Vivian Vance and Bill Frawley, who passionately detested each other. The root of the contempt was Vance's dislike of Ethel Mertz. More than once she told the press that she felt nothing for Ethel, whom she viewed as frumpy, older, and a loser. Vivian's friend from Broadway days, Marjorie Lord (of *Make Room for Daddy*, and mother of *Fatal Attraction* star Ann Archer), declared that Vance "really desired to be a major star." But once the actress, born Vivian Roberta Jones, saw that time was passing her by, she consented to play a supporting role on television, a new medium, about which director Billy Wilder said: "I'm delighted with it, because it used to be that films were the lowest form of art. Now we've got something to look down on."

Vivian had played glamorous roles on the stage and still saw herself in that light, despite the extra years and pounds. According to the latest information, she was born in 1909, which meant she was forty-two in 1951, the year *I Love Lucy* debuted. When Lucille (born 1911) first laid eyes on her she asked what part Vance was to play, then replied, "You don't look like a landlady." It wasn't praise; it was an opinion and also a resistant reaction to Desi having hired Vivian without consulting her. Ball's first choice for Ethel was show biz veteran Bea Benederet of George Burns and Gracie Allen's show and later *Petticoat Junction* (she guested on *The Beverly Hillbillies* as Jethro's mother Pearl). Lucy had recently given birth to her first child, Lucie, and at forty was among the oldest actresses in Hollywood to become a mother. She therefore wasn't as involved in the casting as she would have wished.

"Everyone's heard the story," recalled Mary Wickes, a movie character actress who guested often on Lucy's TV shows.

I Love Lucy: one big, happy family?

"Viv and Bill were cordial for about the first five minutes. In truth, Vivian was in shock from the moment she saw him. She was so disappointed, as everybody found out. The man was in his mid-sixties, so she felt he was much too old to play her husband!

"On top of which, Lucille was definitely reserving any glamour for herself. Ethel had to wear an old bathrobe and curlers in several of her scenes . . . . The two ladies did come to understand each other after a bumpy beginning. But Viv and Bill went from unfriendly to worse, and would bad-mouth each other most opportunities they got. Yet I must say that Vivian never sank to the levels of name-calling that *he* did!"

Lucy made it clear that Vivian was there on approval. She could be written out of the series and replaced at any time during the first season. The chemistry between them and the audience reaction to "Lucy and Ethel" took her by surprise; she gradually acknowledged what an asset Vance was to *I Love Lucy*. By contrast, former vaudevillian Frawley had a lock on his role of Fred Mertz, so long as his heavy drinking didn't interfere with his work; the gruff actor's other passion was baseball (he'd been briefly and unhappily married decades before, no children, and never rewed). What launched the feud was an overheard remark to producer Arnaz that Vivian made, opining that Frawley was "old enough to play my *grandfather*." The exaggeration prompted Frawley to ask Arnaz, "Where did you find this bitch?" The fight was on.

But so was the record-breaking success of TV's most popular show. With it, Vivian Vance achieved the national renown she'd been seeking all her life—against her fundamentalist mother's icy objections. However, she became famous not as Vivian Vance, but as Ethel Mertz. Vance later recalled, "[Ethel] wasn't even a

I (Love) Lucy?

"Brass-bound bitches."—what William Frawley called Lucille Ball and Vivian Vance

"Fat-ass."—what Frawley called Vivian Vance (also "that bitch" and worse . . .)

"That old coot."—what Vance called TV husband Frawley

"A loser."—what Lucy later called her ex-husband

"Please God, I won't have to climb into bed this week with that square-headed little Irishman."—Vance, regarding her TV husband

"Bill and Vivian never got along. He wouldn't speak to her if he could help it. . . . Vivian was very offended by this, until gradually she saw that Bill isn't that crazy about anybody. I'm the only one he really likes."—Desi Arnaz

"The Cuban heel."—what Frawley called Desi Arnaz behind his back

person to me, just an old frump with a technique for stirring laughter. It had never been my ambition to be that kind of a female. Ethel was made of bits and pieces of women I'd known but never admired."

She added, "Mama set her lips in a special kind of hard line whenever she was about to take someone apart." She copied that expression for Ethel whenever the character was about to dress down her husband or her redheaded best friend.

By 1954 *I Love Lucy* was an institution, but that was the first year the Emmy awards included a category for "Best Supporting Actress in a Series." Vivian was of course nominated, and the *I Love Lucy* quartet was in attendance at the Hollywood Palladium. When her name was announced as the winner, Lucy and Desi "hoisted me to my feet and pushed me out of my chair." She climaxed her acceptance speech by stating, "I want to thank the greatest straight woman in show business" (much later adding, "I thought she'd like that"), upon which declaration William Frawley was heard to bellow, "It goes to prove that the whole vote is rigged." (In point of fact, Vance was the straight woman to clown Lucille Ball.)

Of the four actors on the sitcom, Vance had the most legitimate stage training, and was known to occasionally inquire, à la Method, what her motivation was for a line or a scene. As her place on the series grew secure, she ventured to make more suggestions. Desilu executive Bernard Weitzman later explained, "Bill and Vivian came from two different worlds. Viv considered herself literate and Frawley illiterate. She was a stage actress, which she felt put her on a higher level."

For his part, Frawley considered most stage actors pretentious and felt that as an ex-vaudevillian and long-running motion picture actor, he didn't have to take any suggestions from Vance seriously—or, to a lesser degree, from imported musician Desi Arnaz or from Lucille Ball, who was a woman.

Desilu were Frawley's bosses, so he grudgingly did as ordered, although he insisted on learning only his own lines, habitually expressed contempt for "too much" rehearsal, and would listen to baseball games on the radio whenever time allowed, and sometimes when it didn't. Whenever Fred and Ethel had a musical or vaudeville bit on the show, friction invariably occurred. Though Vance had sung professionally, Frawley didn't think much of her vocal talent. "This bitch can't sing worth a damn," he would growl on the set, then asked Desi, "You're going to have her sing again?"

From the first, Desi was Vivian's ally, and later, looking back on *I Love Lucy*, Vance's only words of pure affection were reserved for Arnaz. When Frawley sniped at Vance, Arnaz would come to her defense while more or less humoring the old sourpuss. During one rehearsal, Bill complained, "Well, she bugs me. You know that dance routine she and I are supposed to do next week? Well, this silly broad tells the choreographer she doesn't think we'll be able to do it because I'll never be able to learn it.

"Like it was some kind of Fred Astaire and Ginger Rogers number or something. All we are supposed to do is an old-fashioned soft-shoe routine. Well, for Chrissakes, I was in vaudeville since I was five years old, and I guarantee you I'll wind up teaching fat-ass how to do the fucking thing!"

Vance derided Frawley's nonchalance about preparing for each weekly shooting in front of a live audience. She also shrank from his off-color language and jokes and his habit of unapologetically passing gas. More than once she demanded in frustration, "How can anyone believe that I'm married to that old coot?" Whether he was sensitive about his age or anything else, nobody seemed to know, but Frawley would reply in the harshest terms, such as calling his 22-years-younger costar "a dried-up old cunt."

In the 1950s such a feud was *not* grist for the columnists' mills, as Hollywood was far more of an industry town, and writers who got out of line were frozen out of print. Films and TV series handed out cheerful, often fictitious press releases to dutiful outlets. Plus, Lucille Ball's long friendship with Hedda Hopper, one of tinseltown's two top gossip-slingers, helped keep negative news or dish about *I Love Lucy* out of Hedda's and other columns. Newspaper and magazine readers enjoyed and probably believed the impression of the actors behind the Ricardos and Mertzes as one big, happy TV family. But as writer-producer Jess Oppenheimer eventually disclosed: "We had a generous share of ongoing feuds simmering during *I Love Lucy*, but not a hint of it is to be seen on the screen. Actors might be eccentric, but they're not crazy."

After some friction began to surface during joint interviews with "Fred and Ethel," Desilu brass decided on a policy of separate interviews. Although Frawley exercised restraint during interviews, his on-set language, behavior, and moaning were such that, according to biographers, Lucy, Desi, and Vivian considered having his character written out of the show. But by then Fred Mertz was too integral to *I Love Lucy*. Making no apologies, Frawley explained, "I just say what I have to say when I want to say it."

Some time into the series it was discovered that Frawley had had his agent negotiate two new key points in his contract. First, whatever Vivian earned, he had to earn the same, though fourth-billed. Like Lucy, Vivian would try to up the ante by announcing at the end of each hit season, "I'm not sure if I really want to return for another season . . . ." Second, it was stipulated that if either Vance or Frawley quit, left, died, or for whatever reason was no longer on the series, the other actor would be dropped too—thus further tying Vivian's fate to her detested costar's.

Bill became more alienated from the rest of the cast as Viv's relationship with Lucy thawed and turned into a guarded friendship. "We had our ups and downs," Vance reminisced. "We would fight like sisters, but we also made up like sisters." Ball came to appreciate Viv's suggestions for bits of business and improvements to their comedy routines. The two women constantly rehearsed together and were quick studies who soon tossed away their weekly scripts, which annoyed Frawley no end. He would toss away his script on the very first day, ripping out only those pages that concerned him. Vivian explained: "Right from the start, we knew Bill was going to be a holy terror. He refused to learn one single word of anybody else's lines but his own. He had no idea in the world what the rest of us were saying.... I was being made up one night when he wandered over and said, 'Viv, is this next week's script I just picked up?'

"'We've been rehearsing that all week,' I said. 'We start shooting in fifteen minutes.'"

Vivian didn't always hide her contempt for the seeming lack of professionalism, which didn't affect the televised product but did worry and irritate Frawley's fellow players. Bill may have resented the enthusiastic actress' condescension or—like Walter Matthau in *Hello, Dolly!* toplining Barbra Streisand—the younger female's influence. Or perhaps any actress playing his ball and chain. Said Vivian, "He was mad at me most of the time because I happened to be cast as his wife, and Bill plain hated wives. In a rare calm moment, he told me he'd once had one of his own. Marriage suited him so sorely that he never bothered with the divorce. 'I'll never do it again,' he said." Frawley's secrecy about his marriage caused many to question whether his wife was still alive during the show's run. Vance had four husbands, the last of whom was John Dodds, a gay or bisexual book editor six or twelve years her junior, depending on the source.

Mary Wickes observed that "Viv's self-image was very youthful. She tried to dress and marry youthfully . . . she went in for plastic surgery before it was *de rigueur*. She even dropped hints that she was younger than Lucille, if only by a year or so."

Vivian also liked to give the impression that she—like Ethel—hailed from Albuquerque, New Mexico, partly because she thought her native Kansas was so dull. She once noted, "Dorothy was so happy to wake up in Kansas. Not I! I'd have looked for another cyclone and stood right in its path!"

Vivian Vance and William Frawley

Wickes continued, "It went against the grain of everything she wanted to be known as to be paired with a man so much older than she was . . . someone so, well, rumpled and lacking in any glamorous, sophisticated qualities."

It got to the point where Mondays, on receiving her new script, Vance would comb through it hoping it contained no scenes where she had to hug or kiss her TV husband. Or as she more dramatically put it, "Please God, I won't have to climb into bed this week with that square-headed little Irishman." Despite his own weight, Frawley, like Fred, belittled Vance's figure, comparing it to "a sack full of doorknobs." Actor Richard Denning, who played Ball's good-looking husband on her pre-*Lucy* radio series *My Favorite Husband*, offered, "When you play somebody's spouse, and do it over a length of time, something rubs off. You do tend to imbue the actress with some of your own wife's qualities, and your own relationship on the set becomes closer to that of husband and wife than mere professional colleagues.

"The fact that the public then links you together in their mind makes the working relationship more intense. So that if it's good, it's very good. But if it's poor, it quickly goes from bad to worse."

Which parallels an often-repeated story that Vivian told about Bill Frawley: "Bill fancied himself a singer. He barely tolerated our efforts in that department. In his Dublin barroom baritone, he'd hang on to each note forever, always a stave or two behind the rest . . . Bill insisted that he should handle the repeats, and it was my job to take him aside to convince him otherwise.

"'Lucille has to do them, Bill. She's the star. It'll be funnier that way.'

"He wouldn't budge. I think he somehow got me and the original Mrs. Frawley confused, so very soon the fur was flying. 'Shut up!' I yelled. 'We've got to work this song as we've rehearsed it. Keep still about it!' At last he gave in, but it was no surrender. 'You know what she's going to sound like, don't you?' he growled. 'Like putting a shovel full of shit on Baked Alaska.'"

During one particular rehearsal, Vivian walked on the set in an old blouse, jeans, a bandanna, and no makeup. As was his wont, Frawley saw an opportunity to get at his costar, for the script required Fred to tell Ethel that she looked like Frankenstein's wife. After delivering the line, Bill stopped, stared at the actress and bellowed, "Goddamn, Vivian! You *do* look like Frankenstein's wife!" One of Viv's most dreaded collaborations was the episode where she and Frawley shared a dragon costume while Lucy played a damsel in distress in Scotland. *The Other Side*

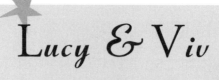 Lucy & Viv

*L*ucille Ball and Vivian Vance never had a feud going. Neither were they the loving, devoted costars that they, especially Lucy, publicly professed to be. The source of the flawed friendship behind the delightful TV collaboration was the imbalance of power between the two women. Ball was a star, the leading lady of dozens of admittedly B movies, and then, resoundingly, the queen of television, the title she still holds posthumously.

Vance was her second banana. When Lucille hired her children to costar in her TV series *Here's Lucy*, Vivian became closer to and protective of Lucie Arnaz, encouraging her stage ambitions and independence. She bitterly advised her not to get caught in the trap of "playing second fiddle to the redhead for the rest of your life."

Ball became friends with Vance only after it became clear that "Ethel Mertz" wasn't going to be competition. Originally, Lucy imagined *I Love Lucy* would be mostly she and Desi, with their neighbors the Mertzes popping in now and then. When she read the first script, she was surprised how often Ethel and Fred were on screen. Then the casting: Lucy had known William Frawley from her movie days and wanted him for Fred Mertz. It was Desi who chose Vivian Vance, hiring her without telling Lucy.

When they met, things were cool. Ball informed Vance, "You're not what I had in mind." Emily Daniels, camera coordinator on the show, recalled, "Lucy's only concern was that Vivian's hair color was too close to hers . . . she wanted Vivian to change it, and that Vivian didn't want to do." But Ball won, of course. Mary Wickes pointed out, "It was *I Love Lucy*, not I Love anybody else, and Lucille knew who was boss. Desi and she, sometimes in that order . . . ." Vance's hair gradually darkened episode after episode. Vivian claimed that Lucy's agent had informed the star, "Her eyes are bigger than yours. You'll have to let her go." Lucy later told this to Viv, who replied, "If I had your looks or your talent, I'd fire that agent, not me!"

Ball did apprise Vance that only *she* was allowed to wear false eyelashes on the show. Script clerk Maury Thompson remembered that one day Lucy stared at Vivian, came closer for a better look, then accused, "You're wearing eyelashes?" "And Vivian says, 'Yes! I've been wearing them for six months. So just leave me alone!' Lucille left her alone. She knew what she had in Vivian, especially after the show was so successful."

As a longtime star, Ball (whom Johnny Carson once referred to as "Lucille Testicle") was used to being deferred to, but Vance was devoted only to Desi Arnaz, who'd hired and stood by her but would later decline into alcoholism and inactivity, while Lucille Ball pressed on and on.

The more Lucy and Vivian worked together, the more Viv stood up to Lucy, who still preferred to hog the laughs. Increasingly, Vance said she would soon stop doing series TV. She told the press, "It's no fun working here. I get up, go to the studio, go home, and fall into bed. It's lonely. If I were Lucy, I'd do what she's doing, but I don't own a studio."

Finally she agreed to return. But at a salary so staggering for a non-star that, in the end, Lucy said no. Some said their relationship never recovered. Others felt that Viv asked for so much money as a way of bowing out without having to say no to Lucy. She'd had no problem when first approached to appear on *The Lucy Show*; one biographer quoted her as insisting, "Not on your life!" After *The Lucy Show*, Vivian sloughed off into sporadic work on stage and television, such as guesting on *Candid Camera*.

Lucy and Viv

The two women did not keep in touch often and grew apart. Years later, Vivian visited Los Angeles with her friend Jay Bell, an actor. She decided to go see Lucy at her Beverly Hills home on Roxbury Drive. Bell revealed, "She got as far as Beverly Hills, turned around, and said she couldn't do it. They were kind of on the outs around this period, but she never said what it was."

Dodds suggested she publish her memoirs. At first Vivian resisted, then began the project. But the result skimped on what the public wanted to read about: Viv and Lucille Ball—and "Fred Mertz." Editor Bill Whitehead stated, "From what I heard, Ms. Vance wanted to detail her

childhood, her Broadway roles, and her psychiatrist . . . . Her *I Love Lucy* years were sketchy, and . . . she painted herself in a very different light from how most people saw her." No memoirs were ever published.

Another publishing insider, who'd also worked in Hollywood, said, "She couldn't very well tell the truth about her marriage to John, not in those days. She did exaggerate the degree of her success on Broadway, possibly as a defensive mechanism to always being compared, less favorably, with Lucille Ball . . . . People who knew her say that it was often painful for her, reminiscing about *I Love Lucy*—which she rarely did. There was such a clash between what she wanted to be and what she was."

One such incident could easily have featured on *I Love Lucy*, but was instead real life, perhaps to be shared with a psychiatrist but not in an autobiography. *I Love Lucy* makeup man Hal King remembered, "We were all standing backstage. Lucy and Vivian were dressed for a party scene. I looked over at Vivian and said, 'Lucy, I'd better go over and tell Vivian that her stockings are wrinkled.' She said, 'Yeah, why don't you.'

"So I went over to her and said, 'Vivian, I want to fix your hose.' She said, 'I'm not *wearing* any.' Fat legs. I didn't know which way to turn."

But a quarter-century later, Viv reunited with Lucy for the last time, for her 1977 hour-long special "Lucy Calls The President," including a cameo appearance by President Carter's mother Lillian. Lucy had recently lost her mother DeDe Ball, eighty-five, who'd always sat in her audiences. Other guest stars included Gale Gordon, Mary Wickes, Mary Jane Croft, Steve Allen, and, as Lucy Carter's husband, Ed McMahon. Lucy was not at her best during rehearsals, according to those present. But neither was Vivian, who was suffering from health problems, including the cancer that would end her life two years later (and John Dodds's in 1986, three years before Lucille Ball died).

The book *Desilu* quotes an anonymous "observer" thus: "Lucy was so incredibly mean to everyone at dress rehearsal. There wasn't a full audience,

just a few people. My seat was next to her off-camera makeup table. She yelled at everyone—the wardrobe lady, the makeup man, everyone. She kept screaming at husband Gary Morton, 'Shut up!' whenever he tried to say anything. Then she would tell him to go away, yelling at him the whole while.

"Once, Vivian Vance came over to her. She didn't look well. It was after her stroke, you could see she was very ill and obviously on some type of medication. Holding up two dresses, she asked Lucy nicely, 'Which one do you think I should wear?' Lucy looked at her with complete disgust and yelled, 'What *difference* does it make? You look like a cow in anything you wear!' Vivian ran away in tears. A few days later, in front of an audience, Lucy was a different person, all sweetness and light and 'My dear Viv.'"

of Ethel Mertz explained, "She despised the idea of being wrapped arm in arm with a man she hated while they were enclosed in a rubber suit.

"She feared that Frawley, known for having flatulence, would at some point break wind. Yet Vivian went on with the scene as written, keeping those concerns to herself."

In the episode "Lucy and Ethel Buy the Same Dress," Frawley had to call Ethel by her full name. He incorrectly called her Ethel Louise Mertz, employing the name of his detested and estranged wife. The director did not cut it.

As the Ball-Arnaz marriage wore down, the series evolved into *The Lucy-Desi Comedy Hour*, longer but infrequent episodes featuring the fab four. Producer Arnaz wanted to star Vance and Frawley, who by that time weren't working as often, in their own spinoff TV series. He knew the penny-pinching Frawley would jump at the idea, but first approached Vance, cautiously yet hopefully. After all, it was a chance to topline in a series where she wouldn't be dominated by TV's most popular actress. He underestimated Vivian's strength of feeling. As Jess Oppenheimer said in the book *Desilu*, "Just because a cast loves working together as professional performers doesn't mean that, as individuals, they can't hate each other's guts."

Vivian did desire one final shot at stardom before it was too late and had repeatedly and enthusiastically hiked her salary up from the original $350 a week in 1951—according to *Lucy & Desi*; other bios quote a higher salary (by the close of *I Love Lucy*, she and Bill were each making $7,500 per episode). But now, at the end of the decade, she informed Desi in no uncertain terms, "No money in the world could persuade me to do a series with Mr. Frawley."

Her biographer added that, "Just the idea of working side by side with Frawley day in and day out made Vivian fear she would have another breakdown from which she would never recover"—referring to a pre-*Lucy* crisis in her life. Besides, Vivian reminded Desi, most of her funniest moments were in scenes with Lucy, not Bill. After Frawley found out that Vance had declined their own TV series—one which could have made him rich for life—he never spoke to her again except in character.

Rather, Vance shot a pilot of her own for Desilu, only to see it rejected by the network and a new pilot shot with younger actress Joanne Dru—in any event, *Guestward Ho!* lasted just one season. Still, it was a crushing blow to Vance's ego, if somewhat of a salve to Bill Frawley, who immediately went into *My Three Sons*, starring Fred MacMurray, of whom fellow cheapskate Frawley said, "He's tighter than two coats of paint!" Though Vivian did do some theater here and there, she was chagrined to find that her next steady job—after Lucille Ball finished starring in the Broadway musical *Wildcat*—was supporting the redhead yet again in *The Lucy Show*, which debuted in 1962 minus "Fred" or "Ricky" (Arnaz produced the series, at first).

Before returning as Lucy's sidekick, Vance got Arnaz to agree that her character would be called Viv and have a better wardrobe than Ethel Mertz ever enjoyed. Arnaz empathized with her, since to most of the public he was still "Ricky Ricardo." The new series was a success, but Vance eventually tired of being number two and commuting from her East Coast home, plus she was concerned about her reportedly platonic marriage, wishing to spend more time with John Dodds—perhaps like Ball with Arnaz, to keep a closer eye on him, although not for fear that he was chasing women. After Viv left *The Lucy Show*, returning sporadically as a special guest star, she was temporarily replaced by Lucy's studio-days friend Ann Sothern. It was at that point that William Frawley agreed to do a cameo appearance on the sitcom. (In the scene, Lucy and Ann walk by a stable where Frawley is sweeping. Lucy says, "He reminds me of someone I used to know.")

While on the East Coast, Vivian and some fellow stage players visited an ice cream parlor. According to Vance's biography, "The owners approached Vivian and said, 'Ethel, Ethel, you play such a beautiful part! Oh, we love you so much, you're so good, and your husband too!' After she'd finished with Ethel Mertz—or so she thought—Vivian grew increasingly annoyed with fans who identified her with the dowdy 1950s character she grew to hate. Eyewitness and friend Dorothy Konrad recalled, 'That finished it! She got furious when they mentioned Frawley. She walked out and screamed, 'I'm leaving, I'm never coming back! Don't you dare ever call me that! I'm not Ethel Mertz! My name is Vivian Vance!' Those two people nearly cried."

After Konrad caught up with Viv, she was still in a rage. "That old son of a bitch! That dirty old man! He was too old to play my husband! They should have cast someone younger to play opposite me!"

Mary Wickes, who specialized in, as she put it, "busybodies, maiden aunts, and old battle-axes," felt that "Viv never got it through her head that Lucy and Desi, or Lucy and Ricky, were supposed to be the attractive, romantic young couple on [*I Love Lucy*]. For better or worse, it's an old tradition that other than the stars of a show or a picture, everyone else has to be funny and, well, rather asexual. Unlike, I might say, the current state of affairs where everyone between sixteen and eighty-six seems to be having them . . . ."

So concerned was Vivian about her true age being discovered that, according to one book, she stole her birth certificate! While in Independence, Kansas, in 1961, being honored with fellow native William Inge the playwright, Vance called on City Hall and emerged with the legal document that she burned as soon as she could. Once married to the younger Mr. Dodds, Viv desperately wanted to exorcise Ethel Mertz. Her girlfriend Pat Colby was there when she tossed all her *I Love Lucy* mementos into garbage cans: "All her life's memorabilia was gone. She said, 'I don't want any part of it.' She took all the film, every segment of it, took it apart and trashed it." Not spared was a scrapbook Lucille Ball had made for her, titled "This Is Your Life, Vivian Roberta Jones."

If William Frawley sometimes blurred his TV and real-life wives, it's possible that he may have been a psychological stand-in for Vance's third husband, actor Phil Ober (who occasionally guested on *I Love Lucy*). The marriage had soured after Viv's success eclipsed his, and then degenerated into wife-abuse. Lucy was quoted, "God, that man! He was terrible. He used to beat her up. Loved to embarrass her. One day Viv came to work with a shiner. That did it. I think I said to her, 'If you don't divorce him, I will.'"

More than a few insiders believe Vivian married a non-heterosexual not only to seem younger and be a part of his glamorous East Coast literary world, but as a reaction against a jealous, insecure husband who'd mistreated her mentally and physically.

In 1966, while out walking in Hollywood, William Frawley fell to the ground and died of a massive heart attack. Vivian Vance heard the news while at a party at Sardi's in Manhattan; a guest told her, and Vivian responded by hoisting her glass and ordering, "Champagne for everyone!" Thereafter, when fans would inquire where "Fred" was, she would usually say, "He's dead . . . . Thank God!"

Producer Gary Tomlin remembered a typical fan encounter. "We were doing a show up on Cape Cod. As we were leaving a restaurant one night, someone said, 'Oh, it's Ethel Mertz! Hey, Ethel, how's Fred?' Vivian said, 'Dead! And it was the happiest day of my life when he died!'"

When fans would ask William Frawley about his costar, he would respond with a mixture of restraint and frankness: "She's one of the finest gals to come out of Kansas, but I often wish she'd go back there. I don't know where she is now and she doesn't know where I am and that's exactly the way I like it."

LAVERNE VS. SHIRLEY

F oes, friends, foes. So went the relationship of the women behind TV's
top-rated sitcom *Laverne & Shirley*.
The characters were introduced on the
hit series *Happy Days*. Penny Marshall was
delighted with the role of Laverne
DeFazio. Previously, she'd acted on *The
Odd Couple* and done gawky bits elsewhere. Her biggest credential was brother
Garry Marshall, who later executive produced *Laverne & Shirley* before turning to
film directing.

Cindy Williams, on the other hand,
felt that she was slumming. She had
appeared in motion pictures, including
the hit *American Graffiti* and *Travels With
My Aunt*. But big-screen roles were now
few and far between, as Williams was a
perky teen type no longer. So she reluc-

Penny Marshall and Cindy Williams

tantly accepted the role of Shirley Feeney while waiting for better offers.

In 1976 the *Laverne & Shirley* series debuted as a midseason replacement.
Marshall was overjoyed to costar in a TV series; Williams cringed at the prospect
of being tied up for five years. Things changed, in more ways than one, when by
the start of the 1977 season *Laverne & Shirley* was the top-rated show on television.
Suddenly, the two were TV stars. And divas in the making. If Cindy hadn't made
it to true stardom on the big screen, she'd certainly made it on the small screen, and
insiders said she was increasingly behaving like a Hollywood star.

"Penny Marshall may not have wanted a bathtub in her trailer, but because
costar Cindy Williams needed a tub, Marshall got one too," explained *TV Babylon*
author Jeff Rovin. "Marshall was also content to drive herself to work until

Williams requested a chauffeur and then they were *both* given limousines." As equals on paper, each had to be treated identically—the "most-favored nation clause" in their contracts was constantly invoked so as not to lose face.

A longtime staffer now working on another sitcom reveals, "Cindy was the real terror at first. She was a frustrated would-be movie personality. She was cute, [but] she wasn't getting any younger . . . . Shouting relieved her of her frustrations. Penny would just watch in astonishment as Cindy vented her anger and frustration . . . . We knew it was only a matter of time until both stars were at it. No way Cindy's behavior wasn't going to rub off on Penny."

It was also said that Williams was a loner while Marshall was more gregarious and took herself less seriously. The staffer continues, "Penny was a homely girl who would never have made a movie star, ever. She knew she was damn fortunate to have lucked into *Laverne & Shirley*, and at first she was having a ball . . . couldn't believe her good luck. And I think at first she was a little intimidated by Cindy's movie credentials."

Probably not for long, though. For one thing, Marshall had a security blanket Williams didn't: apart from brother Garry, Penny's father Tony was producer of *Laverne & Shirley* and sister Ronny was casting coordinator. But Garry had to tend to Cindy, as he told *TV Guide* later. "She didn't think she was in the right place doing television. So I spent most of my time that [first] year consoling her." Which made Penny jealous. As did Cindy's many demands, which gave the impression that perhaps she felt superior to the series and her costar.

In time, each woman became very concerned with parity. TV stardom had honed each one's sense of territory. When each star received her weekly script, she counted the lines to ensure that the other star didn't have more than she. The trade papers reported that during at least one taping, each star's agent was present, armed with a stopwatch to measure how much time each actor got on camera. According to Jeff Rovin, "During the first season, professional insecurity experienced by each blossomed into a personal feud, with Marshall reacting by brooding and Williams by screaming." It got worse when Marshall called Williams names in the press.

Cindy Williams began charging that because Penny's brother ran the show, she was being favored and scripts were increasingly spotlighting Laverne. A former writer on the show points out, "Whatever the case was—and Penny was more inclined to physical humor à la *I Love Lucy*—it was working. *Laverne & Shirley* had golden ratings. No one was about to change the formula, no matter how often Cindy Williams threatened to walk."

As the sitcom turned into a competing camp between two stars, most cast and crew didn't know which way to turn. They feared offending one actress if they befriended the other. Working on that set became a joyless experience for most involved, yet the sitcom continued to attract millions and garner top ratings. The two stars settled into an armed truce, each also isolated from most of her coworkers. Then both women experienced simultaneous personal unhappinesses involving private relationships, with depression for Marshall and extreme nervous anxiety—

"teetering on the edge of a nervous breakdown"—for Williams. Suddenly, the two
found one another.

Penny later remembered, "Cindy had
gone a little nuts . . . we were both real
scared and just didn't know how to accept
the success of the show." They became
friends and confidantes at last. Ironically, it
was widely felt that their amity was spoiling
their comedy. Competition, even hostility,
had supposedly kept the duo on their toes.
Now they were getting soft, their comedy-
play soggy.

Romance intervened, and things
returned to normal after Cindy Williams
wed comedian Bill Hudson of the Hudson
brothers and got pregnant. Sources said he
was trying to make his influence felt on
Laverne & Shirley. Williams and company
demanded that each new script had to refer
to her condition. "I think she believed par-

On the set of *Laverne & Shirley*

alleling her own baby with the baby for Shirley could do for her what it did rat-
ings-wise for *I Love Lucy*," said the show's writer.

Williams also asked that her work schedule be limited to a "reasonable" number of hours during her pregnancy. And she wanted it in writing. But what constitutes working hours? Does time spent in makeup count? Lunch hours? Sulks in the
star trailer? The producers felt Williams's demands were too restrictive and suggested that she not participate in every episode.

The former *Laverne & Shirley* staffer notes, "Laverne had indeed become more
pivotal to the series, and the producers thought if Cindy took some time off, it
would make it easier for her, and also they could save the $75,000 she got per
episode . . . . Not so many years before this, Cindy had been wailing about how she
was now committed to a multi-year run doing television."

But TV stardom brings its own stereotyping, and post-Shirley, Williams would
most likely not be able to return to feature films; by now, she *was* Shirley in the
public's mind and, more importantly, that of movie casting directors. When she
heard the producers' suggestion that she cool it, Cindy was flabbergasted and
reportedly appalled that Penny hadn't insisted that it had to be Laverne *and* Shirley,
not Laverne minus Shirley. In disgust, she decided to walk, and so Shirley Feeney
went overseas with her husband.

After seven highly-rated years, *Laverne & Shirley* was ending on a very publicly
sour note. "What they *really* want to do is to ace me out of the show and finally
give it to Penny," Cindy declared, and filed a $20 million lawsuit against

Paramount for contract violations and discrimination. The Marshalls all denied they were out to dump Shirley/Cindy and put on a happy—but not *too* publicly happy—face about the sitcom's new direction. However, sans Shirley, *Laverne & Shirley* barely made it through one final, low-rated TV season. "If Penny Marshall thought she was Lucy and Cindy was just her Ethel Mertz, she sure found out different," says the writer.

Cindy Williams did not return to the movies and has had a very low-key career since. "Regardless of the righteousness of one's cause," offers the ex-staffer, "actors who sue an employer are generally seen as troublemakers by the show biz establishment and punished. Look at Raquel Welch [who sued MGM when replaced in *Cannery Row* by a younger Debra Winger] or Valerie Harper [who sued when *Valerie's* focus shifted from her to its young male stars]. Litigants don't usually get nice new offers, whether or not they get a nice settlement," the terms of which are rarely made public.

Besides sexism, there's ageism, which hits actresses particularly hard. Neither Williams nor Marshall would be at all likely, post-sitcom, to maintain their on-screen star status, especially the plainer Marshall. But she made the far smarter move: not into motion picture acting, but directing. No longer a self-deprecating "comedienne" or an actor saying somebody else's lines, she became the boss on such varied films as *Jumpin' Jack Flash*, *Big*, *Awakenings*, and *A League of Their Own*.

Garry Marshall explained, "I used to write for Lucy. She would say to me, 'Garry, funny is not enough, you've got to *do* things.' She also used to say that no woman could possibly ever dream about [directing] a movie that would gross over $100 million. Well, my sister Penny has—twice."

SONNY VS. CHER

"I have no belief in the system. So Sonny is perfectly at home [in Washington, D.C.]. Politicians are one step below used-car salesmen."—Cher, upon Bono's election to Congress

"I couldn't believe she made it on her own . . . . When she won the Academy Award for Best Actress, I couldn't believe it even more."—Sonny Bono

"Not unless I have to. We have absolutely nothing in common. I think he's a bit of a sad character."—Cher, about the ex-husband to whom she seldom spoke

"If I hadn't gotten into politics and won, I could never have held my head up after Cher became a movie star with an Oscar and everything."—Sonny Bono

"Sonny wanted recognition and he worked damn hard to get it. You may not have agreed with him, but I admired the length of his journey."—Cher

rue glamour is definitely of the past," wrote columnist Dorothy Manners, former associate to super-columnist Louella Parsons. "In [Hollywood] we had such glamourous and beautiful couples; the fans lived vicariously through them . . . . The best we've been able to come up with in the seventies is Sonny and Cher."

Theirs was a personal and professional marriage that hit it big via television and their joint and individual series of series. In 1964 Sonny Bono, a music promoter with a burning desire to be a VIP, apparently wed his protégé, an unknown singer named Cher—Cherilyn Sarkisian LaPiere. Neil Bogart, head of Casablanca Records, explained, "He had minimal talent, but he was a hustler. He was going to make it at any price. Except that Sonny has always wanted to be, more than anything except rich, a personality in his own right."

So he promoted Cher, and when her singing gained momentum, made himself a part the act. "I knew not to always sing with her," he said. "Some songs were meant just for her. But if they wanted an act, then they got a duo." According to the book *Forbidden Channels—The Truth They Hide from TV Guide*, "Bono kept a

Sonny and Cher

close rein on his young wife, screening her calls, monitoring her leisure activities, and controlling her every career move. More like a strict father than a husband, he did everything but cut her meat."

He even advised her how to dress and make up. Said Oscar-winning composer Paul Jabara, "He was an older man with a long, not terribly savory background, who wanted to create this . . . star. He would be Pygmalion, and she would be his creation [Galatea] . . . . But if you look back, his idea of hip was rather frightening." Singer Ronnie Spector of the Ronettes later admitted, "The first time I saw Cher, I thought she was a hooker."

Sonny allowed, "We looked weird. That was the times. We wore what was 'in.'" Critics, unlike young fans, disdained the couple with the too-loud clothes and the too-long hair. Cher admitted that Sonny got final say over their wardrobe and its details; other women before and after Cher have confirmed Bono's need to dominate: "To me, it's the short-guy syndrome," says an ex of Bono who requests anonymity because "since his death, some segments of the public have almost canonized him." She continues, "Sonny didn't get anywhere very fast. He didn't have the looks, the talent or the height . . . . His height used to really bother him. He felt that it put him at a disadvantage with other guys, that they literally looked down on him.

"And he took this out on whatever woman he was controlling at the time. Everything was by his rules."

Sonny and Cher yielded some saccharin hit songs and made money touring. But by the late 1960s they were old hat, even after shedding the pseudo-hippie threads. Bono was bitterly disappointed that his pet project, a 1967 movie he co-owned titled *Good Times*, hadn't turned Cher into a movie star and him into a mogul. Veteran actor George Sanders recalled, "He is a man of overweening ambition and crassness who believes that being obnoxious is the way to impress people. I think he has hopes of becoming a real producer."

"Singers have a shorter career span than actors," observed Bono. "And Cher has talent. Not for acting, but reacting. I think if I build something special around her, we could really have a hit movie." So he tried again, with *Chastity* (1969), tailoring it specifically to Cher. "I think it will be a big, controversial hit," he advised the entertainment press. To that end, Cher's character would engage in everything *but* chastity as a runaway victim of incest. Later, she would do a striptease and have a lesbian affair.

In the mid–1990s, after her daughter came out as lesbian, Cher publicly revealed that early on she'd experimented with lesbian sex but it hadn't held her interest. At the time of *Chastity*, she got pregnant again, and when her first child was born—she'd previously suffered miscarriages—the couple decided to name her after the film. "It might help our movie," said Sonny. It didn't, and Cher was appalled to learn that he'd financed *Chastity* by mortgaging their thirty-one-room Holmby Hills mansion without telling her. She told *Laugh-In* producer George Schlatter: "Sonny has to be crazy. He shouldn't be allowed out without a leash."

Bono later justified himself, "I was defensive and mad. I wanted to be a part of show business and they wouldn't have me." As shooting had progressed, he backed down from making a controversial film, watering down the script and ending up with a disjointed movie that nobody wanted to see. He foolishly informed the *Washington Post*, "[The title character's] conflict—whether to be a virgin or go ahead and be modern—creates pressures, whatever she decides. It has caused a large increase in frigidity and lesbianism among modern women."

His inane plugging of the movie—for he did nearly all the talking then—helped kill interest in it. He expounded about *Chastity*'s "moral:" "Every woman wants a man to set the limits . . . . Girls don't really want to be free. It makes them nervous and unhappy." Cher reportedly asked friends, "Is *that* what this movie is about?" and later declared, "My husband Sonny Bono is such a male chauvinist. A woman must do what the man says. Walk three steps behind. That's Sonny."

★ ★ ★

During the making of *Chastity* and after giving birth to Chastity, Cher finally began to assert herself and express her opinions, occasionally defying Sonny—except in business; she figured he had a business head and preferred to leave it all to him. Paul Jabara observed, "Many show biz gals who are managed by their husbands are very trusting, very submissive. Cher was all that and more, to an unusual degree . . . . When she finally liberated her soul and her ego, she was bound not only to get rid of such a Svengali, but to put him at the opposite end of the world to her, psychologically."

Times were getting worse for the couple, with more friction between them and a bleaker professional outlook. By 1970 they didn't have a recording label and had lost most of their young fans. For a year they had to work hard on the nightclub circuit to keep the Holmby Hills home Bono had almost lost. Insiders said the pair were ready to call it quits and would have but for Chastity, who was blonde like Cher's mother Georgia, who had left her Armenian-American husband the day after their wedding but eventually married him three times. He was a heroin addict and a convict, and before he died sued his daughter for "not even helping support me, just helping defame my name," as he told the tabloids.

One of Sonny and Cher's gigs was to substitute-host Merv Griffin's TV talk show. The two had honed their act, with Cher playing aloof and sarcastic, putting down the whining but cheerful Sonny. CBS then created *The Sonny & Cher Show* as a summer hiatus series. Network honcho Fred Silverman had stated, "As singers, they're okay. As comics, they're quite funny." One critic wrote, "In the sixties, the Love Couple were unintentionally amusing, Bono trying to act like a flower-powered teenager—in his thirties. Now they're deliberately humorous."

The show clicked and was renewed, bringing the couple out of the musical fringe and into the show business mainstream. Cher biographer Randy Taraborelli quoted a friend on the couple's TV success: "Sonny's feet never touched the ground [at first] . . . . 'See? What'd I tell ya, huh? What'd I tell ya?' he kept saying. He was like a kid in a candy store now that Hollywood had let him in. Cher was as excited as Cher ever is."

She was tiring of Sonny's ongoing control of their personal and professional lives. "He was this Sicilian dictator husband," she later informed *Cosmopolitan.* "I could say *nothing.* I got *suicidal.*" By 1973 when they attended the Academy Awards telecast together, the pair had secretly separated. "If you leave me, America will hate you," Sonny had warned her. As to her own success, Cher marveled, "I kept thinking I must be Dinah Shore. I'm not really very talented, but people like me anyway. There are some people who are respected because their talent is so mammoth—that's a luxury."

She was also increasingly spotlighted in her own right, due to her daring Bob Mackie-designed TV wardrobe—she landed, solo, on the cover of *Time,* captioned, "From Gladrags to Riches"—and a string of Sonny-less record hits like "Dark Lady" and "Gypsies, Tramps, and Thieves." Her individual success was giving her the courage to escape Sonny, which she did during one of their Las Vegas engagements.

"Sonny was more and more concerned with the commercial side of our life together than with our life together," she explained. "I have decided that he is not as good a friend to me as I was to him. And I'm tired of doing it," she told Phil Donahue and audience. But neither Bono nor CBS were about to let her go, professionally. The network threatened legal action if the twosome didn't return to their highly-rated series. They returned, acting the happily married couple for the time being. One critic opined, "The honesty on this series is supplied by their daughter Chastity, who often appears sullen and possibly even aware that she is being used as a symbol of this extremely show biz couple's affection."

The 1974 divorce was one of tinseltown's most acrimonious. Sonny reacted to Cher's leaving him with a $24 million lawsuit for breach of contract. Only then did Cher learn that although Sonny had named their company Cher Enterprises, she was legally just a hired hand and employee of it, "entitled to vacation time she probably never got. And no sick days," according to the biography *Cher,* which in 1986 noted, "Now she believes that Sonny only loved her for the first couple of years, and after that he loved the creation of 'Sonny and Cher.'"

She countersued him for holding her to "involuntary servitude." She claimed he had "unlawfully dominated and controlled my business interests and career" and had violated the Thirteenth Amendment of the Constitution. She informed Barbara Walters, "I felt like a slave who was being set free," and *Rolling Stone,* "If I ever get over living with him, it will be a miracle." Their series ended, and three days after divorcing Bono, Cher wed musician Gregg Allman in Las Vegas. Nine days later, she filed to end the marriage. One biographer wrote, "They separated. They reconciled. She filed for divorce. They reconciled. He filed for divorce." Then she found she was pregnant with their son Elijah Blue.

Their biggest difference was drugs. Looking back, she would say, "Being married to Gregory was like going to Disneyland on acid. You knew you had a good time, but you couldn't remember what you did."

Meanwhile, in the fall of '74 Cher's ex returned to TV with *The Sonny Comedy Review*. No surprise, it flopped immediately. "I lost everything," he said of the split with Cher. In 1975 she went solo with her own series. It started strong but fell in the ratings. CBS insiders said she didn't have the self-confidence to do a series alone and disliked the weekly grind. So she agreed to contact Sonny and do a joint series for 1976. He jumped at the opportunity, but as a condition asked Cher to join him in a personal appearance tour that year, while Cher and CBS requested that he drop his lawsuits against her (by then there were more than one).

Cher in *Silkwood*

The fourth variety series starring Sonny and/or Cher was probably the most eagerly awaited debut of the new season. People tuned in just to see how the exes would relate to each other. Bono's first line to the studio audience that first night went: "Well, folks, I don't know if any of you have heard about it, but Cher and I aren't married anymore." Silence, and then a collective groan. The jokes—she tweaking him about his height, he tweaking her nose (now long since remodeled)—were no longer funny, if they ever really were. Cher was pregnant by Gregg Allman, and Sonny tried to build a comedy theme around his support for Republican presidential candidate Gerald Ford versus hers for Democrat Jimmy Carter.

Despite the hype and initial ratings, by its third week *The Sonny and Cher Show* was down to number thirty-eight. CBS changed the time slot in vain, and in 1977 cancelled the show, "mercifully killing off the weekly prime-time spectacle of Sonny and Cher once and for all," wrote author Penny Stallings.

★ ★ ★

Though Cher's second marriage didn't survive, her career did, more or less, after she left TV and became a solo act. Joan Rivers later marveled about the dark-tressed survivor, "If Cher had been on the Titanic, they'd have cleaned off the ice and kept on sailing." Cher's ability to endure was aided by the public's abiding interest in her, as evidenced by the tabloids and fan magazines which still kept her on their covers. She huffed, "They call me the Queen of the Newsstands. [But] there are not enough hours in the day for me to do all the things they say I do, and with all the people they say I do them with.

"They had me walking down the beach at Acapulco with Jim Brown, and they pasted two photos of us together. They've done the same with me and Paul Newman, Robert Redford, and Elvis Presley, and I never met any of them."

Sonny, by contrast, was no longer in the limelight, though he'd gone on to other women (some said before the divorce). He fumed over the romantic gossip about Cher; said Paul Jabara, "He hated it that she was supposedly dating every other man in show business. He hated it that she was thriving without him. And he especially hated the idea of her marrying again . . . . When she went out with David Geffen, Sonny became more homophobic than ever. When she married Allman, he became more vocally anti-drugs—never mind that he'd done his share, like almost everybody in the music industry."

The media, tabloid and otherwise, were breathless to know about Cher's love life now that she was finally single. They assumed most of it. But as she told *Playboy*, "I have this sex-siren image, but really I couldn't give a shit about that. I am so uninterested right now . . . I really don't care. I feel it's almost like being a bank clerk. I go and do my job, and that's my job, the sex-queen stuff."

One of the topics Cher has not often addressed is the legal status of her marriage to Bono. The pair had claimed to be married since 1964. That wedding didn't legally count, as Cher had performed it herself—in a hotel bathroom (they exchanged $12 silver rings engraved with their names). Of course the public at that time had to be informed otherwise, since only state-sanctioned marriages were tolerated; anything else could have destroyed their careers. Sonny had first divorced in 1963 and was in no rush to retie the knot. "Marriage is a must for a woman," he'd hypocritically pontificated. "But for a man it has its pluses and minuses." By not being legally wed, Cher had less claim on his/their property in California, should they ever break up.

"I think Cher didn't resent Sonny's lack of [marital] commitment until later, after they split," said record mogul Neil Bogart. At any rate, they did make it legal in 1969, immediately before Chastity was born.

Post-Cher, Sonny tried to act, taking assignments on *The Love Boat*, in a B movie made in Europe, etc. It didn't lead to a thespian career, so he became a restaurateur, which indirectly led to politics after he didn't see eye-to-eye with business regulations in Palm Springs, where he went to live. Ironically, he admitted, "A pretty good sign that somebody has had it with show biz or is retiring is when they move to Palm Springs. Its nickname is Death's Waiting Room."

When Sonny became mayor of Palm Springs, it made national headlines, partly because it seemed so unlikely. It was also a case of catching up with Cher. Bono had remarked, "This country deified Cher. She became this huge star. The public turned against me. Suddenly I was just 'that guy' who'd been married to Cher." If "the public" disdained him, he was taken to heart—or pocketbook—by a majority of Palm Springs residents.

Screenwriter, author, and gay activist Paul Monette wrote, "Sonny Bono tried to reinvent himself . . . with a new family and a very business-like, anti-hippie image . . . . He refused to ride in the Gay Pride Parade, and when the sizable P.S.

gay community even dared mention this, he became very angry and critical . . . . I think the reason he's so bitter is that as an entertainer he was finally rejected, so now he runs on negative platforms—he's anti-this and anti-that."

By the time the Palm Springs area elected Bono to Congress, he was on his moral high-horse, intoning, "I think Hollywood can teach Washington [D.C.] a few things about morality. I do." Except when he turned around and lambasted Hollywood or any other groups who irked him or could deliver publicity. As a politician, Bono felt as free to criticize Cher and her perceived excesses of dress and younger men as she did him. His 1991 memoirs were very politically self-serving and included notable gaps, among them true details about his jealous feud with record mogul David Geffen, who had encouraged Cher to stand up for herself and blossom on her own. By the time of the memoirs, Geffen was an openly gay man and possibly the richest person in Hollywood (though not a Republican).

Nor, despite his daughter and their purportedly close relationship, did Bono ever support or vote for any legislation embracing equal rights for gay or lesbian citizens and taxpayers. Chastity had initially avoided the media, and after she was outed in the tabloids denied it. She was trying to be a singer at that time, and her record label encouraged her to stay in the closet. When Chastity did come out, she put music behind her and took up writing—eventually penning her own memoirs, as did Cher after Sonny's death. Chastity also served as a media representative for GLAAD, the Gay & Lesbian Alliance Against Defamation.

She interviewed her father for the gay magazine *The Advocate*. During their session, he evinced total ignorance about the myriad anti-gay laws across the land, which he stated were contrary to the U.S. Constitution. But then he turned around and voted against the rights of Americans like his daughter. Cher, on the other hand, joined P-FLAG—Parents & Friends of Lesbians And Gays—explaining at a meeting, "I'm the mother, and I could have made it so much easier for her," referring to her temporary rejection of her daughter when she discovered she wasn't heterosexual. After Sonny's death in a freak skiing accident, Chastity revealed that father and daughter had been estranged for about a year, not speaking because of his ongoing homophobia.

As for Cher, after winning her Oscar for *Moonstruck*, she backed off from movies, pursuing a variety of interests, including a TV infomercial she later rued. Finally, Sonny's star seemed to be on the ascent while Cher's was dimming. She admitted that she hated aging, and via plastic surgery kept augmenting her looks, once snapping, "If I want to wear my tits on my back, that's my business!" (Record producer Bob Esty disclosed after working with her, "I thought she would be a lot funnier and livelier. But she's very moody and complex. She's not the easiest person to spend the afternoon with.")

Cher continued to wax frequently on the subject of Sonny, for once he became a Congressman, she was asked about him more often. Looking way back: "I thought, 'Either I'm going to leave Sonny or I am going to jump out of a window.'" She objected to his lack of support for women's rights and gay rights, but couldn't seem to let go of their past. Randy Taraborelli asked, "One wonders if Cher will ever work her way through the hostility she still feels toward Sonny Bono . . . . She's been damning Bono, calling him a slave master.

"Part of her therapy seems to be to hang on to all this anger and then to vent it twice a year on television interviews. But it seems that when she's damning him, she's really working on forgiving him." And so she was, for as soon as Bono died in 1998, her tune changed completely. Sometimes it takes death to end a feud, even if it can't quite erase or reverse one.

Clint Eastwood vs. Sondra Locke

Professionally, it isn't smart for an actress to become too closely identified with one actor. Or even, I would say, with one director," said producer-director Alan J. Pakula (*Klute, Sophie's Choice, All the President's Men*). "Their successes will usually be seen as *his* successes, while her outside collaborations, if they fail, will often be attributed to her lack of individual success."

One actress who found this out the hard way was Sondra Locke, who made her Oscar-nominated screen bow in *The Heart Is a Lonely Hunter* (1968), a critical success but not a box office hit. The lovely blonde, born in 1945, floundered professionally until she costarred with producer-director Clint Eastwood in *The Outlaw Josey Wales* (1976). Before filming was over, the fifteen-years-older star had begun an affair with Locke. For thirteen years the two were married in all but name, and Locke worked almost exclusively with her costar and director. At first, Eastwood remained legally married to Maggie, his longtime spouse and mother of their two children. More unusually,

Locke remained legally married to her blond husband Gordon Anderson, who was gay and who became her best friend; the platonic relationship outlasted the turbulent one with Eastwood.

By 1989 when Sondra and Clint made their final movie, *Sudden Impact*, her once brilliant future had evaporated into a career as Eastwood's leading lady. "He's seldom had a strong leading lady," wrote columnist Paul Rosenfield. "He's said to have resented the few times that an actress was billed above him, like Ginger Rogers or Shirley MacLaine . . . . The women in his movies are mostly window-dressing." Locke may not have realized that, according to talk show host Virginia Graham, "If you hook up with a big movie star, girls, when he's through with you and trades you in for a younger model, you won't know what hit you. These big boys play very rough."

In 1997 Locke published a book whose title was a takeoff on an Eastwood movie title: *The Good, the Bad, and the Very Ugly—A Hollywood Journey* about her life with the close-mouthed man of

24

action. In the preface, she acknowledged her lifelong love of fairy tales and the fact that many females would consider it a dream come true to find a Prince Charming in the form of a bona fide movie star. Yet "the Prince was a prince but he proved not to be Charming at all." He had, she said, a "heavy iron door that held his secrets and hid all the shadowed bodies inside. The maiden, whom he called his only love, his Princess, glimpsed behind that door and saw too much. Then he brought all his power and darkness down upon her."

As to why many women romantically involved with actors don't see them as the fallible, often corrupted, powerful men they are, they are, after all, actors. Even less talented ones are adept at presenting a charming or alluring facade. Wrote Sondra, "They all said she had been foolish and naive ever to have believed in him. She was neither, for he had worn a clever mask . . . and she had a trusting heart." She concluded, "There were times I wished I had only read it . . . and never lived it."

Locke discovered that when a movie star and his wife or girlfriend part ways, she loses more than her man does. His friends, whom she thought had become hers too over the years, dropped her. Locke also, by opposing Eastwood in public—in court—lost not one but two promising careers, as a performer and director. For Hollywood stands by its moneymakers only. The strain, the years of litigation, the delays and broken promises, and the frustration, believed Sondra, may have cost her healthwise too. Eventually she had to undergo a double mastectomy.

Chief Dan George, the Native American actor who appeared in *The Outlaw Josey Wales*, jokingly told the *Los Angeles Times*, "Clint's a cool guy . . . but don't ever cross him. There's more there than meets the eye." Locke noted that Eastwood was a wonderful lover but ever the man in control. "For many years the only people allowed at all close to us were, for the most part, the people employed by Clint," e.g., cast and crew of his films—"carefully hand-picked for their discretion"—his lawyer, agent, business managers, and executives from Warner Bros., where Eastwood's Malpaso production company was headquartered.

By contrast, none of Locke's friends were allowed into their circle, except Gordon, who Clint liked—even when Gordon did his Eastwood impression. Sondra eventually found out that Clint and Maggie were not completely through; at one point, Maggie asked him to accompany her to Hawaii to try and patch things up. He went, which distressed Sondra, who'd been informed the marital relationship had ended years before. Eastwood managed to soothe the feelings of "Sweetie," as he called her; she told "Daddy" she was so proud he actually said to his wife that he was in love with Sondra. Locke believed, "I was not like any of his affairs of their past."

The Eastwoods did not divorce until 1984. Sondra later declared that she and Clint hadn't felt the need to validate their relationship "with papers," though that contract enables the discarded woman to more easily collect a larger fiscal recompense. Also, due to Sondra and Gordon's particular situation—he was an artist and spiritual seeker whom she helped support—Sondra remained contractually bound to Gordon, which she thought Clint didn't mind. She did find out that Eastwood didn't like her to work apart from him, which she did less and less, aware however that "I was clearly getting swallowed up in his shadow." When Locke made her directorial debut with *Ratboy* (1986), which won her critical kudos though it wasn't a Warner Bros. hit, it seemed to increase Eastwood's dissatisfaction with their relationship.

Over the years, Sondra—who unlike Clint wrote a book offering her side of the story—claimed to have witnessed several instances of her mate's callousness and manipulativeness, including coldly firing a longtime employee, hiring private detectives, obsessing over minor expenses, or shunning people while they were ill. What Eastwood craved, she said, was "unconditional love, admiration, and surrender." And few questions asked. Their relationship became very uncommunicative, to her frustration, but she didn't like to push and make him angry. Only later did Locke learn about his unfaithfulness, which he treated casually and with no desire to explain or justify.

Sondra believed the one advantage of becoming professionally known as "Clint and Sondra" was that she'd been around the filmmaking process so long and in such depth that she too wanted to direct, which Eastwood made possible, *Ratboy* being a "quirky adult fairy tale." However, Clint made changes which the director didn't wish, and when she tried to use Gordon, a some-time actor and writer, Eastwood charged her with nepotism, which is not only a common tinseltown practice but one Clint frequently indulged in with his children Alison (for whom he created a romance from the book version of *Midnight in the Garden of Good and Evil*) and Kyle (whom he wanted to star and direct in *The Karate Kid*).

When Sondra mentioned this, Clint retorted, "Well, I don't want him in it. He's not mainstream." Locke replied that the film, about a boy who is half rat and half human, wasn't "mainstream" either. Of course Eastwood got his way, "a total control freak" who spent more and more time out of town away from Sondra. By 1986 their problems and quarrels were accelerating. Locke alleges that Eastwood wanted Gordon to break into an ex-employee's house to type a sample note on his machine and see if it matched anonymous hate letters he'd received over the years. Gordon refused: "He can count me out of his suburban espionage, Sondra. I'm not playing cat burglar for him. He's such a coward. Why does he always have to hide while everybody else does all his dirty work? If I were you, I'd start worrying about him. Something is wrong, Sondra. He's warped."

She knew of Eastwood's publicly unacknowledged daughter Kimber, who purportedly caused him a days-long sulk when she requested that her father buy her a used car. Sondra didn't yet know about the woman with whom Clint, during their own relationship, secretly had two children. Even though when Sondra had become pregnant by him, they didn't choose to become parents. Locke opined that by 1989, "He had become little more than a spoiled child. There was no longer any joy. If the least little thing didn't go his way, he pitched a fit." After he was nominated for a Golden Globe but failed to win it, he reportedly told a friend, "Maybe it's time for me to get rid of everybody in my life and start over." Which he shortly did, with Sondra. He changed the locks on the home he'd bought her and which she'd spent years doing over, officially stating that Ms.

Locke had lived there "rent-free" for nine years "with your husband Gordon Anderson."

What exactly caused the breakup is unclear, and as nearly always, each side presented a self-validating version. At the time of the split, Locke was directing a second picture, *Impulse.* Seeing that Eastwood was going to misrepresent her relationship with Gordon, she asked him to surrender all claims on any of her assets that as her legal husband he was entitled to. "In an extraordinary gesture of love and faith in me, Gordon signed away everything without hesitation." According to Locke, who sued him, Eastwood tried to deny that they had cohabited, using the excuse of her non-standard marriage to depict his relationship with her as a casual though long one, the better to avoid a sizable financial settlement. Eventually the megamillionaire claimed Locke was trying to interfere with "my children's inheritance," referring to Kyle and Alison Eastwood. Sondra claimed that he had tapped her phones; Eastwood used the excuse that he did so to find out who was behind what he said were telephoned death threats. Devastatingly, he publicly declared that he suspected Gordon.

Sondra was furious that he would place Gordon under suspicion, and furious about what she said was a lie—there were no phoned-in threats. "All this

Clint and Sondra at the premiere of *City Heat*

showed exactly how much his *money* meant to Clint; why else was he trying to deny our very history, and destroy me, and even Gordon, unless it was to keep every penny of his money, and his 'real estate.'" Gordon had foiled part of Eastwood's alleged plan by not accepting delivery at his home of Bekins boxes full of Sondra's clothes, which would have "proved" that Locke lived with Anderson. Also, said Sondra, "Gordon lived a very private life, and Clint assumed that he would never want to discuss his homosexuality in a deposition or in a trial. And if Gordon hadn't, it would support Clint's claim that Gordon and I were a happily married heterosexual couple."

It was Gordon who found out about Clint's latest offspring—and the other woman in his life. "Clint has two small children . . . right now, in Carmel," Sondra was told. In the four years since the superstar had moved his secret girl-friend into one of his houses, they'd had a daughter and son. Wrote Sondra, "I felt like I'd been slapped in the face. The room I was standing in began to close in on me, like the scene from the old Olivia de Havilland movie *The Snake Pit* . . . . 'I can't believe that's true,' I said." She felt terrible about his double life, the betrayal, and "my pain about my own abortions" she'd had with Eastwood, and her "subsequent tubal ligations."

Eastwood was already involved with actress Frances Fisher, whom he didn't marry but with whom he later had a child in 1993. The legal process dragged on, and Locke tried to prove that Eastwood had bought her home in Los Angeles as a replacement for her. Sondra claimed that Clint refused to return anything from their house to her—"my fairy tale collection, or even Christmas gifts, and birthday gifts, some of which had even been given to me by other people."

She recalled a time when Clint's mother had left a few dollars and change on the kitchen counter with a note that "We made a long-distance phone call. Have fun. Mom." Sondra was amazed that Eastwood "stuffed the money in his pocket and looked impressed that she'd paid—that she hadn't expected a 'free ride.'"

As for *Impulse*, Locke contended that "Despite excellent reviews, Warner Bros. barely released the film." The studio informed her they were "regrettably" dropping the three projects she had in development there. Warners was virtually the only place she'd worked since hooking up with Eastwood. "When Clint 'divorced' me, did Warners go along with the package?"

Later came the mastectomies, the chemotherapy and loss of hair, and temporary lesions on the face resulting from a staph infection. When Eastwood made overtures to meet with Locke, she was hopeful. In return for her dropping all claims against him, he and his people were ready to set up a directing deal for her at Warners. She agreed: "By then I had resigned myself to the loss of my home and all the 'things' in my life and only wanted to move on. The hard way I

had learned that 'things' didn't really matter. Cancer had shown me that."

To make a long story short, the 1990 deal came to nothing. Locke claimed to have brought in over thirty projects "and they said an immediate no to them all." It dawned on her that she was not going to be allowed to remain a movie director. She helmed a TV movie instead, aware that once you've done that you're typed as "just" a TV person. The next blow was finding out that Clint's girlfriend and costar Frances Fisher was pregnant. It reminded her "of the permanent loss I suffered in my efforts to please him . . . . I was later told that Clint had made Frances keep her pregnancy a secret until after the Academy Awards. 'I don't want that kinda thing taking attention away from my Oscar race!' he had said to her" before winning for his latest directorial effort, *Unforgiven*.

Locke sued again, alleging that Eastwood had arranged with Warners to lead her on and get her off his back by arranging a phony directing deal. The lawsuit for fraud, Locke vs. Warner Bros., was filed in 1994. "For me, the reality was that I wasn't working and hadn't worked [in movies] since 1989 when Clint had locked me out of my house." The court found against her. She went back to court, suing Eastwood himself, who had "entered into a settlement agreement with Sondra Locke, settling a lawsuit that was pending between the two of you," and "as a part of that settlement, Sondra Locke entered into a contract with Warner Bros." Locke had originally sued for several millions; she settled with Eastwood in exchange for $450,000 and the modest Crescent Heights house Gordon lived in, and the hollow directing deal.

Locke's attorney told the court that her client had brought suit because "She was defrauded out of her professional reputation, her professional existence, her self-esteem, and her professional identity because she dared to challenge Clint Eastwood." Before the trial ended, Eastwood settled with Locke out of court (she later learned they would have decided in her favor). The amount went undisclosed, as usual. Then, said Locke, Eastwood suddenly decided not to pay due to a perceived technicality, though he soon after did.

Sondra had learned a lesson: "Like so many women, I thought by *not* fighting [during the relationship] everything would work out . . . . 'Daddy' would take care of it all. But I learned 'Daddy' would only take care of 'Daddy.'"

In her 1997 memoirs, Locke concluded with the news that a California Court of Appeals had recently found that her lawsuit against Warner Bros. did "contain proper and sufficient evidence to warrant a trial for fraud and breach of contract." She also noted that six years after meeting a new boyfriend, they were "still living happily together in a real, supportive, and equal relationship." Plus, "always, forever, there is Gordon," who knew and stood by her before, during, and after Hollywood.

P.S. Frances Fisher and Eastwood's relationship also ended badly, despite their child, "his third of record at the time" (he has since married a younger woman with whom he had a child in 1996). Upon O. J. Simpson's acquittal in his criminal trial, Fisher informed columnist Marilyn Beck, "Once again the illusion of stardom has overshadowed a man's infidelity and cruelty . . . corruption and denial take precedence over morality and conscience." Asked if she was comparing Simpson with Clint Eastwood, Fisher replied, "If the shoe fits."

FATALISTIC ATTRACTION:
James Woods vs. Sean Young

"When you get involved with someone in this business, you can also get involved with their relatives or agents or hangers-on, etc."—Gary Merrill, who wed Bette Davis

Sometimes the public perception of a feud is much influenced by the way it's reported and by bias. A prime example was the strange interlude between costars Sean Young and James Woods, who met on the set of *The Boost* (1988), a depressing and little-seen film that was no boost to either's career, let alone their peace of mind for years to come.

In Hollywood it's routine for costars to be romantically linked in the media, whether they are or not. For gay and lesbian stars it's especially useful as camouflage as well as publicity for their latest project. Oddly, in the case of *The Boost*, both Woods and Young later denied any affair.

James Woods was labeled "the most hostile of all American actors" by critic Pauline Kael. Britain's *Neon* film magazine wrote that boxer Mike Tyson "prepared for championship bouts by watching Woods's films, psyching himself up." Producers who "want a psycho, a loser, a deranged cop, or someone who's just downright nasty, call James Woods."

Sean Young was in *Blade Runner, Stripes, Ace Ventura,* and *Wall Street,* in which she clashed with director Oliver Stone and costar Charlie Sheen, who hung a sign on her back reading "I am the biggest cunt in the world." Young later told *Vogue,* "Stone has great difficulty with women. Sheen has had great difficulty growing up. Both of them are intimidated by a woman who has an opinion." Her image was also partly shaped by her encounter with Warren Beatty on *Dick Tracy.*

"I basically was sexually harassed by him. This kind of thing wasn't news to anybody. What *was* news was I blew the whistle on it. I talked about it . . . and boy oh boy! He didn't like *that* . . . . There is one rule in Hollywood you don't break— you don't tell the truth about people in the press. And I broke that rule, and I paid a very, very big price."

When she went after the role of Cat Woman in the *Batman* sequel, Young was portrayed as going too far, even nuts. She dressed up in a cat suit and tried to get producers to see her for an audition, at a time when Cher was the frontrunner for the feline role that later went to Michelle Pfeiffer. Though Young thought it was merely enterprising and creative, perhaps bold, of her, the media depicted her as desperate or a semi-stalker. What didn't make the news was that, according to Young:

"I *was* cast in the original *Batman* and I rehearsed for two weeks in London with Jack Nicholson and Michael Keaton, and I got knocked out of it because I fell off [a] horse . . . . It was after my being fired by Warren Beatty . . . ."

Combustion was in the air when Sean Young then paired with James Woods for *The Boost*, a story about a man who almost destroys his wife via his drug-fueled mania. Woods had told *People* magazine, "I got into this business just to meet women." He informed *Esquire*, "Everyone in this business is scared to death of me because they're all morons and I'm not." On the set, it was rumored that Young and Woods were having an affair that ended abruptly. Whatever did or didn't happen, and whoever ended it and why, is unknown, unlike the aftermath of the dangerous liaison.

Woods said that he received hate mail, including photos of corpses and mutilated animals, allegedly from Young. Then came a voodoo doll left on his Beverly Hills doorstep, accessorized with a slashed neck and iodine for blood. Also, $300-worth of flowers in Woods's garden were destroyed. According to *People*, the following day the actor found "a note on his doorstep apologizing for the delivery [of the voodoo doll], but indicating that the person who had done so had done it at Ms. Young's instruction and that Young was upset because he had not hung it from one of the rafters per specific instruction." The note added, "I think she's rotten. Signed—a friend of Sean Young's."

Rumor had it that at some point the angry Sean Young had Krazy-Glued James Woods's penis to his thigh. Woods had the police question Sean Young, who was on location making a movie, and then he slapped her with a $6 million harassment suit ($2 million, by another account). Woods alleged that Young had made his hair go gray and had given him tinnitus (a ringing in the ears). The suit alleged "intentional infliction of emotional distress" to himself and his girlfriend, Sarah Owen, a blonde horse trainer he'd met at a Chevron gas station in California.

Meanwhile, the divorced Woods and his fiancée Owen hadn't exactly been having an idyllic time. In November 1987, Owen filed a report with the Los Angeles police accusing Woods of verbal and physical abuse, and of forcing her to have an abortion. She'd allegedly demanded he leave her house, but he allegedly returned with a shotgun, forced her

James Woods

Sean Young

to strip at gunpoint, then to lie on the floor and repeat "I am a whore, I am a baby-killer." *Premiere* magazine, in a cover story on Sean Young, said that Owen later dropped the charges. In 1988, Woods moved to divorce Owen after 127 days of marriage (his prior union had lasted three years).

Neon wrote, "Woods hates the Hollywood merry-go-round. His venom's so palpable, you'd think girlfriends regularly leave him for big-shot studio execs. And God help anyone who gets in the way of his art." Woods regularly decried Hollywood for being too commercial, and felt his career hadn't progressed farther because of his high I.Q. Ex-wife and former model Kathryn Greko recalled, "He loved the way I looked, but he never really trusted me. He wanted to control me . . . . Jim thinks his way is the only way."

In 1997 *Neon* wrote that Woods had been "turned down for the first fifteen years of his career" and had not "fit the conventionally attractive Hollywood mold." The book *Sex, Stupidity and Greed—Inside the American Movie Industry* characterized Woods as "manic, a tireless womanizer, and a difficult egomaniac."

In any event, the media had a field day with the Woods versus Young imbroglio, calling it a sequel to *Fatal Attraction*, in which a spurned Glenn Close goes mad seeking revenge against married Michael Douglas. Now it was "crazy Sean," and most sympathy went to Woods, the "wronged" actor and would-be artist. However, Woods dropped his suit when Young and her attorney, according to Young, showed that Woods and Owen had set her up:

"He dropped it because I came up with such incriminating evidence that he went, 'Uh, sorry!' . . . What finally cinched it was that his girlfriend at the time we were making *The Boost* was very unstable, and he's not such a well cookie either, and together they just created this whirlwind and pointed it at me, and then we found out that the woman had been arrested by the Beverly Hills Police Department along with these eighteen other girls when that Madame Alex was arrested. I found out about it from a hairdresser who knew she was, well, a prostitute . . . . It was all stupid and inane, and very hurtful to my career. Probably his too, come to think of it."

Harold Becker, director of *The Boost*, told *Neon*, "I'd ignore anything [Sean Young] says."

In 1992, James Woods told *Entertainment Weekly*, "I love and admire Sean, and she's actually half right," presumably meaning he was not entirely innocent. In June 1989, Young recovered her $277,000 legal costs for defending herself against Woods's suit.

Young had appeared in several popular movies since her screen bow in 1980, and worked with top directors like James Ivory, Ivan Reitman, Ridley Scott, Garry Marshall, David Lynch, Oliver Stone, Joel Schumacher, and Gus Van Sant. But her career's momentum stalled in large part due to the "crazy Sean" episode. In 1997 Ian Grey wrote, "Young still suffers from the effects of a media smear-campaign resulting in this across-the-board perception that she is crazy, perhaps drug-addled, bitchy, vindictive, stupid, unreliable, or worse.

"The case highlights the misinformation and abuse by the entertainment media and the double standard to which women actors are subjected. The power of the media is fierce, and even after a decade, this manufactured image of 'crazy Sean' lingers." Unfortunately, "the press ignored this awkward plot conclusion"—that Sean Young was innocent—"to their *Fatal Attraction* scenario." Since life turned out not to be imitating art (or a popular movie in which the ending was changed so that the female villain is destroyed), the media mostly lost interest in reporting the developments and real ending.

In 1997 Woods looked back: "I was furious with [Sean Young] when I thought she'd done those ugly things."

The same year, Young wrote:

"There were signs all along that this person was really a liar. He would say things, then change the story. I was really innocent. My detectives had found out some bad stuff about him and Sarah Owen. I had rights to all their medical records. She had a police record and he had a whole history of taking medication."

Woods says of his now ex-wife, Owen: "As soon as I was lucky enough to scrape her off my shoe, I never dealt with her again. I've never been treated so evilly . . . . I say to myself every day, 'I know there's a God, because he didn't let her spawn.'"

In June 1997, columnist Jack Martin reported in *Beverly Hills (213)*, "That fine actor James Woods has announced his engagement to his latest fiancée, the twenty-something Missy Crider. Says the often-Oscar-nominated Woods (married twice, engaged occasionally): 'The only two things I ever demand of anyone is that they never hit me and they never lie to me. The relationship is over the second that happens.'" Woods's age, by the way, was fifty.

Woods's professional philosophy is still: "Filmmaking, like sex, isn't a polite enterprise. It involves a lot of mess, sweat, and tears, and the bottom line is, if somebody ain't screamin,' you're not doin' your job." Potential costars beware.

As for Sean Young, the usual progression of getting older has impacted on her career as a romantic leading lady. Not to mention the Cat Woman and James Woods fallout. Young was interviewed for *Sex, Stupidity and Greed*—"Concerning your attempts to get the Cat Woman role, you read about male stars doing zany shit all the time, and *they're* presented as adorable and wacky." Sean replied, "That's true. I really can't say I have an anti-man thing, but what I find is what I call the Weenie World.

"But I also say, life is long, and how much love have I shared? . . . Hollywood is one of those places I try to avoid because those people don't love themselves, they don't know how to *find* it." Young now lives in Arizona with her kids and has her own production company, occasionally appearing in a Hollywood picture to bankroll her own films. She feels Hollywood has become too much about money and anything-for-a-hit-movie. "These deal-makers have hiked all the costs up—it's gone from 'Let's make movies' to 'Let's have a pissing contest.'

"The main thing is to keep working, to have this body of work you can look back on." Her philosophy: "I'm into the long term." And as for the not entirely over past:

"I was really struggling at the time with being told I was crazy, and people believing this obviously insane asshole. It took a lot of wind out of my sails and I lost a lot of blood . . . . It was really hard to get it up when I was now getting breadcrumbs instead of the meal. And it was very disheartening. But I hung in there. I feel I'm a hard worker and everybody knew that, and it's okay that I had a flat period."

Babs Jabs

"I think her biggest problem is that she wants to be a woman and she wants to be beautiful, and she is neither." —Omar Sharif, who costarred with Barbra Streisand in her first movie, *Funny Girl* (1968)

"The trouble with Barbra is she became a star long before she became an actress. Which is a pity, because if she learned her trade properly she might become a competent actress instead of a freak attraction—like a boa constrictor." —Walter Matthau, second-billed to Streisand in her second film, *Hello, Dolly!*

"When we commenced *On a Clear Day You Can See Forever*, I had the mistaken impression that I was the costar. I was Miss Streisand's first leading man who can sing, even though this was her third musical. And I thought she was my leading lady, a partner. I doubt I will choose to work again in Hollywood." —French star Yves Montand, on Barbra in her third movie

"Once was enough."—Walter Scharf, film composer-arranger who worked on *Funny Girl* but declined two subsequent Streisand films

"Of course, she's very talented. But not as talented as she believes . . . . If you work with her, she gives the impression that she's doing you an invaluable favor."—Sir Cecil Beaton

"She's a real kvetch . . . always moaning about something or other, a really hard-to-please lady."—Peter Bogdanovich, who directed *What's Up, Doc?*

"Working with Barbra Streisand is pretty stressful. It's like sitting down to a picnic in the middle of a freeway."—Kris Kristofferson, *A Star Is Born*

". . . ego to the *n*th degree, and the sensitivity of a starving elephant."—Frank Pierson, who helmed Streisand's hit *A Star Is Born*

"Barbra is working on a tree—you know, only God and Barbra Streisand can make a tree."—songwriter Paul Williams, who with Streisand won an Oscar for the song *Evergreen*, from *A Star Is Born*

"Some people like her as a singer but not as an actress. I like her as a person—she has done many fine, caring things over the years. She is not as selfish as she's made out to be. Except as a performer; then it's me-me-me-me . . . the demon diva."—director Martin Ritt (*Nuts*)

"For a woman whose career was launched and maintained by gay men, she's been the next thing to homophobic until she discovered her only son is [openly] gay. Then she did a complete turnaround. I guess until it concerns her personally, it doesn't really matter to her . . . . Sometimes Barbra tries, and sometimes she's just trying . . . ."—Joe Layton, choreographer and musical director

"I'm the only man who was top-billed over Barbra Streisand . . . but she got $4 million despite it being a much smaller role . . . . Wouldn't you know, it was a flop and almost nobody saw it!" —Gene Hackman, *All Night Long*

"Streisand kept insisting I should be thin, I should look good . . . . Sometimes I wondered, Who is the leading lady here?"—Nick Nolte, on his *Prince of Tides* costar and director

"She's sort of tough to work for." —son Jason Gould, who played Barbra's son in *The Prince of Tides*

"Barbra Streisand was my opening act in Las Vegas. She was multi-talented from the start, but with the social instincts of a landlady. Barbra is interested in Barbra, and her only marriage that will survive is the one between her ego and her career."—Liberace

"My toughest job was being married to Barbra Streisand."—Elliott Gould

Bette vs. the Boys

"I directed some pretty tough customers, John Wayne, Clint Eastwood, and Ronald Reagan among them. But the toughest star I ever directed, in a film titled *Jinxed*, was Bette Midler." So said Don Siegel. Viveca Lindfors, the Swedish actress who was briefly married to sometime actor Siegel, felt, "Don was like many men . . . hated not being in control. He loved being a director, the big boss.

"And heaven forbid any actor, much less an actress, should stand up to him. The effrontery of such a performer!"

Bette Midler called *Jinxed* (1982) "the worst professional experience of my life. . . . It took me ages to recover from that, and I still can't believe what I went through." Not only did she have an antagonistic, outspoken director, but an adversarial costar, Ken Wahl, whom she'd picked and given his big break. She told *Rolling Stone* that the first words out of his mouth when he met his leading lady were, "I want you to know, I hate niggers and faggots." Midler lamely explained, "I had no idea why he said that, because we had neither of those in our picture."

Wahl was unhappy that a female star had creative control over the movie he had agreed to be in. Bette's first film had been *The Rose*, for which she was Oscar-nominated, then a concert film, and then the aptly titled *Jinxed*. Bette also picked director Siegel, and like many stars offered screenplay input, which seemed to offend Siegel, who had gotten involved in some blowups with John Wayne, helming Wayne's last movie, *The Shootist*. "She didn't trust me, I don't think," he later

allowed. "I think she's very insecure," which many stars are, even the more wooden ones (Siegel directed Clint Eastwood in *Dirty Harry*). "I don't like actors to think they can direct," said Siegel. Viveca Lindfors eventually admitted, "Bette Midler must not have known what a hard case Don could be . . . or she believed she was up to fighting him."

Sexism, according to many on the scene, played a big part in the discord. "Bette was nervous, yes. She was all business," volunteered friend Kenny Sascha. "She was following up her debut movie and at the beginning of her screen career. She is a perfectionist, and she wanted it to be as good as possible."

Bette had commented on Ken Wahl's "animal magnetism" and thought they could share on-screen chemistry. But Wahl called her "hard" and informed the press that the only way he could "force himself into kissing Midler on-camera was to pretend that he was kissing his dog." He complained that the person in charge was Midler, not Don Siegel. But after all, she had director approval. "She believed it would be a collaboration," said Sascha. "Siegel thought it would be just him giving orders, and the 'girl,' as he always called her, meekly following them."

"A man can yell on the set," stated Bette. "Men do yell on sets, it's not unusual. But let a woman yell . . . ." One particular male studio executive sided consistently with Siegel, but United Artists vice president of production Anthea Sylbert noted, "Everyone got into the habit of blaming everything on [Bette]."

She declared that there hadn't been so much talk of diva/director antagonism since Barbra Streisand made her screen bow. Sylbert said that Siegel's contention that Midler was ordering retake after retake—as

Bette Midler

had been reported with Streisand on *Funny Girl*—was untrue: "The dailies were consistently wonderful . . . . [Midler] is an extremely hard worker and conscientious . . . . We're talking about a director who spent most of his career dealing with men . . . . There may have been resentment for a woman having some kind of power."

Viveca Lindfors added, "Don was toward the end of his career. I think he felt he was entitled to an unrealistic amount of respect." Bette also liked more rehearsal than Siegel or Wahl did. Said Midler, "I was trying to make the best movie I could, and I was resented for it. When somebody gives you that much money to make a picture, you can't short-change them. But these people, there wasn't a single one of them who wasn't out to stiff the studio—they're lazy and uncommitted, and they resent you for being so square. They didn't want to work that hard."

Eventually she disclosed that the director had "*slugged* me! We were filming a scene he didn't want to do . . . . We started to fight over it. It got pretty ugly. He started calling me names, and he jumped out of his trailer and I followed

him. His wife—she's very large, about six feet tall—grabbed me because I was getting ready to haul off and hit him. She held me from behind, and instead of me hitting him, he hauled off and hit me. I was livid. It was terrible, just traumatic."

Midler claimed most of the crew didn't like Siegel either. "Part of the set was a dungeon with an entrance from above and very little room underneath. One day the crew pushed him into it, locked it, and went to lunch."

When shooting was finished, Siegel and Wahl announced they would never work with Midler again. They kept bad-mouthing her, and she threatened to sue. Her lawyer stated, "My client has been more cooperative than anyone has a right to be. She waived her overtime . . . . I don't understand why Siegel is on this vendetta." As a director and an industry veteran, he could better afford to keep criticizing Bette. Wahl soon ceased, eventually starring in the TV series *Wiseguy*, where his hard, negative attitude became common knowledge. A potential star, attractive on the outside, he seemed to sabotage his own career, leaving the series and becoming involved with substance abuse and reported violence, today a faded non-star.

Bette was haunted by articles like "Trouble on the set of *Jinxed*? You can *Bette* on it." Negative publicity hurt the film, which lost $20 million for the studio and stalled Midler's movie career until her Disney comeback. Siegel kept talking: "If I could have my name taken off [the film] I would. I wish to God that I hadn't made it. There were many things I expressly wanted to do but they were all blocked by those two women who work there," including UA president Paula Weinstein. He added that Bette "wasn't happy with how she looked, though the cinematographer did a good job." As for her rewriting certain scenes, he complained, "All this from a girl who made two movies, one of them a bomb."

Columnist Marilyn Beck called *Jinxed* "a crushing defeat for Bette, because flawed as [it] might be, it is not bad enough to deserve the whipping that it is receiving." Bette claimed a nervous breakdown after *Jinxed*. "I was sick for a good three months . . . . I couldn't get out of bed. I just cried for weeks on end." But for a year, she didn't talk against her director and leading man. "I couldn't

believe they would bite the hand that fed them—our movie! Our movie that we worked so hard on!"

It was two years before Midler, suddenly labeled "difficult"—unlike Siegel or Wahl—was even offered a secondary movie role. She remembered, "I kept thinking, If I can just get through one more day—one more day of having to face them and their awful hatred . . . . I had always been 'one of the boys.' I never thought about being a woman in this business. For me it was always, This is how it is, and if you don't like it, goodbye.

"A lot of times during the women's movement, I would think, what's all the fuss about? If you're smart, you go in and say what you want and that's that. Well, that's *not* that. This picture opened my eyes to the world. I said to myself, I'm not the only woman who has gone through this." Bette later formed All Girls, her own production company. And like the Sondheim song says, she's still here.

SUPREME RIVALRY:
Diana Ross

"Diana [Ross]'s attitude has earned her the nickname of Miss Cute. I noticed
Diana standing in the wings watching us [a young Gladys Knight & the Pips] I
knew trouble was brewing . . . . The next day the word came down from Motown
that we were yanked from the tour."—Gladys Knight, in her 1997 memoirs

"I was far from the biggest celebrity visiting [Diana Ross] in her dressing room
[after a concert]. There was a very famous actress, trying to be gracious, and the way
Diana snubbed her was embarrassing for me and everyone else in the room. I've never
seen anything like it, and I don't believe there's any excuse for it."—James Coco

I have forgiven Mary . . . but I no longer consider her a friend," wrote Diana Ross
in her 1993 memoirs, referring to former Supreme Mary Wilson and her tell-all
book *Dreamgirl—My Life as a Supreme*, which became a 1986 best-seller and
yielded a 1990 sequel. "Dealing with Mary Wilson's book was a journey in
which lightness triumphed over darkness. I was depressed for a while," noted
Diana, who sighed, "I had to allow our friendship to fade away."

"Diane Ross does not have the gift of friendship," opined Michael Peters, who
choreographed Michael Jackson's *Thriller* video. "I give Diane credit for going a
very long way on relatively little . . . . She's exciting for audiences, but not for the
people who thought they were her friends." Peters used Diana's real first name, as
did Mary Wilson throughout her books, which was said to have infuriated the
Detroit diva who remade her image from lucky girl out of the Brewster housing
projects into predestined entertainment goddess.

"My story has often been referred to as classic 'rags to riches,' but . . . the
Rosses were never raggedy," she wrote in *Secrets of a Sparrow*. If her rise wasn't
raggedy, it was described by many who were there as very pushy. Show biz chronicler Penny Stallings stated that "Diana Ross never stopped in the name of love or
anything else when it came to trampling over the other Supremes to grab the spotlight." After Diane moved to Mary Wilson's neighborhood from Alabama, the two

The Supremes (*left to right*): Florence Ballard, Mary Wilson, and Diana Ross

became sort of friends. Mary later said, "Though I didn't know her well, I admired her enthusiasm about things."

Another neighbor was Florence Ballard, one of twelve children, nicknamed Blondie because of her relatively light hair and skin. She was also much bustier than Diane and Mary, and when she was a teenager she was raped and suffered what she described as "mild paranoia and indecision about my singing career." The consensus was that Flo was the best singer of the three, while Diane had the most commercial sound and definitely the most drive. Flo, a year older than Mary and Diane (both born in 1944), explained, "Some of the times, I thought they were just kids, and sort of taking this girl group thing a bit too far."

In 1959 Flo and Mary formed a singing quartet called the Primettes. When one girl departed, Mary talked Flo into accepting Diane into the group. Florence, who'd instigated the foursome, wasn't sure. "Mary liked her better than I did, singing-wise." Though she had pressure at home to devote less time to music and more to her education, Flo stuck it out and the group evolved into the three-member Supremes. "Luckily, [none] of us fell in love with a boy who was a pimp or a gang member. The girls who did ended up in trouble."

The Primettes had auditioned for Motown founder Berry Gordy, but to no avail. However, Diane got an office job and began to cultivate an incipient relationship with Gordy. It would turn the tide in her favor. "She learned about the business and how the power builds up by just being there and keeping her big eyes wide open," said Marvin Gaye. Diane persuaded Gordy to let her group sing background now and then. Finally, he reluctantly signed the Supremes, a name devised by Flo. But when Gordy chose Diane—by then "Diana" like the goddess of the hunt—as lead singer, Mary and Flo were disappointed (for some time, Mary believed they'd eventually get to share the lead) and Flo was hurt. She later reflected, "I think I could have been an opera singer. If I only had more training." She was known as a fine soprano. "As it was, none of us learned to read music."

The trio was not an instant success, and was dubbed the No-Hit Supremes by detractors. As they spent more time together, they became friendlier. Said Mary, "Diane was always very intense about things. When she wanted to go, she wanted to go, and I enjoyed being caught up in the enthusiasm." She added, "Even at that age, I could see that Diane was trying to build up her own self-confidence. Her haughtiness was just a front; deep down, she believed that she wasn't as pretty as the other girls. She craved attention, and in her attempts to get it, she could seem almost ruthless. Sometimes she would throw a childish tantrum." Mary explained that when, say, Diana criticized her or Flo in public, being "lady-like" was then deemed more important than trying to call her on her faux-pas or settle the score.

Rivalry reared its ugly head when Mary became engaged and "Diane began dropping hints" that she wanted Mary's man. "Diane was one to covet anything that belonged to anyone else, and as we got older, those things could include men." Diane, said Mary, would complain that other girls didn't like her, and treated her badly. At first she sympathized, later wondering if Diana's treatment was the result of an overly aggressive, competitive manner. One reason the infighting between Diana and what became the-other-two didn't come to light was Mary and Flo's fear that negative publicity would curb the group's success or even split it up.

By 1964, the girls, two of them barely twenty, earned $300,000, and in 1965 appeared on over two dozen TV shows. Each girl bought her family a house, all three on the same Detroit street.

The 1966 rumors of trouble within the Supremes were too widespread to ignore. But mostly they had to do with Florence and the after-effects of the rape. She had been a virgin, and the knife-wielding rapist a boy she'd known socially. Friends said Flo became increasingly cynical and afraid. "The man who raped Flo killed part of her that night," wrote Mary. "My friend was never the same again." Flo, who had planned on becoming a nurse and whose voice had made her feel special, was growing disgusted with her diminished status as a backup singer to Diana Ross, especially as she had founded the Primettes and then the Supremes. When it became Diana Ross & the Supremes, she apparently decided that continuing in the same well-paid rut was no longer worth it.

Diana would recall, "It got to be too much for her," ignoring the slaps Flo's ego had taken en route. "She wouldn't show up for recording sessions. She wouldn't show up for the gigs . . . . Yes, she was drinking . . . . But the problems were mainly in her head. She was tired. She didn't love what she was doing. She wanted out. Florence was buying a lot of furs and fancy cars, but she wasn't having any fun."

Berry Gordy, said most insiders, didn't show enough compassion or patience with Flo. Instead, he issued ultimatums. When he proposed replacing her, Mary and Diana protested, and Flo, when she found out, was bitterly disillusioned and hurt. In time, her absences and disorientation threatened the Supremes' future. She was increasingly seen not just as a third wheel but a liability. She wrote to Diana and Mary that she was leaving the group for good, which she did in the summer of 1967. She was replaced by Cindy Birdsong, but by then she could have been replaced by almost anyone, for the two in the background—"& the Supremes"— were little more than a backdrop for Diana Ross. Sometimes they didn't even sing on her songs.

Soon after quitting, Florence married, then had twin daughters in 1968, then a third daughter. Reportedly asked half-jokingly by a friend if she'd like her girls someday to form a singing trio, she answered, "No, sir! I love all my girls." Flo and husband divorced, and she was left career-less with three children to support. Rumors had it that she lived in a dilapidated apartment, was on welfare, and spent her days watching TV with her kids and mother. Two years after leaving her group, she determined to come back as a solo. She signed with ABC Records, but her few singles did poorly, and in 1971 she sued Motown for $8.7 million, charging that she hadn't been paid any royalties since her departure. Motown claimed that Ballard had accepted a sizable cash settlement at the time in exchange for relinquishing future claims. Flo lost the suit.

In 1975 the rumors made it into print. The former glamour girl, bloated and lethargic, was indeed living on welfare. She told the press, "I've been through so much . . . so much anguish over so many things. Now I just let things happen. I hope things will turn out all right, but I just don't know." Stories said she'd been working as a maid before returning to welfare. The publicity got her some job offers, but she lost her nerve. "Flo knew if she went back [on stage], everyone would be staring and inspecting her," said R&B singer Charles Brown. "Her looks, her voice, the whole way she acted, everything would be under a magnifying glass."

Mary and Diana contacted Flo during the publicity swirl, offering help. Flo still had her pride, and refused. She died of a heart attack in 1976, the year after Motown moved from Detroit to Los Angeles. Mary and Diana were shocked, saddened, and angered. "I'll be damned if I'm going to end up like Flo," said Mary. "She had it all, and she threw it away," said Diana. "She quit the Supremes, we didn't quit her . . . . Florence was very important in my life, but I'm not dead. She did this to herself." Berry Gordy did not attend the funeral, which Mary Wilson arranged and which many reports said was upstaged by Diana Ross. "She was grief-stricken," said Charles Brown. "But not so much [that] she wasn't about to show everyone that she was the biggest star at the funeral, and the champion survivor. She stole the show like a . . . what's the opposite of a shrinking violet?"

After Diana's impromptu speech at the services, which infuriated Mary, mourners filed out as the organist played "Someday We'll Be Together." Mary commented bitterly that this "Diana Ross & the Supremes" hit—their much publicized last one—was one that neither she nor Flo had sung on. After the stars arrived for the less public burial at the cemetery, Mary realized "Diane wasn't there. Regardless of what had passed between us, we were the only two people who had shared Flo's greatest moments. For that reason alone, Diane should have been there. But she was gone."

★ ★ ★

While Diana was working her way to the top, she was gaining more enemies and adversaries. "If ever there was a queen bee, it's her," stated singer Carmen McRae. "She'll defer to men or flirt with them or ignore them. With other women, she'll ignore them or arch her back like a cat." Post-Supremes, Mary Wilson revealed, "Over the years, Diane's spats with Mary Wells, Gladys (Horton), Dee Dee Sharp, Brenda Holloway, and especially Martha Reeves were company knowledge." If Diana was asked about her fights and feud-lets, she'd say, "They're picking on me." Mary disagreed: "Once when Mary Wells suggested helpfully that Diane wear a girdle on-stage, Diane flew off and started insulting her."

Other Motown acts resented the trio because of Diana's direct line to Berry Gordy, who fathered her first child—she too had three daughters, and later two sons by her second, very rich Norwegian husband. For years, her first-born was credited to husband Robert Silberstein, a Hollywood PR man and son of a wealthy garment manufacturer. How had they met? For years, Diana said *shopping*, later advising reporters that "how we met is just something we don't discuss with other people." As for Gordy, he made it known that though he loved Diana, marriage was out. Her biographer Randy Taraborelli noted that Gordy was aware that living with Diana would not be easy.

Mary was often caught in the middle. As a Supreme, she had to outwardly side with Diana's statements and actions. Though Diana could disagree with Gordy, Mary could not. "He believed that artists should never be allowed to think for themselves . . . he just thought they should stick to making music." Marvin Gaye pointed out, "Diana always said, 'Do what Berry says.' But sometimes she didn't . . . . But when the other girls would get out of line, Diana'd be the one to go tell Berry what was going on behind his back."

Gladys Knight later disclosed, "[The Supremes] had an aura of class that made them more of a lady group than a girl group. Off stage, it was a bit of a different story . . . . The first time we performed with them . . . they weren't headliners . . . . I shared a dressing room with the three of them and I could see how Florence and Mary were very close and caring of each other while it seemed that Diana already considered herself to be above them as a performer." Knight noted that if a Supremes performance didn't go smoothly, Diana would blame her fellow performers afterward. "Minutes later, though, . . . Diana was back in character, poking her head out of the sunroof of their car, giving the star wave, showing that famous 'stretch-limo' smile."

The next time Knight encountered Ross and company, it was Diana's act and "Diana was still as competitive and driven as ever." Ross had Gladys and her Pips pulled from the Motown tour: "Diana had seen the enemy and it was us. As the headliner, she wasn't about to have an opening act outshine her." Gordy didn't hide the truth when the unlucky group returned to Detroit. He chuckled, "I hear you were giving my act a hard time."

Some insiders believe Diana was insecure. As Gladys put it, "She [was] not the most talented of the trio or, for that matter, the cutest." A genuine talent like Martha Reeves, whose backup group was the Vandellas, may have seemed threatening to the ambitious woman who eventually ordered most everyone to "call her Miss Ross." British singer Dusty Springfield was a fan of Reeves, and told the UK music press in the late sixties, "She should have been farther along than she is now. But . . . it's not always a question of talent. It's also company politics and a question of who your rivals are." Springfield helped introduce Reeves to British audiences. In the 1980s she apprised *Music Maker*, "You have to remember that most of us didn't think being a [female] singer could last forever . . . . I think a few of us like Barbra Streisand or Diana Ross were planning for the long term, about remaining a singer and becoming an actress.

"But most of us imagined, somewhere in the back of our minds, that it would all be over by forty, with most of the girls choosing to have a husband and children."

She may have looked to the long term, but Diana Ross was often unforgiving of what she perceived as insults here and now. She was also sensitive about her being skinny at a time when fuller figures were more fashionable. Gladys Horton of the Marvelettes once made a comment, "Oh, her dress looks like a nightgown!" Diana tried to get Flo riled: "Did you hear what she said? She said our dresses look like nightgowns!"

"Diane, I didn't say *their* dresses—I said *your* dress!" clarified Horton.

Mary Wilson remembered, "Later that evening, as we were leaving the theater, Gladys was helping a little blind boy named Lee across the street. She was headed for the station wagon we all shared on the tour, and Diane was sitting behind the wheel. The minute Diane saw Gladys, she pulled out, hit the gas, and stopped just a few feet short of Gladys and Lee. Gladys left Lee standing in the street and ran over to the car screaming, 'Go on and hit me!' Diane gave Gladys the finger, rolled up the window, and sped off."

The next day, Diana apologized, under pressure from both Berry Gordy and her formidable mother Ernestine.

"We all heard horror stories," confessed Charles Brown, who in the early nineties toured with Bonnie Raitt, who "rediscovered" him. "Especially Diana against Martha Reeves, 'cause she and the Vandellas went higher than the Supremes did—at first." Why didn't the stories see the light of print? Gender and race. Flo explained, "With the Supremes it was always 'best foot forward.' We couldn't goof off or make any trouble like, say, the Four Tops or the Temptations . . . . And all the little colored girls looked up to us." The Supremes had to be role models.

"Flo and I would get caught in the middle," said Mary, "and though we both liked all the Vandellas, our relationship with Martha was strained by her feuds with Diane [who] was in our group, and solidarity was crucial, right or wrong." In the Detroit area, Gordy and Motown were powerful enough to quash negative publicity, while nationally, the media didn't want to seem negative or possibly racist by publicizing the success-at-any-price behavior of one fast-rising black star.

Early on with the Supremes, Diana would sing her lead, then join Mary and Flo to record the background. As she grew away from them, she stopped singing background. Said Mary, "Besides being upstaged, Flo and I also felt that the records suffered; our three-part harmonies were so beautiful; we should have recorded more of them." Many felt that the higher the trio ascended, the bigger the slice Diana wanted for herself. Anthony Perkins, who costarred in Ross's second of three films, *Mahogany*, recalled, "This is not a person who shares . . . . At first she was impressed after she met me—'You were in *Psycho*, that movie's so famous!' The next day, I'm a competitor, and from then on it's her trying to make clear to *me* that I'm in *her* movie and I'd better not do anything to detract from her in our scenes together.

"I've heard people say that stardom spoiled Diana Ross, but in my experience people with her personality act like stars no matter what level or profession they're in."

Even when the two Supremes were relegated to the background, Diana's competitiveness did not diminish. On the contrary. Where the trio had usually worn matching gowns, Diana would check ahead of time on what Flo and Mary were wearing so she could wear something contrasting. "I'd lent her clothes of mine, often," said Mary, "but she began to refuse to lend me any of hers." The two resented that the woman they thought of as a lifelong friend was behaving like a superior. It took time for Mary to become aware that "our friendship was a means to an end, a license for Diane to behave exactly as she chose."

The pair's off-stage behavior came under increasing scrutiny from the diva, who felt they reflected on her soaring public profile. Mary was flabbergasted when, at a restaurant, Diana became very angry with her because she'd eaten too slowly. "Mary," she snapped, "you did that just to make us look bad." "I couldn't believe my ears, and the look on Diane's face was hilarious. Would someone deliberately eat slowly to make someone else look bad? I didn't think so."

When Cindy Birdsong joined the trio in Flo's place, Diana had one less longtime rival. A newcomer necessarily has to dance more carefully around the star turn. An anonymous friend of Birdsong's who is still in the business explains, "In public relations, secrecy is the preferred way . . . it's public relations that makes a star. When the three of them would be interviewed, Diana would answer most of the questions, even the ones not addressed to her. I was there, I saw it happen."

Flo recalled the time Diana said to a journalist that, yes, her real first name was Diana. "She'd come up with things, and the first we'd hear something would be with the rest of the public . . . things she and Berry came up with, instead of letting Mary and me know ahead of time, so we'd be there like bumps on a log and hear about it for the first time when [Diana] would open her mouth and make like royalty or something . . . . No question, she did become Berry's spokesman."

Motown publicity and Diana Ross had it that she'd "discussed" her going solo with "the girls." Mary says she first found out about it when a British journalist asked her how she felt about Ross's imminent departure. The question took Mary back in time to Berry's assuring her, "Changing the name doesn't really mean anything, except that you girls will be making twice as much money . . . . Now we have two entities: Diana Ross, and the Supremes." He added, "And I want you to remember, Mary—no matter what happens, I will always take care of you."

In 1969 Gordy decided to launch a massive publicity campaign for his new act, the Jackson Five. Gladys Knight and her brother Bubba had heard Michael Jackson and his brothers sing for them. She then "got on the phone to our manager at Motown. When it became apparent that the Jackson Five were going to be superstars, Berry Gordy decided their discovery should be credited to another one of his biggest stars . . . none other than Miss Cute, Miss Diana Ross." In the late 1980s, the myth that Ross had discovered the Jacksons would be exploded by

Diana's on-again, off-again friend Michael Jackson, who had instructed his chauffeur to call him "Miss Ross" but who wasn't as close to Diana as both had wanted the public to think.

Ross and Jackson became rivals once his stardom matched and then outstripped hers. Insiders said he felt she didn't pay him enough respect and was too competitive with him. Others said that at least Diana was upfront about her aggressiveness, unlike Michael, who usually maneuvered indirectly or behind the scenes. When Diana's second son by Arne Naess was born in 1988 (the first, ten months before, was named Ross), she invited Michael to the christening. He declined. The party was attended by a throng of Scandinavians while Diana had only one "personal acquaintance" there, according to author Randy Taraborrelli.

For whatever reason, Diana took Michael Jackson's declining her invitation hard. She pulled out of a Showtime cable-TV salute to Jackson; she'd been due to host, but suddenly refused to be involved in any capacity. Michael retaliated by editing her out of most of the "memory footage" of the two of them together. On the special, Motown executive Suzanne de Passe allowed that "it seemed like a good idea at the time," to credit Ross with the Jacksons' discovery. In the following clip, Ed Sullivan introduced Diana from the audience as their discoverer, "and she stood up and bowed graciously as everyone applauded," wrote Taraborelli. "The way Michael Jackson had this version edited made Diana Ross look like a liar. She had to be insulted."

★ ★ ★

In 1969 when Supreme Cindy Birdsong was kidnapped by her apartment building's maintenance man but escaped from him a few hours later, it was said that Berry Gordy felt the action was directed at him. "The whole thing about Motown being one big, happy family," says Cindy's music business friend, "was baloney. It worked. It was effective. No one dared contradict it. But it was dog eat dog there, and the bottom line was always money—and Diana Ross. Everyone else had to scramble . . . and keep waiting for the next hatchet to fall."

Diana Ross & the Supremes' final appearance occurred on January 14, 1970, at Las Vegas's Frontier Hotel. The theme song for the evening, which was packed with celebrities, Motown employees, and their families, was the ironically titled "Someday We'll Be Together" (background was sung by the Andantes, Motown's house background singers; even so, it became an anthem for Diana Ross *and* the Supremes). Before the show, Diana was in the wings; Mary and Cindy shared champagne by themselves in their non-star dressing room. Cindy commiserated about how hard it must be for Mary, who'd been with the group since its inception. She replied, "Hey, don't talk like this is a wake. Just because *she's* leaving doesn't mean we're dying. This is a happy night. The Supremes aren't dead."

As the pair left their dressing room, they passed Diana, who had been joined by Berry, around whose neck she had her arms, while he clutched her by the waist. They heard him telling Miss Ross, "You're a star, baby. This is your night. Forget about the girls."

Cindy looked at Mary, who said nothing but straightened her shoulders and moved on.

The performance, said people present, was just that: Diana playing hostess and dispenser of loving nostalgia and regretful parting. She totally dominated the evening. Ed Sullivan sent a telegram that was read by a senator from Nevada. It elicited raised eyebrows and suppressed guffaws by announcing that the success achieved by the three Supremes exemplified what could happen when individuals "working as a team" did so "without backstabbing and hypocrisy." Jean Terrell, the replacement for Diana Ross,

Diana Ross

was introduced while Diana smiled and cooed love and encouragement.

Cindy Birdsong later stated, "It was all acting—the smiles, the tears, all of it. Just acting. Afterwards, there was a big scene backstage, an argument over something I don't remember."

That night, at 3 a.m. in the morning, Mary Wilson got a phone call in her hotel room. It was Gordy, asserting, "I want to replace Jean." Half-asleep and totally unbelieving, she didn't reply. "Mary, you hear me? I want her *out*."

She realized he was serious. He ordered, "Wake up, damn it. This is important. I'm gonna replace her with Syreeta" (another Motown artist, Syreeta Wright).

"You can't do that. We just made the announcement about Jean. What happened?"

"Never mind what happened. Syreeta's a better singer anyway—sounds more like Diana. We'll just say we changed our minds."

Mary then said what most people in her place would have, but what most of Motown considered a fatal mistake. "No way! We want Jean in the group, so you can just forget it!" For emphasis, she added, "And that's final"—something maybe only Diana Ross could have said to Gordy without ill consequences.

"Fine, then," he began to shout. "You're on your own. I wash my hands of the whole goddamn group," and he slammed down the phone.

Before the Supremes finally disbanded in 1977, they enjoyed several hit records in spite of Gordy's "lack of interest in our career," as Mary put it. But nothing to compare with their success in the mid-sixties. In 1972 Cindy Birdsong left the group—returning later, then leaving again in 1976—and in 1973 Jean Terrell departed. When Mary Wilson went out as a solo act post-Supremes, she had to legally fight Motown for the right to billing as a former Supreme. Finally she lost that right.

Singing on her own again, admitted Mary, seemed strange. "It had taken ten years of singing 'oohs' and 'aahs' in the background for me to lose my confidence; it would take some time to get it back." As with the post-Diana Supremes, Mary found she was much more popular in Europe and Australia than on home ground. A critic in Sydney explained, "The cult of stardom is less established here than in the States, where the solo star who left behind her former mates is admired but those left out in the show biz cold are not. It's the American winner-take-all mentality."

Another prickly chapter was added to the Diana Ross & the Supremes saga in 1983, when Motown celebrated its twenty-fifth anniversary with an all-star reunion TV special. Of course, the business of show is about perception, not reality, so most of what happened the night of the taping was never seen by TV viewers, though it was written about at length by Mary Wilson and others. It was the first time in thirteen years that Wilson would share a stage with Ross and Birdsong. Mary and Cindy had decided to try and stand up to Diana during the reunion, but she had her own plans for taking center stage.

While Britisher Adam Ant was singing his version of the Supremes' first number one hit, "Where Did Our Love Go?," Diana slinked out onto the stage doing a bump and grind, wowing the audience. The surprised Ant was briefly caught off guard, but moved toward the superstar and danced along with her until she slinked off. Comments from the wings and audience included, "How could she just jump up there while someone else was performing?" and "I can't believe Diane would do that!" and "The Supremes were always so classy, why would she act like that?"

Then, while the Supremes clips were running, Diana walked solo up the aisle and onto the stage, tossing her white fox stole on the ground while she beamed during a standing ovation. Backstage, Richard Pryor teased, "Step on that fur, Mary!" and a female voice urged, "Kick it!" Diana did an emotional speech, then the very symbolic song "Someday We'll Be Together" filled the hall. First came Cindy, out to join Diana, and then Mary entered, "doing my slowest Detroit strut, just like we used to do in the Projects." The crowd applauded, and when Diana stared at Mary, she temporarily stopped singing, which gave Mary the chance to pick up the lead, though not for long, for then Diana introduced them. "This is Cindy Birdsong," and "*That's*," she pointed, "Mary Wilson."

Before the performance, Mary had instructed Cindy to follow her every move, as anything could happen. So when Diana took a few steps forward, Mary and Cindy, instead of hanging back behind the star, moved forward with her. Diana again moved forward, and so did her partners. On the third move forward in unison, "Diane suddenly turned and pushed me. The audience gasped. In a flash I saw something in her eyes that told me she knew she'd crossed the line. Of course, this was later cut from the tape." Richard Pryor, Smokey Robinson, and Billy Dee Williams were all rushed onto the stage before the song was half over, to distract from the potential fight.

Diana did not want to share the stage with an entire congregation, so before the next song, her "Reach Out And Touch (Somebody's Hand)," she yelled, "Stand back! Everybody stand back!" "I could tell she was angry, and she even tried to push people back, but there were too many of us, and we all pretty much ignored her."

Mary kept singing, then beckoned the audience to stand up. Diana made another speech, a tribute to Gordy. When she finished, Mary called out, "Berry, come on down!" but Diana wanted to be the one to invite the Motown boss on stage, and "The next thing I knew, Diane forced my left hand down, pushing the microphone away from my mouth. Looking me right in the eyes, she said loudly, 'It's been taken care of!' On the tape all you see of this episode is Diane turning around and calling out to Berry."

Once Gordy got on the stage, Diana hopped up and down on the edge like a child, waiting her turn to kiss him. He kissed or embraced several people. While he stood with Diana and the Supremes—who were never introduced as such—Ross stood behind him, "poking him in the head and pinching his rear end like she would," said Mary, "when we were teens."

When Gordy moved to Mary, he whispered in her ear, "You finally learned how to sing, huh?" referring to her temporarily taking the lead. "The next thing I knew, Diana ran to the back of the stage and climbed the orchestra platform, so that she was standing high above the rest of us." When the song ended and *Life* magazine's photographer began to take a group picture on stage, Diana "scurried down from her perch and pushed her way to the center of the stage. She grabbed for Stevie Wonder and kissed him. When the photo ran, sure enough, she was smack in the middle."

Diana's greed for the spotlight never abated over the years, but had never been so obvious. Mary later wrote, "In the earlier days, Diane would do things like this, but never in public . . . . But tonight of all nights, why did it have to be this way? This was to be a joyous reunion. Even people whose parting with Motown had been less than amicable had returned with nothing in their hearts but love . . . . Deep in my heart, I knew [the public] were anxious to see a cat fight. That Diane had so foolishly given them that satisfaction hurt me deeply. Her actions seemed to say that the Supremes were unimportant . . . . What a terrible way to end an evening, a career, a friendship."

Perhaps in response to comments that she seemed not to get along with women, Diana Ross wrote, "I'd love to have more girlfriends at this time in my life, but I guess I don't trust very easily."

Five years after the 1983 behind-the-scenes debacle of the reunion, Mary Wilson attended the ceremonies at the Waldorf-Astoria hotel when the Supremes were inducted into the Rock and Roll Hall of Fame, along with the Beatles, the Beach Boys, and others. The only other female celebrity present was Yoko Ono, accepting for the late John Lennon. Mary noted, "Diana Ross had decided that she was far too busy to even acknowledge the group that had made her a household word . . . . Since she left the group . . . she's gone out of her way to pretend that the Supremes never existed and that our phenomenal success was hers alone."

But much of the public remained fascinated with the Supremes, and when it came time to do the sequel to her tell-all book, Mary prefaced it with "The Supreme Answer" to her adversaries' neglect: "I cannot idly stand by as Diane, Motown, and Berry Gordy Jr. try to crush all I have worked so hard to preserve. Everywhere I go, people tell me what the Supremes meant to them, and I am gratified to know that we touched millions of lives. They remind me of what Diane and Berry seem to have forgotten: that the world first fell in love with *three* young black girls from the Detroit projects, not just one."

Divo vs. Divo:
DAVID BOWIE AND ELTON JOHN

David Bowie was the first big music star to come out in the early 1970s. First he said he was gay. Later he said he was bisexual and told *Playboy* that he and wife Angie had met when they were both seeing the same man. Later still, Bowie claimed he was heterosexual all along, prompting comments that he was the first celebrity ever to go back *in* the closet.

By contrast, Elton John didn't declare himself for the longest time. Nowhere as publicity-seeking as Bowie, he did fewer interviews, was less flamboyant—at first—and worked harder, eventually eclipsing Bowie as a singer, composer, and star. From the start, Bowie seemed inclined to jealousy, commenting for example that Elton's "Rocket Man" was a rip-off of his "Space Oddity." Mick Ronson, Bowie's famous guitarist, offered, "A lot of David's act is flash—the costumes, the glitter, the shock value . . . . When Elton began wearing the outlandish sunglasses, David thought he'd gone and copied him."

Doug Weston, Los Angeles club owner and founder of the Troubadour, said, "Elton took longer to hit because substance takes longer to recognize than mere dazzle. I think Elton's fancy threads are a cover-up for a guy who was never terribly handsome or thin, but his music has stood the test of time. Unlike Bowie's, really . . . . It didn't take long to see that this guy had the real goods."

Like many celebrities, Bowie had some respect for those who came before him. He became friends with Mick Jagger, a relationship that endured (*more* than friends, according to ex-wife Angela Bowie, whose divorce settlement entailed a gag order of ten years, ending with her 1993 tell-all book, *Backstage Passes*). By the mid-seventies when Elton had easily caught up with him, David was making public comments against him. One of the hottest—and perhaps most hypocritical— was when he labeled Elton "the Liberace, the token queen of rock . . . I consider myself responsible for a whole new school of pretensions—they know who they are. Don't you, Elton?"

It was apparently Bowie's way of trying to *out* John. Music chronicler Philip Norman wrote, "How Elton's [homosexuality] had not leaked out into the British press must count as a minor miracle of news management. Certainly, it was known to every national journalist who covered pop . . . . We find a parallel with the Beatles, whose human aspects were resolutely ignored by [journalists] . . . the stories that sold papers were about cuddly mop-tops, and so those were provided, whatever evidence might crop up to the contrary."

Elton's route was, on the surface, opposite to Bowie's: he gradually came out as bisexual, then wed a woman, later admitting that he'd been homosexual all along and the marriage had been a misguided attempt to change his sexual and affectional orientation. Elton rarely retaliated against Bowie's criticism, though he did crack, "The towel bills that David Bowie must run up dyeing his hair . . . ," and explained, "I try not to be bitchy, even though at times we're all bitchy in conversation. Saying it in print is another

Elton John

thing . . . . I didn't retaliate when Bowie said I was a token queen, even though he's had a couple of go's since. Because I know what's happened to him. I'll always remember going out for dinner with him and Angie when he was Ziggy Stardust. It was a fabulous evening, and over dinner he admitted to me that he always wanted to be Judy Garland, and that's the God's honest truth."

Keith Moon, drummer for the Who, felt, "David has more images than any singer, ever! He can be anybody, because at heart he's nobody." Long after he'd insisted to the mainstream press that he was heterosexual, Bowie informed gay *Out* magazine, "I don't think there was much ambiguity. I was fairly forthcoming about being bisexual." Singer Peter Allen stated, "Bowie wanted to be a star, period. Anything it takes. He got into movies, hoping to extend himself. Didn't work . . . . Elton knew he wasn't movie material, and except for that wonderful bit [as the Pinball Wizard] in *Tommy*, he's avoided them. But David's plugged on, from one film fiasco to another."

Beatles Battles:
M((ARTNEY VS. LENNON

Paul: John and Yoko are not cool in what they're doing.

John: If we're not cool, what does that make you?

Paul: I like . . . *Imagine*, but there was too much political stuff on the other albums.

John: So you think *Imagine* ain't political, it's "Working Class Hero" with sugar on it for conservatives like yourself!—McCartney and Lennon in Britain's *Melody Maker* magazine

Musically and popularly, the Beatles' central figures were John Lennon and Paul McCartney, whose union was harmonious in melodic terms. But their friendship wasn't as ideal as fans might have imagined. Lennon later revealed, "We were never really close . . . . We were working so hard and so long, that's all we were ever doing . . . . Ours was the sort of relationship I imagine soldiers develop during wartime. The situation forces them together, and they make the most of it."

Paul was more driven than John, who could go for periods without working. Beatles producer George Martin said, "Paul needs an audience, but John doesn't." Lyrically, the more talented was John. "I have the soul of a poet," he explained, "which is not necessarily what I'd wish on myself." Paul's tunes tended to be more commercial; "I don't think he's particularly proud of this," said Martin, who acknowledged that collabo-

rating with Lennon made McCartney try for deeper lyrics and more lasting material: "But for meeting John, I doubt Paul would have written 'Eleanor Rigby.'"

Early on, the individual Beatles were labeled by their fans, and John came to resent the "wonderful Paul and crazy John" image. Beatles biographer Peter Brown characterized the behind-the-scenes McCartney as "a control freak." When Yoko Ono became not only John's romantic but also professional partner, a resentful Paul told Lennon, "Either she goes or I go." John replied, "She's not going." Paul had also resented John's closeness to the Beatles' manager, Brian Epstein. "Brian was virtually the fifth Beatle," explains music columnist Joey Ferrario, "the mover and shaker. And Paul worried that somehow John might get the upper hand over the rest of them through 'Eppy.'" Much like the Ross/Supremes nightmare.

Beatles biographer Geoffrey Giuliano characterizes a McCartney tune as "bouncy, toe-tapping, family entertainment. Infectious, but largely one-dimensional and ultimately lyrically inconsequential." It was expected that post-Beatles, Paul would enjoy the greatest individual commercial success. But it was the Lennon-McCartney collaboration that made the Beatles musically immortal. Lennon's tunes were less upbeat but more penetrating, like the winsome "Julia" or the cynical "Glass Onion," versus Paul's "Ob-

La-Di, Ob-La-Da." Although Lennon's latter image seemed to connote drugs at times, it was McCartney who got famously drug-busted in Japan, and John who explained:

"There's been so much gobbledygook written about *Sgt. Pepper*. Even now I just saw Mel Torme on TV the other day saying that 'Lucy (In the Sky with Diamonds)' was written to promote drugs and so was 'With A Little Help from My Friends,' and none of them were at all."

Beatles legend has it that Ono, the wife who wouldn't stay in the background, was the catalyst who broke up the Fab Four. The reality was of course more complex; however sexism—and racism—did play a part. In 1971 John told the press, "They despised her. They insulted her and they still do . . . but I was always hoping they would come around . . . . They all sat there with their wives like a fucking jury and judged us . . . . Ringo was all right, so was Maureen, but [Paul and George Harrison] really gave it to us. I'll never forgive them . . . although I can't help still loving them either."

McCartney was the acknowledged businessman of the quartet, the one who worried most about sales and was the first to urge the group back into the recording studio. John became embittered when in late 1968 he and Yoko released their album *Two Virgins*, which would compete with the Beatles' White Album. Four years later, John said, "Paul and . . . all of them were in collusion to kill *Two Virgins*. They had meetings where Paul said, 'Let's kill it.'" John and Yoko's album peaked at number 124, while the White Album was a huge hit. The day it was released in Britain, November 21, Yoko endured a miscarriage with life-threatening complications.

When Paul left Jane Asher for American divorcée Linda Eastman, his fans didn't like it, due to her nationality and marital status (as with Wallis Simpson, who'd married England's former king). But fans—and fellow Beatles—were more upset when John paired with Yoko. Some celebrities were outright racist when talking about her, like Truman Capote: "I hate her—the Jap." Within eight days of each other, John and Paul got married, McCartney explaining, "I think we spurred each other into marriage.

Paul McCartney

[John and Yoko] were very strong together, which left me out of the picture, so then I got together with Linda and we got our own kind of strength. I think they were a little peeved that we got married first." Among celebrities, being first is inordinately important.

Lennon later admitted that his professional activities with Ono did drive a wedge between him and the other three. McCartney admitted, "I was beginning to get too producery for everyone. George Martin was the actual producer . . . ." John was disappointed with the shallow content of their latest offering, *Abbey Road*: "What was there to sing about?" he later asked. "Mean Mr. Mustard and Polythene Pam . . . . When I get down to it, I'm only interested in Yoko and peace." As an antidote to John's dissatisfaction, Paul suggested a 1969 tour; the Fab Four were already starting to go their separate ways, "but Paul would be the last to call it a day," says Joey Ferrario.

John abruptly informed Paul, "I think you're daft. In fact, I wasn't going to tell you, but I'm leaving the group. I've had enough. I want a divorce, like my divorce from Cynthia." It was agreed to keep the news under wraps, partly so not to hurt the potential sales of Paul's first solo album, *McCartney*. Paul wanted a release date that would conflict with the group's upcoming album, *Let It Be*. Soon, Paul wasn't speaking to his bandmates. Ringo Starr visited McCartney as an intermediary, but "[Paul] went completely out of control, prodding his fingers towards my face, saying, 'I'll finish you all now! You'll pay!' He told me to put on my coat and get out."

In conjunction with his solo debut, Paul revealed that the Beatles were disbanding—being the first to make the announcement and giving the impression that *he* was leaving. John was furious: "The Beatles were my fucking band. I put the band together, and I took it apart!" In 1964 he threatened to disband the group when Brian Epstein was offered £100,000 for it. "I told [Brian], 'If you sell, we'll never play again. We'll disband.' The funny thing was, when it was all over [in 1970], Paul wanted credit for breaking up the band. 'I'm leaving,' he kept saying. But he couldn't, because I had already left."

In 1986 McCartney allowed, "When I look back on it, it looks very hard and cold . . . . I think maybe the manner of doing it I regret now. I wish it had been a little kinder or with the others' approval."

March 11, 1970, marked the release of the Beatles' final single. When Paul sought to break officially with Beatles manager Allen Klein, he found he had to sue the group's company, Apple Corps Ltd., which meant suing The Other Three. It took almost five years for the split to become legal, but the lawsuits dragged on, and in 1988 when the Beatles (and the Supremes, the Beach Boys, and others) were inducted into the Rock and Roll Hall of Fame, a publicist announced that Paul wasn't attending (Yoko Ono accepted for her late husband, who had been fatally shot in 1980) because "[Paul] was still mad at George Harrison, Ringo Starr, and Yoko Ono, because of a pending lawsuit over royalties from the Beatles' former record company."

At the induction ceremonies at the Waldorf-Astoria, Beach Boy Mike Love put in his two cents: "I think it's sad that there are other people who aren't here, and those are the people who passed away [meaning John Lennon, Beach Boy Dennis Wilson, and Supreme Florence Ballard], but there are also . . . people like Paul McCartney, who couldn't be here because he's in a lawsuit with Yoko and Ringo . . . that's a bummer, because we're talking about harmony . . . in the world. It's also a bummer when *Miss* Ross can't make it."

Soon after the split, George Martin commented on the fans' how-could-they-split-up hysteria: "They don't say it's amazing how long they lasted together." Fans also mourned the end of the Lennon-McCartney collaboration and their friendship. The two had once bond-ed through their music, the loss of their mothers, and their global success—which also drove them apart. "Because they were so often teamed as a pair," notes Joey Ferrario, "they were positioned as rivals. *One* of them had to stand out," as indeed in any group, be it duo, trio, or quartet. Paul was said to resent John's image as poet and number one Beatle, and later his involvement with peace and equality causes, which many celebrities with a social conscience supported in the 1960s. All the more so when John and Yoko's activism made them media dar-lings: in Paul's song "Too Many People," he commented on John's outside inter-ests, later acknowledging, "He'd been doing a lot of preaching and it got up my nose a bit. That [lyric] was a little dig at John and Yoko."

By the late sixties, their rivalry had gone quite public, with Paul of all people calling John a "maneuvering swine" and John comparing Paul to Englebert Humperdink with his ballads. McCartney was unhappy when Lennon beat him to the solo charts in 1971 with his hit "Imagine"—in the Beatles' early days, John's output had also dominated the charts. Paul got a chance to shine when John took a five-year hiatus to stay home with Yoko and enjoy raising his second son—and first with her—Sean. It was said that just as Yoko influenced John to become less conformist, Linda McCartney influenced Paul to become more bour-geois. Furthermore, much of Paul's solo success came when he teamed with the likes of Elvis Costello, Danny Laine, Stevie Wonder, and Michael Jackson. Writer Geoffrey Giuliano feels, "It was his jeal-ousy of John Lennon that motivated much of his great work."

Today, many of the best remembered Beatles' songs are those from Paul McCartney. However *the* Beatle remains John Lennon, who became not just suc-cessful—as did Paul—in his own right, but a symbol of an era and a generation, and of striving for something more than banal fame and fortune. How tragically ironic that John's life was shot away in New York City by a fame-craving and shallow fanatic.

BORIS KARLOFF MEETS BELA LUGOSI

"Poor Bela. Sometimes it seemed as if the fates were conspiring against him."
—*Boris Karloff*

"Those damned English! They all think they're so superior."—*Bela Lugosi*

Never did two stars so thoroughly dominate a film genre, or for so long, as Bela Lugosi and Boris Karloff. The kings of horror became world-famous in the early 1930s as, respectively, Dracula and Frankenstein's monster. Each served a long apprenticeship as an actor, and both broke through thanks to luck. Lugosi had starred on the stage as Bram Stoker's *Dracula*. But the film version would almost certainly have starred Lon *Man of a Thousand Faces* Chaney had he not died prematurely of cancer in 1930.

Even then, Lugosi wasn't second choice to enact the undead Transylvanian count. However, the Hungarian eventually nailed the screen role, at a modest fee, and with it global stardom along with lifelong typecasting. His heavy accent and limited acting ability (at least in English) made almost all his roles seem Dracula-like.

Ironically, it was Lugosi's ego that allowed the Englishman born William Henry Pratt to become renowned as simply "Karloff," as he was sometimes billed after playing the ultimate figure of terror in the 1931 classic *Frankenstein*. Lugosi was first choice for the monster role, having triumphed the year before as *Dracula*. But Lugosi, the stage veteran who'd portrayed Jesus Christ and diverse characters like Armand in *The Lady of the Camellias*, declined the role in a huff. For the nameless monster, a creature composed of partial corpses, had no lines. "Anyone at all can play this *thing*," he reportedly explained. "I am an *actor!*" Lugosi also felt that the requisite heavy makeup, padding, and elevator boots would render any actor playing the monster virtually unrecognizable.

Karloff, who'd played dozens of small, usually villainous roles in silent and then talking pictures, gladly shouldered the assignment. *Frankenstein* was at least as big a hit as *Dracula* and today is universally considered the better film, due in large measure to its director James Whale, an imaginative and flamboyant Englishman. It was the first horror movie to engender a sequel, the 1935 classic *The Bride of*

Frankenstein, deemed by many the best horror film ever made, and also helmed by Whale, also starring Karloff. When *Dracula* spawned two sequels, *Dracula's Daughter* and *Son of Dracula*, neither included Bela Lugosi, whose post-*Dracula* success waned rapidly and whose subsequent films were mostly forgettable.

By contrast, Karloff soon made another, different classic, *The Mummy*, which in the 1940s yielded several sequels, none featuring Boris, who was busy elsewhere. Karloff acted in several prestige projects in Britain and the United States, and eventually was in much demand for recordings. Meanwhile, Lugosi quickly developed a reputation for taking any old project so long as he was placed stage-center. The more lines and screen time, the better.

The crux of the difference between Lugosi's and Karloff's cinematic fortunes was that Bela truly was a foreigner, with a thick accent and wavering command of English, but "Boris" was an Englishman with an upper-class accent and a refined, eerie lisp ideal for offbeat and sinister roles. At the time, Hollywood idolized British culture. Tinseltown's stars were trained to shed their regional American accents and acquire a pseudo-English sound. Brooklynite Barbara Stanwyck was taught to say "good ahfternoon," and nearly all non-British star surnames were anglicized so that the actors wouldn't be correctly identified with their German, Italian, Slavic, etc., backgrounds.

Karloff's daughter Sara recalls that the language difference was crucial to her father's taking quick and permanent precedence over his rival. Bela Lugosi was born Bela Blasko (he adapted his surname from his home town of Lugos). In addition, the American attitude at the time toward Slavs, particularly Russians, was that they were a semi-savage, war-like "race," less cultured and accomplished than Mediterranean and especially Nordic people.

Ironically, the English Mr. Pratt took the Russian name Boris Karloff when he became an actor. Back in Hollywood's heyday, actors were seldom asked anti-image questions, so interviewers and actors alike avoided the topic of real names. Over time, Karloff alluded in passing—the key word being *passing*—to having some Russian ancestors. Sara Karloff, however, has stated on TV that she knows of no Russian ancestors on either side of her father's family.

But William Pratt had a secret, and during the racist climate of the time he had to hide it. He was of part-Indian descent, from at least one British ancestor who'd served in the "Raj" and married locally. Since Hollywood deprecated all heritages other than European, part-Indian individuals with high aspirations had to, as it were, closet themselves. Merle Oberon passed off her Indian mother as her maid when

Bela Lugosi and Boris Karloff

she went to England to become an actress. After her mother died there, she buried her in an unmarked grave, then headed for Hollywood, ever after claiming to be from Tasmania, a conveniently remote spot off southernmost Australia.

Family photos of "Boris Karloff" and his brothers revealed the unmistakable Indian heritage. As he grew older, he looked increasingly like an Indian gentleman of darker coloring. To explain away his exotic looks, Pratt devised a Russian moniker reflecting a remote heritage, yet categorically European. Like Oberon, he spoke flawless English which in the United States ended curiosity; it was widely believed that if somebody *sounded* like that, they must be, well, kosher.

Karloff was never an avid interviewee—the rather English-challenged Lugosi was far more willing to speak to the press—and rarely spoke of his private life. About the only strong opinions he ever expressed were his dislike of Method acting and the term "horror movie." He felt it connoted a "horrible movie" and much preferred "terror movie"—but the media and fans didn't follow his suggestion.

Karloff and Lugosi both excelled at playing brutes, and their "sadistic"-sounding names suited their images. Blasko legally became Bela Lugosi, but Pratt never legally became Boris Karloff—nor a U.S. citizen. Lugosi did, rather noisily, in keeping with his theatricality and what some have called his right-leaning politics. (Charles Chaplin remained a British subject and incurred much media wrath—from columnists Walter Winchell and Hedda Hopper—primarily because of his left-wing politics. Karloff was guardedly apolitical but did staunchly support Britain during World War II.)

As thespians, the difference between the rivals was that Boris could also enact gentle and kindly men, particularly as he aged. Lugosi on the screen was invariably a character one didn't trust. Neither actor was initially sought for non-horror roles; Universal, which survived the Depression and near-bankruptcy thanks to its horror cycle of films, saw both men as repeating money machines. But Karloff created a diversity of terrific characters, and when the horror cycle dried up—partly due to Britain's anti-violence ban against such movies—he was able to find employment as a varied character actor.

Karloff moved into historic and costume films, also onto the stage, as in *Arsenic and Old Lace,* where his name was part of the script, or *Peter Pan,* as Captain Hook. In golden-age Hollywood, an English accent enabled an actor to essay any historical nationality. For instance, most Imperial Romans had English accents, yet no one would have cast a Hungarian actor as an English king, a Caesar, or an Egyptian pharaoh.

Arthur Lubin, director of the Karloff-Lugosi picture *Black Friday,* explained, "If you said the name Boris Karloff, Hollywood people would first think of ghouls and horror. But then most would concede he could do other things. But if you mentioned Bela Lugosi, Hollywood said or thought only one word: *Dracula.*"

In later years Karloff admitted that he avoided playing vampires. "I don't like blood," he grinned. Said Lugosi of *his* most famous role, "Perhaps I played him too well." He so incarnated the vampire that no one since has truly taken over his cape or mantle. By comparison, the Frankenstein monster has been played by umpteen actors, including Bela. As the kindly, charming Boris grew older, he became less closely linked to the monster. Bela, on the other hand, kept wearing the Dracula cape at every opportunity and was even buried in it. This only reinforced the stereotyping, also recalling the ex-star's glory days once he was reduced to such vehicles as *Bela Lugosi Meets a Brooklyn Gorilla* (1952; the British title was *Monster Meets the Gorilla*).

★ ★ ★

Because Lugosi became a star first, and due to Karloff's rapid stardom, a rivalry was inevitable. The two were constantly compared and rated in the business and by the fan magazines. Besides horror, what did they have in common? Each actor had but one child in an era when big families were the rule. Each man was the youngest in his family, and as many youngest offspring do, rebelled against paternal authority. Bela, born in 1882 and Boris's senior by five years, longed to be an actor. His father violently objected, so the teenager ran away for good.

Billy, as Karloff's family called him, objected to following his father and elder brothers into a career and life of diplomacy, so he headed for Canada to pursue his theatrical bent (Lugosi made silent movies in Germany before approaching Hollywood). Both men had more than one wife, but Karloff was reticent, even

Bela vs. Boris

"Bela Lugosi was a very domineering sort. He resented Boris Karloff's manners and culture . . . and the way bigger, better roles came his way. Boris was a true professional. I think Bela was more of a ham."—Vincent Price

"Boris Karloff! He acts with his eyebrows . . . and he lisps. In his own language, he lisps!"—Hungarian Bela Lugosi

"I don't think poor Bela even knew what typecasting was. I don't think it concerned him. Until the money stopped coming in. Then he believed that the system had done it to him."—Boris Karloff

"All I know about that Lugosi-and-Karloff feud is they hated each other's guts. Except that Boris Karloff was successful enough to pretend he didn't give a rat's ass."—John Carradine

"Mr. Karloff wants to be liked by everyone. But he is ambitious also, oh! . . . We never see each other outside the studio. It is for me already a big sacrifice, working together."—Bela Lugosi

"[Lugosi] used to admit that he beat his wives and once even bragged about it. He said he suspicioned his then-wife of having an affair and that . . . he would strangle her if he found out it were true. I was appalled and made it known. He laughed that demonic cackle of his and shrugged, 'Ah, the English!'"—Boris Karloff

secretive, about his private life and past. Nearly everyone agreed that he was a gentleman on the set and off. A shy, modest man, he treated all women like ladies as a matter of course.

Lugosi was much more the ladies' man: flirtatious and domineering, more apt to categorize women as "virgins" or "whores." At least one wife alleged that Bela used to beat her regularly. (There were five wives.) Wife Lillian, the fourth, has described how Bela often asserted himself "head of the family . . . he was this, he was that." Screenwriter Curt Siodmak (*Black Friday*) told the press Lugosi "was always out for himself. His career, his libido. Didn't believe in public service. Like most people drawn to Hollywood, he went there to grab what he could." By contrast, only hardcore Karloff fans are aware that Boris was one of the thirteen founders of the Screen Actors Guild, at a time when any pro-union activity was greeted with hostility by the studios.

Siodmak apprised a Lugosi biographer that Bela "could never act his way out of a paper bag!" Lugosi's black-or-white outlook on life was matched by his generally unsubtle performances. In contrast, Karloff could make you hate him or feel sorry for him, sometimes simultaneously. In 1935 he played twins in *The Black Room*, one predictably all good and one all bad. He made them not only distinctive but also three-dimensional, and when the evil twin impersonated the good one, created a third character.

Since Karloff survived well into the television age, his talent extended itself into such projects as a transvestite in "The Mother Muffin Affair" episode of *The Girl From U.N.C.L.E* and the voice of the Grinch (its expressions modeled on Karloff horror films) in the Dr. Seuss classic "How the Grinch Stole Christmas." Both are highlights—the latter now an annual event—of 1960s American television.

Bela continued to see himself as a romantic leading man. Screenwriters in his orbit were pestered to come up with scripts that pictured him as terrifying to men and irresistible to women. On the other hand, Boris never considered himself a romantic figure, but a character actor, gauging his prospects more realistically than Lugosi. From the onset, he realized that despite the fine speaking voice, his looks restricted him to the unusual. Coworkers said he enthusiastically considered each new role as a challenge, even in the often repetitive horror genre. Karloff's professionalism was renowned in Hollywood, though often he himself would put a temporary stop to production at four o'clock: teatime.

When Karloff broke through as Frankenstein's monster—he would correct fans who called him *Frankenstein*—he was surprised and grateful (daughter Sara listed it as his eighty-first film). Bela Lugosi took his belated film success—nowhere as belated as Boris's—as merely his due. Yet within two years of *Dracula*, Lugosi's star had dimmed. Roles and billing were shrinking, and his salary was never royal. He'd signed low with Universal to star in the film of *Dracula*, and the studio never forgot how desperate he'd been to star.

When it came time to combine Lugosi and Karloff for maximum box office returns in *The Black Cat* in 1934—using Edgar Allan Poe's original title—the Englishman was automatically billed over the Slav. (One critic tellingly wrote that whereas Boris's accent was "high-class," Bela's was "weird" and "occasionally difficult to comprehend.") Before filming, the two stars were assigned by the studio to supposedly audition black cats for their film—a publicity stunt. The two men never socialized, perhaps partly because as early as 1932, Universal had been comparing and pitting against each other its two masters of the macabre.

On the set of *The Black Cat*, the first-billed Karloff requested and readily got his cherished tea breaks. Lugosi professed to dislike tea, preferring cigars and some degree of solitude during the breaks. To those who would listen, Lugosi sometimes mocked Karloff as affected, sneeringly ridiculing his veddy British

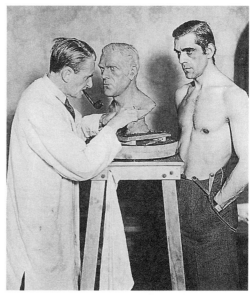

Karloff, having his bust done in the 1930s

tastes. Sports-wise, the men differed too: Boris was a devoted cricket fan; Bela loved soccer.

Each man socialized within the confines of his particular ethnic community, Karloff in the sizable and prestigious Anglo one, Lugosi in the far smaller Hungarian community. But where Boris socialized moderately and modestly, Bela entertained lavishly and showed off with frequent parties boasting generous food and drink. He also loaned friends and hangers-on money that wasn't always repaid. It was said that with Bela, the money went out soon after it came in. Karloff was much more careful with finances.

With the success of *Frankenstein's* sequel, Boris was earning twice what his continental rival did. This angered and hurt Bela, who complained that though in their several films Karloff always received top billing, "I vas the big cheese before he vas." When they re-teamed in *The Raven* (1935), Karloff was given first choice of roles. To Lugosi's delight, Boris declined the more dignified doctor, instead playing the pitiful victim. Bela's pride was satisfied until the film came out and reviews came in, awarding all the acting kudos to Karloff. Boris was usually more concerned with a good part than how he rated image-wise.

In their third joint effort, *The Invisible Ray* (1936), the Englishman earned four times what the ex-Dracula did: $3,000 a week to Bela's $4,000 for the entire picture. By the 1939 *Son of Frankenstein*, Karloff was getting almost $4,000 a week, Lugosi $500 a week—half what he'd requested; Universal knew he'd recently lost his house and used the knowledge against him. In their fifth collaboration, *Black Friday* (1940), Bela's part reportedly had to be completed by another actor. His declining fortunes were tied to his diminishing health and escalating substance

Karloff (*left*) vs. Lugosi in *The Black Cat*

abuse. In 1945 the two technically costarred in *The Body Snatcher*, but it was a Boris Karloff movie and Bela made only a cameo appearance in it.

Karloff's shadow had all but swallowed Lugosi by the time Bela finally enacted the Frankenstein monster in 1943, after Boris passed on it. Later, on stage, he inherited Karloff's role in *Arsenic and Old Lace*. By the 1950s Boris was living in England again and working solely when he wished to. When he traveled to Hollywood to film, he resided at the Chateau Marmont. But by the 1950s Bela's career was a joke. Seldom sought even for interviews, Lugosi's questioners typically focused on *Dracula* or the Karloff-Lugosi movies. When one journalist asked Bela's favorite of their films, he answered, "*Black Friday.*"

"Why?"

"We had no scenes together." After a pause he added, "So it made concentrating easier."

Lugosi lived in a drab utilitarian apartment, glad of attention from teenage fans. Supposedly he was afraid of being alone too often, sometimes finding he'd passed out drunk. Worsening health put him into more than one hospital, and he became addicted to morphine as a painkiller. Lugosi's last project, *Plan 9 From Outer Space*, has been called the worst movie ever made. After he died in 1956 at seventy-three, his role was completed by director Ed Wood's wife's chiropractor.

Karloff continued working until the end (1969), even from a wheelchair, and lived to eighty-two. Most of his final films were far from classics, but compared to Lugosi's last efforts were class acts. Besides which, Boris appeared in films tailored for and starring him. One of his last, *Targets* (1968, directed by newcomer Peter Bogdanovich), traded on his status as a horror icon—named Byron Orlok—and has become something of a cult movie. Karloff lived long enough to experience and enjoy the TV-fueled rediscovery of 1930s and 1940s horror movie classics. In several interviews, he admitted to having had "jolly good luck" over the years.

Theirs was a one-sided feud, an increasingly peripheral one for "Karloff the Uncanny" (as he'd also been billed), but an increasingly bitter one for 'Lugosi. Horror authors have stated that Karloff wasn't inclined to feuds or competition and had no reason to hate Lugosi. Plus in those days, disparaging comments about costars didn't usually make the newspapers or magazines, let alone books, TV-yet-to-come, and so on.

Fans of terror and the macabre have mythologized the rivalry between the two kings of horror. Books have been written about the "pair," even though due to the times they lived in, Bela's envy of Boris could not have resulted in the same colorful and public cracks that eventually sparked between Bette Davis and Joan Crawford. Lugosi must have realized that he could only lose by excessive public criticism of Karloff's talent, luck, popularity, and king's English. A clash of the titans or a duel of the divas is one thing, but a faded star raging at a rival who's stayed on top makes the has-been look pathetic and seem undeserving.

A postscript to the "feud" between the two merchants of menace occurred with the 1994 movie *Ed Wood* starring Johnny Depp as Lugosi's last director, with Martin Landau playing Bela down and out and not in Beverly Hills. The screenplay of the black-and-white film had Lugosi refer to Karloff more than once as a "cocksucker." Over the decades, rumors have persisted about Boris's sexuality: was he secretly gay or bisexual? Whatever the truth, *Ed Wood* stooped to anti-gay and anti-English stereotyping to belabor the obvious point that Lugosi was jealous of Karloff.

What Boris privately thought or said about his number two remains a matter of speculation. But Karloff and Lugosi's haunting *public* relationship—their collaboration in over half a dozen motion pictures—is out there for all the world to see, on big or little screens. Together and separately, they embodied thrilling characters in "terror movies" which have never been topped and rarely equaled.

Family Feuds!

ERIC VS. JULIA ROBERTS

"I gave her her first break. My sister got her first movie because I was right in the middle of it . . . . Her career skyrocketed . . . you notice she hasn't asked me to be in any of her movies. Not that I'd necessarily accept, but she could ask."—Eric Roberts, on kid sister Julia

Julia Roberts's first screen role was *Blood Red*, a forgotten 1986 D movie. She played the sister of the lead character played by Eric Roberts, who'd made his big-screen debut in 1979 in *King of the Gypsies*. By the mid-eighties he was no longer starring in A movies, but his sister who was eleven years younger commenced a superstar movie career which would in every way eclipse his. Still, hers wasn't quite the overnight success often pictured by the media. At seventeen the would-be model had photos taken, but modeling agencies were unimpressed. One told her she was "too heavy." When she turned to acting she was Julie Roberts until the Screen Actors Guild made her change it, as they already had a Julie Roberts on their rolls.

She'd been born Juliet Fiona Roberts in Georgia in 1967, but was called Julie at home, and later Jules by her close friends. She was the third child of the former Betty Bredemus, a would-be actress who joined the Armed Services in 1953, where she met Walter Roberts and gave up her dream. Preceding Julie's birth was a largely unhappy and impoverished twelve-year marriage. Walter yearned to be a famous writer, director, and producer—"Actors are mindless," felt the father of three future actors—and held on to his dream, which never came to pass. He thought ordinary jobs were beneath him, and being both arrogant and argumentative, couldn't hold on to a job for long.

It was left to Betty to work and support the family. Money was such a problem that the bickering couple waited almost ten years after Eric to have a second child, Lisa. That same year, 1965, Walter opened an Actors Workshop in the living room of the family's apartment. He'd already worked as, among other things, a theater publicist and a wholesale milk salesman. Though in love with the theater and show biz, Walter was doomed to frustration, for he didn't want to leave Georgia!

By fifteen, Eric had participated in some eighty stage productions. He idolized his father, "my best friend, my teacher, my dad, and I loved him." But in 1971

Betty sought a divorce. At about that time, Walter realized he'd never make it big; for a time, he had his own TV kiddie show in Atlanta. Julia recalls, "My dad ended up selling vacuum cleaners and my mom got a job as a secretary." After the divorce, Betty took up with a man named Michael Motes, while Walter got a girlfriend. However, in May 1972, Eric got into a fight with his mother's boyfriend, and two nights later, "on a rainy Saturday night, Betty ordered Eric out of the house" she was sharing with Motes in Smyrna, thirty minutes from Atlanta, according to Julia's biographer Aileen Joyce.

Eric was sixteen at the time, though he has said the family broke up when he was twelve. He has also said in interviews that after the altercation, his father (whom he couldn't reach at first because he was out on a date) had Motes arrested. But there is no record of Walter Roberts ever pressing charges, and the cause of the fracas has remained a family secret. When Eric returned to school after that weekend, he told classmates his parents had died in a boating accident and he was now living with an aunt and uncle. In early Hollywood interviews, he declared that his mother was dead. After completing his sophomore year of high school, Eric went to London to study at the Royal Academy of Dramatic Arts during a summer session.

That fall, Walter sued to gain custody of the three children. The court awarded Betty custody of their daughters and Walter custody of Eric. Julia and Lisa were living with their mother in Smyrna when she wed Michael Motes, eleven years her junior and eleven years older than Eric. "We lived as a family unit until I was twelve. Then Mom took the girls away." Long after, Betty, by then best known as Julia Roberts's mother, called the marriage to Motes "the worst mistake of my life." In 1974 Walter married Eileen Sellars; he was forty, she was twenty-eight and ten years older than Eric. After remarrying, Walter again tried to gain custody of Lisa and Julia, again in vain. Three years later, Eileen really did die in a boating accident.

Two and a half months after his stepmother's death, Eric's father died of throat cancer—he'd entered the hospital two months before and never left. Exactly ten years after Walter Roberts died, Eric, by then a fading movie star, was arrested in Manhattan for assaulting a police officer. "He was drunk and incoherent," said Aileen Joyce, "and was found to be in possession of two glass vials of cocaine . . . ." Among the many bizarre statements Eric made to the arresting officer that night was the comment, 'My father died ten years ago today and he was cremated.'"

By the time Walter had died, Betty and Michael had a daughter, Nancy. Ironically, Walter and Eileen's deaths benefited the Motes household, as Eileen had died without a will, so her estate—her mother had died eighteen months before her—went to Walter, who had signed a will while in the hospital leaving his estate to his three children, with Eric as executor and directing that he be made guardian and trustee of the girls. Three weeks after Walter's funeral, Eric petitioned the court as an adult to become his sisters' guardian—Lisa was twelve and Julia ten. His mother filed an objection on behalf of Lisa and Julia. She also sought to have herself named guardian and trustee of her late ex-husband's property. Her petition claimed, "Eric Anthony Roberts is not a fit and proper person to serve as guardian and trustee. He is a New York City actor with no regular income, and caveators

Eric Roberts

[Lisa and Julia] fear the waste of their inheritance."

Eventually, Eric, Lisa, and Julia each received some $90,000, due to Eileen Sellars Roberts's mother's holdings. Mother and son had called a truce; he became executor of his father's estate, and a Cobb County attorney was appointed the two girls' legal guardian. Eric tried to become closer to his two sisters, but, says author Dr. Abraham J. Twerski, "Siblings tend to organize themselves into twosomes, and in families where there are three children, two are likely to form a special bond, leaving the odd one out." How much more so when the two are the same gender and far closer in age? Besides which, friend Sandy Dennis explained, "Eric can be very intense . . . at times he can frighten people off." For some while, Dennis had Eric Roberts living with her.

While he dwelled in Manhattan, Eric sometimes had either of his aspiring-actress sisters stay with him. But eventually the girls moved in together. Eric was the first to achieve success. Two years after his father died, he costarred opposite Susan Sarandon in *King of the Gypsies*, sad that Walter never got to see him make it big. Ironically, Sarandon, who played his mother, would become a close friend to Julia, to whose wedding she was invited, while brother Eric was not. In 1998 the women costarred in and coproduced the movie *Stepmom*. Eric became known as a heavy stellar presence in films like *Raggedy Man*, *Star '80*, *The Pope of Greenwich Village*, and *Runaway Train*, for which he got an Oscar nomination for Best Supporting Actor.

According to one biographer, though, Eric Roberts also became known as "an angry young man" off the screen, "routinely savaging his body in a series of accidents, heavy drinking, and drugs . . . fleeing his inner demons on motorcycles, Jeeps, and horses." By the mid-1980s he'd alienated several producers, directors, and talent agencies, and his star was quickly descending (in the 1990s there would also be reports of spousal battery). Sandy Dennis once noted, "Eric has a problem respecting women. I think it goes way back." In 1985 he told *Playboy*, "There has never been a relationship between us. I just don't like the woman," referring to his mother.

★ ★ ★

Unlike Eric, Julia didn't start out in a starring role. In fact her role was tiny, and she was cast on the strength of her resemblance to Eric Roberts, by then no longer a major star. Who got her the job? Conflicting reports. But then, according to her biographers, conflicting reports and claims are not infrequent in a family that has tried not to air its dysfunctional linen in public. The Roberts's soap operatic background only came out in stages, and Julia in particular is loath to discuss certain aspects of her past, or her brother. (She reportedly hired an attorney for her sister-in-law when she was divorcing Eric and trying to gain custody of their child.) Betty and Motes's 1983 divorce came through just weeks before Julia left Smyrna behind for New York City.

She experienced a frustrating first year before making her negligible screen debut. Eric said he got her the role, and at first she gave him credit. Years later, she informed the media that having had a film star brother had never really done much for her career. In 1988 Julia costarred in *Mystic Pizza*, a minor cult movie. Then came her breakthrough role as Sally Field's dying daughter in *Steel Magnolias*, featuring an all-female-star cast. Julia got the role partly because she'd met Field through her then-husband, a producer, when Julia appeared in a film called *Satisfaction*. *Magnolias* was a hit and yielded a supporting Oscar nomination for Roberts, who achieved superstardom in the next year's megahit *Pretty Woman* (1990). It landed her a lead Academy Award nomination and costarred Richard Gere.

In *The Runaway Bride*, her 1999 reteaming with Gere, Roberts was the bigger star, and earned a reported $20 million, the highest salary ever paid to an actress. Her fee for *Magnolias* had been $90,000, then $300,000 for *Pretty Woman*, and $550,000 for *Flatliners*. By the time of the Peter-Pan-themed *Hook*, she was earning $7 million a picture. In *Hook* she played Tinkerbell, but by then her temperament had earned her the name of "Tinkerhell," and immediately after *Hook* she took nearly two years off, focusing on the male celebrities in her life. Columnist Liz Smith wrote, "I think it would be great if she concentrated on her career and not on the men in her life."

And when Julia returned to moviemaking, she experienced a string of non-hits that was finally broken by *My Best Friend's Wedding* (1997). By then she'd become a celluloid diva, noted for her demands and attitude. "I don't like having to explain myself," she explained. "I resent having to make it comfortable for other people to understand. My job is not being in the public eye. My job is acting." She also stated that when somebody praises some particular gesture or manner of hers, it makes her want to do the opposite next time.

Volatile is a word that has been applied to Julia increasingly, on the set and off. In 1991 Barbara Walters asked if she really

Julia Roberts

thought she would spend the rest of her life with Kiefer Sutherland. "Yeah. Forever love. I believe in that, and I believe this is it. We live together and we are happy and we are in love with each other—isn't that what being married is?" Eventually they decided to contractually marry. Julia insisted, "He is the person I love and admire and respect the most in the world. Kiefer is probably the most wonderful, under-standing person I have ever met." Then she called the wedding off.

Said actor Ray Liotta, "Poor Kiefer and what he had to go through [afterward]. I worked with him on *Article 99*, and I think that's why I've stayed away from going out with actresses." (However, it was said that Sutherland had become jealous of Roberts's Oscar nominations and greater success.) Julia's next surprising move was in 1993 when she wed long-faced country singer Lyle Lovett, whom she hadn't known long and didn't stay married to long. Mother Betty acknowledged to reporters, "Julia's brother Eric wasn't there. He wasn't invited. Julia was afraid he would make trouble."

By then, Betty, Julia, Lisa, and Nancy had become quite close, with Julia invit-ing her mom, sister, and half-sister to visit her on sets and locations, and shower-ing them with gifts, including paying for Nancy's orthodontia. "The girls are very close to each other," said Betty. "They both keep in close touch with Nancy, who says she has three mothers, which is sort of true . . . . We still have a lot of fun together, the girls and I . . . ." Eric was not a part of this feminine family unit, and told the media that he'd only spoken with his mother once since age fourteen, but had bonded with actress-director Lee Grant, whom he met on the set of *It's My Party* (1996), in which she played his mother: "And now she's what I call my sur-rogate mother."

Julia has always been publicity-shy, understandably in light of her background, which she has tried to characterize, when at all, as fairly normal and happy. She especially dislikes questions about her boyfriends or her brother. She once snapped, "People seem surprised that Eric and I act so differently. Well, we're two different people. We share the same last name, but that's about it." Fortunately for Julia, the press doesn't inquire much about Eric Roberts anymore. By 1992, according to the biography *Julia*, she was "no longer discussing Eric, even in the remotest of terms, and had requested that Eric do likewise where she was concerned. What no one then knew, other than Julia and Eric, and those people closest to them, of course, was that by then the two siblings also were not speaking to each other."

Now it's Eric who almost invariably gets asked about kid sister Julia Roberts, when he is interviewed at all or is willing to be interviewed. For the most part, he has tried to say positive things, probably aware that in knocking her he would appear the villain of the two—likewise, regarding his mother—no matter who is more to blame. It has been suggested that Eric may, somewhere down the road, pen a tell-all book about Julia, Betty, and the rest of his family, or at least the first two. But such tomes usually come toward the end of a career, like Joan Fontaine's book about her sister, parents, and stepfather, or after an acting career has been traded in for something else, like Buddy Foster's 1997 memoir in which he outed sister Jodie, who then characterized her elder and only brother (she has two sisters, further paralleling the Roberts family) as "a distant acquaintance motivated solely by greed and sour grapes."

Buddy Foster, a regular on TV's *Mayberry R.F.D.*, had helped kid sister Jodie get her first big break, on his show. As with Eric Roberts, it may or may not have been a move he later regretted, but it was one that did little if anything toward cementing family solidarity. Hard-driving mothers, unhappy brothers, volatile kid sisters . . . too often, the family that play-acts together doesn't stay together.

Warren Beatty vs. Shirley MacLaine

*I*f it wasn't for their parents, who they're each devoted to and sort of compete over, I don't know if Shirley [MacLaine] and Warren [Beatty] would ever see each other much," said writer-director Colin Higgins, who did the TV mini-series of MacLaine's book *Out On a Limb*. A gay Australian, Higgins often escorted Shirley to parties and public functions. He also helmed *Nine to Five*, *Foul Play*, and *The Best Little Whorehouse in Texas* and wrote *Silver Streak* and *Harold & Maude*.

"They won't usually admit it, but Shirley and Warren are pretty competitive." Insiders say they always have been. Shirley, the older (1934 vs. 1937), was a naturally domineering child, a self-professed tomboy who then had to share the spotlight with a more reticent and pliable child who was nonetheless a boy. "I think he eventually rebelled at Shirley getting so much attention, and just went his very separate way," felt Natalie Wood. The two costarred in his first film, *Splendor in the Grass* (1961). Shirley had begun her screen

career in 1955, after taking her mother's birth name of MacLean and adapting it (Warren kept his father's surname but amended it from Beaty, since Beatty also doesn't rhyme with "meaty," despite the jokes over the years about his private life).

Unlike Natalie Wood's younger sibling, Warren could more realistically aspire to stardom in his own right, since between a girl and boy there would be fewer comparisons and no overt competition. Both their parents had harbored show biz aspirations before giving them up. Said Shirley of her mother, "With all this great talent that she had, she didn't do a lot with it. I was always wishing that she'd get out more and live more." Of her father, the outspoken actress later said, "I saw that he was such a spectacular disappointment to himself for having never tried it . . . he realized I didn't want to be like him."

Shirley got the acting bug early, unlike Warren. She turned to dancing and Broadway. Warren has admitted that when he saw his sister becoming a movie star—minus the extreme good looks he would later manifest, especially after letting his hair grow—he realized it wouldn't be impossible for him to become a successful actor. Shirley declared, "Warren has been prettier than me from the age of three." Although he was offered football scholarships to college, he declined, partly for fear of physical disfigurement. He too headed to Broadway, each sibling of course winding up in Hollywood. Until he also achieved superstardom with *Bonnie & Clyde* (1967), it was often said of Beatty that he resented his big, established sister not giving him a helping hand in Hollywood, including a role, however small, in any of her movies (Shirley was one of the first actresses to earn $1 million per movie).

Rather, he had to do television work, for instance a romantic rival to *Dobie Gillis*, or in support of older woman and star Joan Fontaine on *One Step Beyond* in 1959. Beatty was considered and sometimes tested for male film leads which instead went to established stars like Troy Donahue and Anthony Perkins. Shirley and Warren have never worked together, although since her brother attained an equal level of fame, MacLaine has from time to time voiced a desire to costar with him, which he seems to resist—obviously, since as a producer and sometimes director of various of his films he has the power to cast anybody he wishes. "Shirley is ten times as articulate as Warren," offered Colin Higgins. "I imagine he would fear her dominating anything they did together, and not just because of her red hair or infectious grin."

In the sixties, Shirley and Warren—at that time, always in that order—were often contrasted with Jane and Peter Fonda. The Fondas costarred—romantically—in the French film *Spirits of the Dead* (1967). Jane and Peter got along and were not notably competitive, except perhaps for the love of their distant and oft-married father. As with MacLaine, Jane became a star first; unlike with Beatty, Peter didn't become a superstar, and has remained close to his older sister. The major difference between the Fondas and MacLaine/Beatty is that the latter didn't have a superstar father. Henry Fonda's daughter and son were each fairly assured of an acting career of sorts due to the family name and their individual good looks. Shirley and Warren had to scramble for their big breaks.

Beatty at first also had to experience comparisons to MacLaine, the big star in the family. Jane and Peter were compared not so much with each other as with their father. They were allies, children of wealth and privilege. Both had to compete with their father's giant shadow, which neither probably expected to equal, although Jane did. Another difference between the four is that Jane is much more guarded in interviews than Shirley is. Perhaps because she grew up knowing what it's like to be commented on or compared to a celebrity, Jane thinks before she speaks; likewise, she and Peter are both careful what they say about each other.

According to biographer James Spada, Warren and Shirley have had a "curious, skittishly wary relationship" that has included "years of total separation." One cause is Beatty's resentment when his sister has referred to his private life, particularly during his sex-full heyday. For instance: "I haven't seen Warren naked since he was six. I'm really curious to find out if he really has what they say!" During the 1960s, he told a journalist, "We haven't been close for the past seven years." *She* stated, "I only know what I read in the papers about Warren. We rarely see each other anymore. I've tried to reach out to him, but he just doesn't seem to want to communicate with me."

Shirley MacLaine and Warren Beatty

for his behind-the-camera directing, he never won an acting Academy Award, unlike his sister, and has not generally been considered a talented actor. Questions about his sister's talent have often irritated him. He once snapped at an interviewer, "She has great talent. Let's just leave it at that." As Beatty slowed his pace of

Asked if there were bad feelings between them, Shirley said, "Yes, there is some feeling. But I don't want to discuss it . . . . Why rehash old things? It's my life now, and I want to forget the past." Rarely has Shirley evaded discussing most topics; Warren once asked a reporter, "Did she *really* say all those things stated in your article?" A rift reportedly occurred when Beatty offered box office star MacLaine the female lead in his *Bonnie & Clyde*. She declined and publicly joked, "That would be adding incest to injury!" After the film became a megahit, he was the bigger star, and she would declare, "I'd love to do a kissing scene with him, to see what all the fuss is about!" Later, when he became known for liaisons with younger women, Shirley kidded, "I keep my daughter as far away from Warren as possible!"

Although Beatty would win an Oscar

moviemaking, Shirley—sometimes nicknamed Mac the Mouth—noted, "I'm much more decisive than Warren . . . . Also, I tend to trust people more . . . . Warren seems to be quite enthusiastic about sex, to put it mildly . . . ." On at least two Oscar telecasts, she quipped cutely about what some called his sexual addiction—much to his displeasure. Another barrier between them has been Shirley's books, which have not dwelt on Warren but have offered her views of their parents. Her brother disagreed with her portrayal of their parents as conservative and provincial, declaring that they had reared Shirley with "a good, healthy, early feminist point of view." Beatty has so far not chosen to write his memoirs, and allows that there is an entire range of subjects that the siblings do not discuss, due to personal differences. "They share a political viewpoint that's for the underdog.

Both believe strongly in fairness," Colin Higgins informed the *Sydney Morning Herald*.

"They have more in common than not . . . they even look quite a bit alike when Shirley's not wearing makeup and except for her dyed hair. They close ranks when anyone criticizes the other; they have an underlying loyalty that has grown as they've aged and their parents have aged. But each hates being queried about the other; each thinks they're so fascinating, so why should she or he talk about a famous sibling instead?"

Shirley once explained, "We both love being king of the mountain . . . so we can't resist giving each other the needle about the other's foibles . . . . It takes time to work out childhood rivalries." Warren acknowledged that he sometimes felt overwhelmed by the energetic and very verbal Shirley: "I think I just learned

to talk to my sister later than anyone else."

Most individuals who become actors have fragile, needy egos. Competition may be a prerequisite of acting, but comparisons are odious to most actors, particularly stars, and particularly two stars who have been compared since childhood. Although Warren hasn't asked her in years, or decades, about working together, Shirley has made it known, "He's a very strong, and good, producer. But it's all got to be *his* way . . . . I don't think Warren and I are ever going to costar . . . [and] I don't like his chaos."

She has also clarified, "We only feuded in spurts. I'd lose my temper, or he would, and then we wouldn't see each other . . . . We never got together in public, mostly at his insistence, because he resented being called Shirley MacLaine's kid brother." In a nutshell.

THE PARENT TRAP

Fathers vs. Daughters

It's been said that when fathers and daughters feud, it's usually due to control—his lack of it—rather than rivalry. There isn't the same feeling of comparison or competition as between same-gender parents and children, or as siblings. "Most girls have a crush on their fathers, at first and to some degree . . . sometimes all their lives," believed Tennessee Williams, who was noted for the well-rounded female characters in his plays.

"Women make little gods out of their fathers," said the talk show host and author Virginia Graham. "If a girl's father was nice, she adores him. If he wasn't there, if he's dead, he's still a huge presence in her life—the missing god. Look at Barbra Streisand. Isn't this her theme in *Yentl*? In real life she lost her father young, so this is her quest . . . . If a girl has a lousy father, they either make amends later, or she ignores him and cuts him out."

Two actresses seem to be examples of the latter: Nastassja Kinski (*Tess, Cat People*) and Rebecca De Mornay (*Risky Business, The Hand that Rocks the Cradle*). Each has or had a difficult man for a father. Not that that's unusual. As former Congresswoman Bella Abzug put it, "A man spends a minute or two of pleasure, has an orgasm, contributes the sperm for the egg, bang, he's done.

"But the woman's job has just begun. Nine months, to his few minutes . . . yet the child gets *his* name, only, and afterwards Mother does 90 percent of the work rearing the child, but still the father—present or not in that household—gets the credit."

Nastassja Kinski's father Klaus acted in a reported 160 movies, including *Dr. Zhivago, For a Few Dollars More*, and the aptly titled *Venom*. He was famous in Germany and much of Europe. He was also infamous to those who knew or worked with him. "I don't hold anything in," he boasted. Nastassja's father was always there, for better and mostly worse: "I have never met a man like my father," she later explained. "He is so mad, terrible, and vehement at the same time. Because of him, I never knew anything other than [anger]. When I began to meet other people, I saw that it wasn't normal."

As a teenager, Nastassja was discovered by Polish director and lover Roman

Nastassja Kinski in *Paris, Texas*

Polanski, who cast her as Tess in the eponymous movie, a made-in-England *succès d'estime.* "As a director he was ten times more wonderful than as a lover." Nastassja's father wasn't hypocritically prudish but had little positive to say either. In one French interview he huffed, "Unless she has talent her career won't last . . . . They use up these young actresses very fast."

When she was compared to Ingrid Bergman and Audrey Hepburn—she somewhat resembled the former, but neither vocally—he said, "It takes more than looks, as I can tell you!" Klaus was cast as a rat-like vampire in a 1979 remake of the silent horror classic *Nosferatu.*

Unlike his daughter, Kinski had trouble establishing himself as a star in non-European pictures. His confrontational qualities discouraged directors from working with him again; Werner Herzog declared, "He's not aging well. The best thing to happen to his career is for him to die immediately." By then, Nastassja was living in the United States, her career faltering due to flop movies and a talent level which critics might properly disparage, but not a father, even if undoting. Toward the end of his life (he died at sixty-five of an apparent heart attack) he admitted:

"Sometimes even I get enraged with myself. My standards are too high. I cannot meet them . . . . But is it too much to ask and insist on loyalty and obedience from a wife, a daughter? In choosing a woman who was shaped by the East, I have been wiser, and our son is growing up very differently from what has been with me before."

Although his comments about her were more frequent and scathing than hers about him, Klaus told a reporter, "My daughter Nastassja has never forgiven me. For what, I don't know, because for years she won't speak to me. She blackens my name in the press and makes me think abortion is an excellent idea."

Asked in London's *Sun* if he was "feuding" with his daughter, he replied, "People feud every day of their lives. Then it stops. Until another day or week. If it does not stop, that is bad . . . this is how it is with Nastassja and me. I don't think it will ever stop, unless she comes back to me and my ways." It apparently didn't stop, and Klaus died in 1991. A family friend told the German press, "He wanted so much to have an apology [from Nastassja]. He didn't hate her, but he felt she owed it to him as his child . . . he believed he was right." Regarding the feud, Nastassja was heard to say, "In the U.S., we don't like to criticize our fathers."

The father of Rebecca De Mornay (born 1961) is longtime ultra-right TV talk host Wally George, based in conservative Orange County, California, where he spouts sexism, homophobia, and other still-acceptable prejudices to a small but loyal viewership and a small-minded studio audience of angry young white males. Asked on somebody else's talk show why his daughter and he were estranged, he placed the blame on her shoulders, and on a favorite scapegoat's: "Well, she fell in with Jane Fonda and that crowd."

George and De Mornay are reticent about their "feud." It wouldn't reflect well on the "family values" host if his image were dominated by the rift with his beautiful movie star daughter.

Geraldine Page, who won an Oscar for *The Trip to Bountiful*, in which De Mornay had a small and atypically non-sexy role, said, "Rebecca is a dear. Her defenses are up—she's been hurt, not just by strangers . . . .

Rebecca De Mornay

I've coached her [in acting], but I don't pry into her relationship with her father. One is afraid that it might cause her hurt or embarrassment, despite my conviction that the fault lies elsewhere than in Rebecca."

Actresses who indulge in feuds are no rarity. But for their own sake, they're not supposed to square off against authority figures, usually male, or parents. "The best feuds," wrote Louella Parsons, "are the ones between evenly matched opponents— two actors or two actresses." Even today, a younger actress doesn't want her relationship, or lack of it, with her father to dominate her publicity or mar her career ascent.

De Mornay's most recent comment when asked if she had changed her opinion about her intransigent father was, "The answer is still no. I have no reason to change it."

As Dr. Benjamin Spock said, a father can only become friends with his son or daughter when he concedes that the individual is now an adult, with an individual life and mind.

Mothers vs. Sons

Mother-son feuds are rarer than father-daughter ones. Fathers generally expect to hold more influence over their female children than mothers do over their sons or daughters. A father may turn on his rebellious daughter or disown her if her beliefs or habits run counter to his. Likewise, some sons resent mothers who don't know their "place." The emperor Nero's mother Agrippina was crucial to his attaining the throne. Yet when she tried to influence his decisions and the empire, he forgot his debt(s) to her and three times tried to have her assassinated, before succeeding. It took the Roman army to vanquish the formidable Agrippina, who when her murderers arrived, told the soldiers to aim their daggers at her womb.

Some mothers alienate sons by swamping them with control or even sexuality, as with gay actor Tony Perkins. Others by turning against their gay sons, like Nina Capote. Or their son's male partner, as with Nina Vidal, who excoriated Howard Austen—who liked her better than her son did—in Gore's presence. Gore asked her to leave the two men's home, whereafter she wrote him a poisonous letter, which he destroyed—only his friend Paul Newman's wife Joanne Woodward read it. He then wrote his mother, "I shall never see you again as long as I live." He didn't, and she died twenty years later—"This was a savage Medea who meant to kill," he wrote, long after she took to the bottle. Meanwhile, she showed her son's letter to as many as 1,000 people.

Among the odder show biz stories were those of the singer-actor Bobby Darin (born Walden Cassotto) and Jack Nicholson, whose mothers turned out to be their "sisters." Both grew up thinking their grandmothers were their mothers and their mothers were their sisters. "Stranger than fiction," Darin described his short life; he died at thirty-nine following heart surgery. Nicholson found out through a *Time* investigation.

Tony Curtis's mother used to beat him and was jealous of his beautiful face, which he later admitted she tried to damage. Some friends and biographers attributed Errol Flynn's sleeping with countless women and treating most like prostitutes to his contempt and hatred for his mother.

It has been theorized that mothers can affect a man's outlook and relationships, if not his sexuality (a largely discredited myth). In Europe it's often said that a boy who loves his father more tends to become conservative, while a boy who loves his mother more tends to become liberal. But of course the unique individuals who aim for and grab the spotlight are exceptions to most rules.

"I haven't talked to my mother since I was fourteen, except once. I went through all those years without a mother. But when I met Lee Grant [who played Roberts's mother in *It's My Party*, 1996] . . . we really bonded. And now she's what I call my surrogate mother. What's wonderful about it is, I got to choose her, which doesn't happen often with mothers."—Eric Roberts, who is also estranged from younger sister Julia

"My mother was like a vulture. She wanted every part, she couldn't get enough . . . . She'd throw herself at people. She was always right . . . always crossed the boundaries. She is frightening, and years later, when I worked with older or aggressive actresses, I would see something of my mother in them . . . . My mother just would not let go of my life."—Tony Perkins

"I never liked my mother. Which is too bad, but that's how she was. I have nothing good to say about her, so why expound on it?"—Errol Flynn

"Most of the time, I didn't hate my mother. Only because I tried very hard. What made it tougher on me was those times when she could be kind. They were few and far between after I stopped being a kid, but there were just enough of those moments that made her awful times harder to bear and more difficult to understand . . . . The adult is already formed when the child is born. It's up to him or her to provide some consistency and stability. Parents are loved to the extent that they're lovable.

"Time made my mother harder and more bitter, not more mellow. Like many women, she lived too much through her son, instead of herself. I had to be myself and what she wanted me to be, and that just wasn't possible. She loved her vision of me more than me, and finally I had enough of that, and enough of her."— Truman Capote

Fathers vs. Sons

Mothers are typically proud of their sons' accomplishments. Most fathers are too, if not always as whole-heartedly. But sometimes, especially if the son follows in dad's footsteps, it can get complicated. Nowhere more so than in Hollywood, which has always worshipped youth and paid age less than its due. Prime example: George Westmore, cofounder—for, there was a woman behind the man—of the Westmore "dynasty" of movie makeup men.

In 1917, George established the first studio makeup department. His sons would go on to head the makeup departments of Paramount, Warner Bros., RKO, Universal, and Selznick. Some of them gained additional renown by marrying actresses. Perc Westmore wed beautiful Gloria Dickson, who later died in a fire. Bud married Martha Raye, who reputedly kept a gun hidden under her pillow so that her new husband wouldn't get too perky with her; he soon after married actress Rosemary Lane instead.

George had taught his identical twin sons Perc and Ern the craft of wigmaking before they were ten. He and son Mont did the makeup for Cecil B. DeMille's biblical epic *King of Kings*. Mont went on to pluck and redo Rudolph Valentino's very active eyebrows. The younger Westmore also vaselined the Latin Lover's lips for maximum impact and may have created his slicked-back hairdo and angle-cut sideburns. After the successful *King of Kings*, father George opened his own salon on Hollywood Boulevard, at that time a fashionably swank location. He hoped the movie capital's feminine stars would flock to his salon. But no.

The stars as well as the studios preferred a younger hand. In 1926 he'd been bypassed to head up Paramount's expanded makeup department, in favor of son Wally, who was all of twenty years old. George's salon did not thrive, as Max

Factor's did later, in the 1930s. Westmore Sr. hoped to head up RKO's makeup department—but that position went to son Ern, who in 1931 earned an Academy Award for his work on *Cimarron*, the only western to win the Best Picture Oscar until *Dances With Wolves* in the 1980s. Weeks after son Ern got his award, George realized that personal recognition would not be forthcoming.

So he committed suicide by drinking bichloride of mercury; it took him four days to finally die . . . .

The law tends to punish children who murder their parents, for instance Lyle and Erik Menendez or Lizzie Borden, but not necessarily fathers who kill their offspring, for example the father of singer Marvin Gaye (unsurprisingly, the law usually does punish mothers). In 1946 Wilfred Buckland didn't have to worry about the law when he shot his sleeping son in the head with a .32 caliber Mauser automatic. Buckland was Hollywood's first art director of note and though virtually forgotten even within the industry—only famous murderers are remembered—he was called "the founder of Hollywood cinema art." When Cecil B. DeMille hired Buckland, it was the first time the established director, who was known for not sharing credit, had used someone specifically to design sets. Buckland had previously worked on Broadway, and once employed by DeMille, often worked eighteen hours a day, seven days a week, for years.

Buckland is credited with pioneering the use of klieg lights and revolutionizing interior lighting in American films. Before Buckland, moviemakers used sunshine. Buckland brought in arc lamps. He designed everything from staircases to bathtubs, and earned about $75 a week from DeMille. In the mid-1920s he left C. B.'s employ. But with the Depression his life savings disappeared, and his only child, Wilfred Jr.—aka Bill—who attended Princeton, had a reported nervous breakdown. A contributing cause was said to be his mother's death from cancer— she was actress Vida Buckland, a beauty in her day.

Complicating matters between father and son was the elder's homophobia and the fact that Bill was gay. His father instilled in him further guilt than the times and society already had, and Bill became an alcoholic. After he was found drunk on Hollywood Boulevard, he was committed to Camarillo, a state asylum for the insane. There, he was forced to undergo electroshock treatment, which left him worse off. He was released and, through connections, given a gofer job on a movie set. After the job ended, Bill was back on the bottle.

Wilfred despaired of his son ever kicking the bottle or "becoming" heterosexual. By then, he was in his eighties and jobs were hard to come by for him too. So on July 18, 1946, while Bill slept, Wilfred—an expert marksman (a 1917 issue of *Photoplay* had stated that "His hobby is shooting . . .")—shot his son dead, and then himself. He left a suicide note: "I am taking Billy with me." Like father, unlike son.

Mothers vs. Daughters

"I will not do an interview if I'm asked to go into my relationship with my mother."—Meg Ryan, who is estranged from hers

"My daughter has *nothing* to do with me or my life, so don't you dare ask me any questions about her!"—Martha Raye

"My mom's out of my life now, yeah."—Roseanne, who is estranged from her parents and siblings

Barbra Streisand (*right*) with mother Diana and half-sister Roslyn Kind

"My mother was a mother!"—Gypsy Rose Lee, whose memoirs, *Gypsy*, focused on Mama Rose

"We were bought and used, and when our usefulness was over, we were dismissed. I was sent to boarding school at ten and never lived at home again . . . . I did everything I could, so that after she died I had not one instant of guilt. Zero. I still don't. Now I feel quite neutral toward her, though it's taken fifty years to get there."—Christina Crawford, fifty-eight, about her adoptive mother Joan

"I did not write my book to get even."—B. D. Hyman, who wrote two books about Bette Davis

"She lived off me, and I lent her husband money to start his own business, and they have both conspired against me . . . I, who was not the best mother in the world, but in *no* way abusive . . . and I always tried my best!"
—Bette Davis, on the Hymans

"I cannot imagine why she wrote this book."—Loretta Young, whose daughter Judy Lewis publicly admitted she was the love child of Clark Gable and Catholic activist Young (aka Attila the Nun)

"When I was very young, without my consent, my ears were pinned back [via plastic surgery] so that I wouldn't share that famous physical trait with my real father."—Judy Lewis

"It seems as if, if you don't want a book written about you, don't have a child! . . . I would have made a terrible parent. The first time my child didn't do what I wanted, I'd kill [it]."—Katharine Hepburn

"I'm not child-less, dahling. I am child-free. "—Tallulah Bankhead

Liza Minnelli with mom Judy Garland

"Nearly everyone wants babies. But not everyone wants children . . . ."—Lee Remick

"What if you have a daughter, and she is prettier than you? Or she is ugly?"—Gina Lollobrigida, who had a son

"Don't have an actress for a mother."—Maria Riva, daughter of Marlene Dietrich

"My children come first . . . . I never feel competitive with Mia, who is a fine actress. Except when I see her on the screen. That's when I think, that should be *me*. And in a way, it is."—Maureen O'Sullivan, Mia Farrow's actress mother

"My mother became my best friend. After she lost any other ones she had. I'm it, by default, and we see each other regularly only because every year there's that darn Thanksgiving."—Gypsy Rose Lee

"My mother can drive me up a wall better than anyone I've ever known . . . . We're not too close at the moment."—Cher

"When my mother criticizes my clothes or shoes—like, I like men's shoes 'cause they're more comfortable—it's real easy to get back at her because of the clothes she wears . . . . But we are good friends."—Chastity Bono, Cher's daughter

"My mother said to me, 'You're revolting. And on top of that you're not even very feminine.' Well, that led me to the stage, which is an accepting and comfortable place. So in a way I have my mother to thank."—Carol Channing

"My mother said I should become a secretary or a teacher. She discouraged me from acting, because she said I wasn't pretty enough."—Barbra Streisand

"Barbra is too busy to have friendships or care much about people. She doesn't have much time for her own mother."—Diana Kind, Streisand's mother, in the 1980s

"My daughter is living the career I put in front of her . . . that *I* could have lived, if I had been born later . . . . But with a daughter usually, sooner or later, the husband comes between."— Romilda Villani, Sophia Loren's mother, who didn't get along with her son-in-law, producer Carlo Ponti

"My mother was constitutionally incapable of being the loving, kind, devoted mother you see so often in the movies."—Joan Crawford

"Our mother believes firmly that being selfish is good for you . . . it makes you ambitious and successful. She is a wonderful example of that philosophy." —Eva Gabor

"I don't think most girls get along worse with their mothers than boys do . . . or guys with their fathers. It's just that we're more open about it. Somehow it's not such a taboo to bitch about your mother."—Emma Thompson

"My mother was the *real* Wicked Witch of the West."—Judy Garland

"She was a friend of mine—a trying friend, but a friend . . . . She never denied herself anything for me . . . she did what she wanted to do. And I have no right to change her fulfillment into my misery."—Liza Minnelli, Judy Garland's daughter

"If I thought I'd have to have the same life my mother did, I'd kill myself!"—Elsa Lanchester (*The Bride of Frankenstein*)

THE PRINCESS AND THE PLEBE:
Natalie Wood

I f a girl is exceptionally pretty or talented and wants to stand out in show business, she shouldn't have an older sister who is herself quite attractive or talented. Not if the older sister gets there first. Otherwise, the younger sibling will dwell in her shadow and be doomed to a frustrating lack of major opportunity. Examples abound, as with the talented singing half-sisters of Barbra Streisand and Liza Minnelli. Or such good-looking actresses as Natalie Wood and her full sister Lana.

Lana Wood is best remembered for the small but well-endowed role of Plenty O'Toole in *Diamonds Are Forever*, a 1971 James Bond movie. She tells Sean Connery, "Hi, I'm Plenty"—he ogles her and assures her that she is.

Natalie's half-sister, Olga, was the first and oldest child of Russian Marie Gurdin, whose husband later emigrated to the United States. Two years later, Marie followed him to America, only to find him living with another woman. End of marriage.

Marie's second husband was one she could rely on—to pretty much do as she wished. In 1938 she had another daughter, Natasha, who grew to look like a child star, with large, expressive brown eyes. Marie was determined to get her into the movies after a movie company came to Santa Rosa, California, to film, and put out a call for extras. Marie and five-year-old Natasha were among the first to arrive. Olga, thirteen, would have loved to have been an extra, but she was in school. She went on to study drama, but in show business the breaks often happen to those not seeking them.

The director of that 1943 film, *Happy Land* (starring Don Ameche and Frances Dee), was Irving Pichel. In 1945 he asked for Natasha to do a screen test. She did, and he wasn't pleased. Marie managed to talk him into a second test; it worked, and she moved the whole family to Los Angeles, finding her husband a job at the studio as a carpenter. The seven-year-old made her official screen debut in *Tomorrow Is Forever*, starring Claudette Colbert. She also got a new name: Natasha was Americanized to Natalie, and Gurdin was dropped in favor of Wood after Pichel's friend, the director Sam Wood. In 1945 Natalie Wood made another movie for Pichel, and in 1947 costarred in the hit *Miracle On 34th Street* (titled *The Big Heart* in Britain). She became an established child star.

Meanwhile, Olga started to drift away from the family. Lana, born in 1946, later revealed, "Olga felt increasingly out of place in our family. Mother's entire energies were focused exclusively on Natalie," plus there was Lana, eight years younger than the family's biggest breadwinner, to look after. Additionally, the

Lana and Natalie Wood with Jack Warner

Hollywood rumor mill had created whispers that Lana was the illegitimate child of Olga! The economic situation was lopsided and led to Olga leaving home within Lana's first year, to be with her father's family, who were also in northern California. When Natalie got ballet lessons, Olga had wanted the same, but her mother refused. Due to child-star laws, most of Natalie's money was put in trust and the family had to live on Mr. Gurdin's modest salary (he switched to the studio's special effects department).

Ironically, it was with Olga that Lana would remain close all her life, especially as adults. Her relationship with her rich and famous sister would be more problematic. But although Natalie was the center of attention, her life was strictly bounded by rules imposed by Marie and the studio. She was permitted hardly any friends and no boyfriends at all until she rebelled at fifteen, once she got a sense of her own power (she compensated with numerous affairs in her late teens, including much older director Nicholas Ray of *Rebel Without a Cause*, 1955).

Lana had far more freedom, and less parental attention. She invariably looked up to Natalie, who was making the rare transition from child star to adult star. "Natalie was my surrogate parent," she recalled. "I was in awe of my sister. An entourage surrounded her, attentive and solicitous. A smile or caress from Natalie, or a talk with her—these were the highlights of my life." Natalie had more affection to give than Marie. "Mother rarely touched me," and the mystified sisters had been instructed to sleep with their hands always outside the covers.

When it became apparent that Lana was also an attractive and personable—if not quite as perky—girl, Marie began pushing her toward acting. Lana, however, was fearful of auditions and had little thespian interest. Her reluctance may have been due to the overshadowing example of her older sister, and fear of having to compete with her or be compared to her. "[Mother] pushed, I resisted." Like Lilian Fontaine, Marie Gurdin hoped to have two movie star daughters. Both sisters later admitted that Marie was a true stage mother, and proud of it. Lana would write that such women's "drive comes from a desperate effort to escape the life they find oppressive and unhappy." And that: "[Mother] believes if I had done as she told me to do, I would be a star today. It is a subject we no longer discuss."

Lana eventually threatened to run away if she had to keep auditioning. She informed Natalie, by then married and living in Beverly Hills, who took her side and temporarily took her in. Marie was furious, "and that strengthened Natalie's resolve. Natalie was now in control, and Mom did as Natalie demanded." Natalie promised her sister that she wouldn't let Marie try to mold a new star against Lana's wishes.

Lana had done some professional acting, but without a natural inclination, without an exerted and ongoing effort, and with no studio building her career, she didn't click. It was as a young adult, when *she* felt ready—and was better able to appreciate Natalie's stellar lifestyle and fringe benefits—that Lana decided to tackle an acting career. She got a contract with Natalie's old studio, Twentieth Century-Fox. But where Natalie had conquered the movies, Lana would primarily be seen on TV. She was cast in a series based on the film *The Long, Hot Summer*, in the Lee Remick role as a sexpot, which would become her stereotype, for Lana was bustier and less innocent-seeming than her older sister.

At the time, 1962, Lana had already experienced "a marriage gone wrong," and frequently turned to Natalie for advice. Natalie was the poised and confident one. While Lana was making the series—which soon died from low ratings—Natalie had just completed *Gypsy* and was due to commence *Love With the Proper Stranger*, which would yield her third Academy Award nomination. Lana sighed, "She was as secure as I was edgy."

With the cancellation of her series came a stunning realization: when Lana asked to use Natalie's guestroom, she replied, "No, that won't be possible right now. Look, Lana, why don't you go get a job as a stewardess? The pay's good, and you get to see the world." Lana left Natalie's home in tears. "She wanted to get me on the first plane out of town. I was an embarrassment."

Once Lana was an adult, she found her relationship with Natalie more difficult. They were more like peers, more potentially competitive, and minus the parental referees. The only time Lana had heard her "shouting full force" was when Natalie confronted her mother over the strict dating rules. The mature Natalie "had what I came to think of as her Queen Victoria attitude: if you gave the slightest offense, Natalie made it clear she was not amused. There were no accusations, no verbal assaults, no sharp remarks, just a withering look and a back turned in your face . . . . You crossed Natalie at your own peril."

Behind the lifetime spent in front of the camera, Natalie had her own demons. Both sisters underwent tumultuous relationships with men, though Lana wed more often. And by 1966 Natalie's star was dimming. Shortly after making an unsuccessful comedy titled *Penelope*, which she coproduced, Natalie tried to commit suicide. It was Lana who assisted in the cover-up; Natalie insisted that her mother not come to the hospital (Marie was afraid of hospitals). Their mother was becoming jealous of the sisters' closeness, which endured primarily because Lana nearly always gave in to Natalie's wishes.

★ ★ ★

From 1965 to 1967 Lana appeared on the TV hit *Peyton Place*, which made movie stars of Ryan O'Neal and Mia Farrow, the daughter of Maureen O'Sullivan (Tarzan's Jane) and director John Farrow. Lana and Ryan had an affair, but he objected to her curly hair, which she may have affected to contrast with her sister's. After three years away from the movies, Natalie returned in the 1969 hit *Bob & Carol & Ted & Alice*. Yet, as Lana would write in her semi-autobiographical memoir *Natalie*, the older actress showed her competitiveness for the first time not because of Lana's work, but because Natalie was in between men and "At last I was deeply involved with a decent man who was a success." The friction occurred during a party at Natalie's where, presumably, Natalie made a move on Lana's man. Lana became "furious with my own sister. We did not speak for some weeks after that, and when we finally did, the strain took some time to go way. I never asked her why, no doubt out of my lifelong training to avoid troubling Natalie."

In 1971 Lana appeared in *Diamonds Are Forever* and also nude in *Playboy*. Her mother actually approved the idea, according to Lana, but when she wondered "if Natalie would do anything like that," Marie exclaimed, "Absolutely not! *She* doesn't have to." Natalie was noncommittal when Lana asked her opinion, yet "made her disapproval known to everybody, but not to me." The following year, Natalie married for the third time, again to first husband Robert Wagner. Lana was married again, and her husband, also an actor, took several wedding photos. Marie reportedly convinced Lana to allow the pictures to be published in a fan magazine. This enraged Natalie and especially Bob Wagner, who blamed Lana and her husband. They didn't blame Marie because she begged Lana not to "make trouble for me" with Natalie by revealing Marie's role in the deal.

Natalie and "R. J." refused Lana's calls and attempts to make peace. "It was well over a year before I spoke to or saw Natalie again." Unlike Natalie, who'd been in analysis for years, Lana didn't visit a psychiatrist until, during their estrangement, she began questioning "over and over, [why] had I placed so much importance on our relationship, why was it I so wanted Natalie's approbation and love?" By the end of several weeks, the shrink informed Lana that she would do virtually anything to remain part of her sister's life.

By 1973 when Natalie was pregnant for the second time—and first time by Wagner—Lana "realized that for the first time in years I was totally envious of Natalie. Here we were, scraping to make ends meet, and there was Natalie, pregnant, with her beautiful home and her servants, leading the charmed life." When Lana became pregnant again with what would be her first child, she wrote Natalie, saying she hoped they could be friends and sisters again. "She was, I wrote, such an important part of my life that I hoped she would be a part of my child's life too."

Natalie did reply, offering congratulations on her sister's impending maternity but declaring that she had no time for a mutual friendship. But if Lana was willing to go to a psychiatrist, Natalie would gladly pay for her (ongoing) analysis. "I started weeping. Then I started screaming." Lana wrote a letter back—saying she'd been to a shrink and didn't need one, and took responsibility for her own mistakes but had merely written Natalie out of a desire to re-connect, not to be told there was something wrong with her. However, the letter didn't get mailed. Perhaps because it might have upset Natalie or driven her further away.

Perhaps the brouhaha over the wedding photos was just a smokescreen, thought Lana. Perhaps Robert Wagner didn't want her around. "I knew too that Mom was having some trouble with Natalie and was being made to keep her distance. Mom, of course, did exactly as Natalie wished. But then, I thought, I did too." A star usually gets her way.

Shortly before she gave birth, Natalie decided on a reconciliation. She conveyed the request to meet for lunch via Marie, who was already invited. The date was also Lana's birthday, although it wasn't acknowledged. "I didn't say, 'Tell Natalie to go to hell.' I didn't say, 'Why can't she call herself?' I didn't say, 'Not until we discuss a few things.' What I said was, 'What time and where?'" As a gift, Lana made two diaper bags out of old Levi's—one for Natalie and one for herself—from a pattern she'd seen in a women's magazine:

"Considering I had not been exactly the domestic type most of my life, I thought my diaper bag was a triumph. I wanted to give Natalie something original, something special, and this was it. Many years later, I discovered she had thrown it away upon arriving home."

In 1975 Natalie and her mother invited Lana and her daughter Evan to the first birthday party for her own daughter Courtney. "Once again the question was in the back of my mind, but it never came out of my mouth: Why didn't Natalie herself call? I was being . . . summoned . . . and of course we went. The invitation did not include [husband] Richard, who had neither seen nor spoken to Natalie or R. J. since he took the last picture of them on their wedding day."

By then, Lana was becoming aware that her acting career would never take her very far. And her marriage was disintegrating. Before long, she wound up with Natalie's old flame Warren Beatty, even moving into the Beverly Wilshire Hotel at his invitation. "Because he wasn't making Natalie unhappy now, I could look upon him in a different light." After leaving her physically abusive husband and taking Evan with her to the hotel, Lana called her mother. "She listened to my story, and when I was done, had only two things to say. 'I'll be right there. And don't tell Natalie.'" At the time, said Lana, she had $50 to her name.

Eventually Lana landed one of her last sizable roles, in the TV movie *Nightmare in Badham County*. But the bill collectors were snapping at her heels, and she had to borrow money from Natalie, and then wed a producer in his fifties "because I was broke and my prospects for making a good living were dim indeed." Marriage number five lasted under six months, but didn't end messily. The sisters gradually became closer, but Natalie would now and then become upset with Lana, who declared she didn't always know why. She rarely asked and when she did, "my hand sweating as I held the telephone," Natalie would usually "explain" as to why she hadn't returned her sister's calls for weeks:

"I don't have any problem. If you think there's a problem, then perhaps it's your problem."

It wasn't until she approached forty that Natalie moved away from her Hollywood training of almost never admitting to nor discussing her problems. She finally admitted to Lana that she was terrified of going on TV talk shows because she wasn't used to speaking words that weren't pre-scripted. She confessed her method for handling the ordeal: "I pretend I'm you." She told her younger sister, "I have always been envious of [you]. You've always got something to say. Usually funny."

"I always thought you were the one who knew what to say."

"Fooled ya," laughed Natalie.

Natalie became more sympathetic to her sister, a single mother rearing a child "with little in the way of financial help from Evan's father." Natalie "never offered me money," but always lent an ear. Despite her dwindling movie career, Natalie and Robert Wagner were richer than ever, for they owned a healthy slice of the 1970s TV megahit *Charlie's Angels*, and Wagner's faded movie career had been followed by his TV series *Hart to Hart*. R. J. and Natalie's friend Mart Crowley, the playwright who penned *The Boys in the Band* but little else, was made a producer of *Hart to Hart*. In her very candid *Natalie*, Lana revealed that the lucrative producing "position [was one] both he and I sought, and for which Natalie and R. J. arranged for him to be chosen. It caused some awkward moments between us, but our friendship survived"—Lana and Crowley's. Like many celebrities, Natalie and her husband probably thought it best to avoid potential business entanglements with relatives.

★ ★ ★

In 1980 the two sisters' father died. "Mom, true to form, went into hysterics and it required the services of a doctor, nurse, and all three of her daughters to get her going again." The two sisters almost clashed over Natalie's eulogy and plans for the funeral—almost, because Lana didn't want to create a family crisis during a time of grief. She later resentfully wrote about his final days, "Pop wasn't dead yet and here was Natalie already planning his funeral. Film friends were to be present. She looked on this as a performance."

Natalie would read a poem from her film *Splendor in the Grass*. Lana noted that the man never cared for poetry or fiction. "I realized she was indulging her private feelings rather than attempting to express what Pop was all about." Also, Natalie wanted a simple wooden coffin, in keeping with the simple working man who had once been a carpenter; Lana thought, "Why not give Pop something better?"

Natalie had previously bought a condominium in West Los Angeles and allowed her parents to live there rent-free. Lionel Stander, who played Max on *Hart to Hart*, told the press after the 1984 publication of *Natalie*, "[Natalie] had her faults, like any of us, and was more complex than her happy-go-lucky image. But basically she was a good kid.

"I think it's fair to hear both sides of the story before making any judgments . . . . Her sister Lana had some tough breaks, but just because she didn't get to be a star doesn't automatically make her spotless or any morally superior."

After the death of her husband, Marie expected to stay with her daughters, one at a time. Natalie soon tired of what Lana called her "elaborate intrigues." Less than half a year after Marie was widowed, Natalie reportedly threw her mother out. She'd warned her not to keep playing off one daughter against the other, and both against her famous son-in-law. Marie telephoned Lana from the Beverly Hills bus stop. "I jumped in my car and found Mom, my tiny Mom, standing with two suitcases, blowing her nose." Marie complained about her ungrateful star daughter's mistreatment, "and I listened, knowing full well that Natalie was forgiven no matter what she did."

Lana took her in, but within days Marie was quarreling with Lana's daughter in the small apartment. Natalie phoned and asked, "Promise me that whatever happens, you'll never let Mom live with you. She's taken care of. If she lives with you, there will only be trouble." Lana promised, but then said she couldn't find the nonheart to kick her mother out. She moved back to the condo and occasionally lived with Lana.

Both Marie and her middle daughter were fond of and used to exercising control. Mart Crowley, who remained Natalie's friend to the end, revealed, "You can take one step, just one, to either side of the line Natalie draws for you. But if you take two steps, you're in big trouble . . . . Natalie likes to be in control. Or else."

By the late seventies Natalie's movie career had mostly turned to TV work. Lana's latest acting effort, in "a horror film in every sense," convinced her to seek steady work, since she had to support a gifted daughter attending a private school. Lana and Natalie drew up a list of Lana's skills, and production work seemed the logical choice. When her sister suggested that she could go to work as an assistant on *Hart to Hart*, Natalie made no response but said, "With all the people you know, finding a job shouldn't be too hard." Lana knew that "the credit sheet for (*Hart to Hart*) was chockablock with their friends. It would not, however, contain the name of any blood relative." Not that nepotism is by any means frowned on in Hollywood.

Natalie's mother explained that nobody would ever be able to say that Lana Wood got a job because of her famous sister (Joan Crawford used the same excuse when her daughter Christina became an actor). Lana noted that Natalie and R. J. would often pick up the phone to help friends. Nonetheless, Lana found herself a job, assisting Ron Samuels, who was Lynda "Wonder Woman" Carter's husband and producer. She worked on several Lynda Carter TV specials and began learning about show business from behind the camera.

For Thanksgiving 1981, friends and family, including Lana and her daughter and mother, joined Natalie, R. J., and their three daughters (one together and one apiece via each second marriage). Lana would posthumously relate that it hadn't been like prior get-togethers. Something had felt wrong, and Natalie had not seemed her old self. Before the night was over, she had invited several of those present to join her and R. J. on the *Splendor*, their yacht, for a weekend. Natalie's costar in her current sci-fi movie *Brainstorm*, Christopher Walken, would be joining them. All the invitees declined. Lana pointed out:

"Natalie did not issue me an invitation, though she certainly knew I loved boats, fishing, and diving. It was a part of her life in which my side of her family was never included." Some of Natalie's friends said keeping her sister at arm's length was her way of retaining control and showing who was still boss. The irony is that had Lana been invited and accepted, Natalie Wood might still be alive.

Though the sisters' differences were mostly ironed out before Natalie's untimely death by drowning at forty-three, the fundamental difference between them could not be bridged. Natalie's assistant Tommy Thompson, later a best-selling writer, stated, "In Holly-

Natalie Wood in *Brainstorm,* her last movie

wood, power is the name of the game, and any advantage is fully exercised. The only time a star ever relinquishes any degree of power—maybe—is with her husband, while things are going good.

"With Lana, Natalie tried to be there for her. But she never for a moment lets her forget she's the big sister, she's the big star. From the beginning, that was so inbred into their relationship, I doubt Natalie always realizes when she's being controlling."

Natalie bequeathed to Lana all her clothes and furs, a considerable collection. But Lana was hurt when she found out her sister's will stipulated that should Wagner die, Marie Gurdin was to raise their daughters; if Marie was deceased, then Natalie's older half-sister Olga would be guardian; and if Olga died, Mart Crowley and a friend named Howard Jeffries would decide the girls' living arrangements. Lana was not mentioned in any contingency.

Lana took possession of the clothes, but for sentimental reasons R. J. wanted to keep the furs and offered her a fair price for them. However before the check was issued, she had to sign a release declaring that her claims against Natalie's estate had been satisfied. Lana found the procedure cold and unfamilial. When Lana sold Natalie's clothes, Wagner was reportedly surprised and furious. The relationship virtually ended. Marie refused to try and play peacemaker for fear of losing access to her two granddaughters. Although Evan was still allowed to visit her cousins, Lana revealed, "I was not to be allowed to have the telephone number at R. J.'s new house" (. . . in 1990 he married former actress Jill St. John).

In her 1984 book Lana stated that their mother "is living in Natalie's past," and, "She sees Natalie's children; I do not. She sees Robert Wagner, Natalie's last husband; I do not. I have asked her many times why it is I'm not allowed to see my nieces, why my former brother-in-law does not return my phone calls or answer my letters, yet my own daughter is taken by her grandmother to see her cousins (but only when I am at work and not aware the visit is about to take place) . . . . I have been convicted of a crime. I don't know what the crime is, but that doesn't seem to matter to anybody but me. I still see our mutual friends, and they profess to know nothing about it. I stopped asking them long ago."

Actor Dack Rambo, a friend of Lana's before he was on *Dallas*, said in 1989, "In a way, royalty is fairer than movie stardom . . . . Lana was a good friend of mine, and I always thought she could have made it in this business, except for what she couldn't help—whose kid sister she was. I guess her situation is like having a princess for a relative. But instead of being a younger princess, it's more like having a princess and a commoner in the very same family."

The Gabors

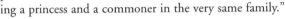

The three Hungarian-born Gabor sisters in some ways paralleled the Russian-born Marie Gurdin's three daughters, of whom Natalie Wood became a star. Supplying the Gabor engine was the indomitable Jolie, who lived well into her nineties. Family legend had it that after she presented husband Vilmos Gabor—who was twice her age—with Magda, their first child, Jolie told him she was leaving to become an actress. He demanded that she stay and produce a male heir. A second child was born, a girl named Sari (later Zsa Zsa), and again Jolie said she was off to become an actress. Again Vilmos ordered her to stay.

She then gave birth to a third girl, Eva, and informed Vilmos that three children were enough, no son was forthcoming, and now she must try her luck as an actress. To which the patriarch replied, "Now you are too *old* to become an actress!" After drying her tears she asserted, "Then I will live my life through my daughters. They will be rich, famous, and successful, and *I* will push them to the top!"

Jolie sought to make her daughters fearless and competitive with one another. As small children, she reputedly took the girls to a nearby lake, rowed them out to the middle, then dumped in a daughter at a time, ordering her to swim back to the boat. As the child approached, Jolie rowed the boat away from her, forcing her to stay afloat and keep moving toward her goal. "Now my daughters swim beautifully and are afraid of nothing," Jolie would boast in her palatial Palm Springs home.

In her book *One Lifetime Is Not Enough*, Zsa Zsa noted, "I phone up excitedly and say, 'Mother, I have got a wonderful new part in a movie.' And instead of just saying, 'Great,' Mother's answer will invariably be something like, 'Great.

Zsa Zsa Gabor

husband which in 1953 catapulted Zsa Zsa Gabor (who's Sari now?) to national fame or notoriety. She created a fashion sensation and media-wide sympathy by showing up at a press conference with a decorative eye patch where the Latin lover had supposedly hit her.

But did you hear that Eva got that part in . . .?' . . . She believes that competing will only make us better. That is how she has made us world famous."

The least known Gabor is the eldest sister, Magda, a redhead who declined to go blonde like her brunette sisters. Nearly everyone says she is the nicest—or the nice one, depending—and she's had the fewest marriages and dabbled least in the limelight. In 1970 she followed in Zsa Zsa's footsteps when she married Zsa Zsa's favorite ex, actor George Sanders, who according to some was hard up for money (Magda became rich via her marriage to a plumbing millionaire who died). Within six weeks, Sanders drove off and filed for an annulment, later stating that he must have been "out of my mind" to wed more than one Gabor.

Sadly, Magda suffered a major stroke in the 1960s that limited her ability to speak. Of the threesome, she was closest to her mother and was said to dislike competition with her juniors. Zsa Zsa has been the most competitive and avid for attention. By not being as selective or prudent as she might have been, she has regularly reaped negative publicity, although it was a then-scandalous affair with heiress Barbara Hutton's impending

However, Zsa Zsa has gotten into far more columns than movies, and could more accurately be described as a professional guest star—or talk show guest—than an actress. Her best known film is *Queen of Outer Space* (1958) and her best known role a glamourous housekeeper: "Darling, I'm a wonderful housekeeper," she often says. "Every time I get divorced, I keep the house!" Asked how many husbands she's had, she once quipped, "You mean apart from my own?"

In 1982 Zsa Zsa apparently wed for the eighth time. Her younger husband (one directory gives her birth year as 1919) was said to be a Spanish duke. The wedding party, in Puerto Vallarta, Mexico, included a few requisite VIPs like director John Huston and Vivian Vance's ex-husband Phil Ober, and received international press coverage. But it turned out that the handsome fifty-two-year-old was a Mexican realtor, and the man who married them had no authority to do so. Plus Zsa Zsa was still legally married to number seven. Her latest husband is a German who reportedly bought the title of "prince" which she coveted so that she could call herself Princess Zsa Zsa.

Except for Eva Gabor's TV series *Green Acres*, Zsa Zsa was the more famous sister and the better known "actress." Ironic, because Zsa Zsa always wanted fame and fortune but harbored few acting ambitions. "Since Eva was five," she explained, "she has prepared to be a star . . . . Whereas I really wanted to be a vet. So when I became an actress by accident, my career came between us." Zsa Zsa admits that Eva "has never approved of the things I do. I'm too wild for Eva."

In the 1940s Eva was under contract to Paramount, which dropped her, and in 1942 became the first Gabor to get a divorce, initiating a long and successful family tradition (despite their twenty or so marriages, the three sisters produced only one child, Francesca Hilton, from Zsa Zsa's marriage to the famous hotelier who later boycotted one of Eva's marriages because the groom was Jewish!). Eva resented the massive publicity conferred on Zsa Zsa during the 1950s; one of her own publicity stunts was an alleged affair with gay or bisexual star Tyrone Power—not the last time Eva would be "romantically" linked with a gay celebrity.

In the 1960s she lucked into *Green Acres*, which had been designed for B-list film stars Eddie Albert and Martha Hyer (it was said that for movie casting, the Gabor sisters were Z-list). Hyer wanted too much money, so Eva became famous, if not as a serious actress, then as zany Lisa Douglas on the long-running sitcom. One biographer has written that on the set "one of the few things that drew her ire was *any* mention of Zsa Zsa. Fellow actors learned quickly that her sister was taboo as a topic of conversation."

In 1976 Zsa Zsa and Eva were costarred in a playhouse production of *Arsenic and Old Lace*. The "spinster" characters were glamourized, and audiences flocked to see the two together. Pamela Mason, a some-time friend of Zsa Zsa, noted, "To her horror, Eva found that in no way could Zsa Zsa control her appetite for hogging the stage . . . . She upstaged her at every turn, showing her natural bent as a comedienne. All the Gabors are comediennes, if they but only knew it." Zsa Zsa improvised so many new lines for herself that her role became notably bigger; therefore, Eva filed an official complaint with the theater's management.

During Zsa Zsa's last publicity circus, her trial and 1990 jail sentence for slapping a Beverly Hills cop, Eva angrily avoided the subject in interviews and was the sole Gabor not to attend the trial as a show of solidarity. Nor did she visit Zsa Zsa in the clink, though she telephoned. Pamela Mason had long since explained, "Zsa Zsa and Eva would be permanently on the outs if not for Jolie. She keeps that family together . . . . They are all devoted to the idea of Mama Hungarian Hen and her three not so young chicks."

Eva told Zsa Zsa that if she hadn't "talked so much," the trial wouldn't have become such a farce. Atypically, Eva once admitted in print, "It is very trying to be someone who wants to really achieve something, but to have an outrageous public image hanging over my head, and it's not even my own!" Neither sister liked being mistaken for the other, which happened often. For instance, on a quiz show, a photo of Zsa Zsa appeared, with the question: Name this famous Hungarian actress who starred in *Green Acres*. Answer: Eva Gabor—the more serious sister, who hated seeing her identity submerged in that of her flamboyant older sister. Zsa Zsa didn't mind such mistakes as much, for Eva maintained a slimmer figure and looked younger.

Columnist Lee Graham recorded one case of mistaken identity. "Eva's face, hands and forearms were completely covered, but her body was bare, as she sunbathed in her garden. Her waist and legs are on the thick side, otherwise she might not have minded so much that when she rose to take a dip in her pool, two men from the utility company were staring at her, over a fence. She froze, and one man said, 'Hi, Eva!' She smiled shyly, then suddenly beamed, 'Not Eva, darlings—*Zsa Zsa.*'" Eva died unexpectedly before her older sisters, and with her passing and that of mother Jolie, Zsa Zsa has seemingly withdrawn from the public eye.

SISTERS UNDER THE SKIN:
Joan and Jackie Collins

You can understand what Jackie Collins is about when you remember that she's a younger sister of an actress who tried in vain to be an actress herself," said Daniel Massey, a member of an acting family which included father Raymond and sister Anna. "Joan was already a success, and prettier, so Jackie turned to writing. It took time, but she did become a success with her novels. Then what happens? As Joan is towards the end of her leading lady period—which she had a wonderfully long run with—*she* turned to writing novels! How do you think Jackie would feel?"

Vanity Fair magazine, when it did a joint profile of the sisters, noted that each had to be treated exactly like the other—in other words, Jackie demanded all the same perks as Joan, who would get them anyway. When Joan declared, "I'm bringing a woman's point of view to novels, which is rather revolutionary," she completely overlooked Jackie, not to mention Jacqueline Susann (*Valley of the Dolls*), Margaret Mitchell (*Gone With the Wind*), and hundreds of women from Jane Austen back to Murasaki Shikibu, generally credited as the first *person* to write a novel, the Japanese *Tale of Genji*.

When Joan sued publisher Random House to tremendous publicity, and then won, it couldn't have overjoyed Jackie, who has said she's not read her older sister's books. "Jackie began with no fanfare, like any new novelist," explained professional biographer Gerald Frank. "But when Joan got into publishing, it was all celebrations and publicity and praise . . . even if part of it was on the order of, 'Oh, Joan can actually write. Will wonders never cease?' And there was some friction back there when both sisters were [temporarily] at the same publisher."

As with any celebrity who has a relative who's an actor, there can also be friction over the actress spilling too many beans. Jackie has been a chronicler, fictionally, of the rich and famous; though now herself rich and famous, she reveals little about herself. Unlike Joan, in or out of her tell-all autobiographies which chronicled Warren Beatty's sexual insatiability and how Joan's first husband wanted to rent her for a night to a wealthy Arab sheik. The more modest Jackie confesses things like, "My weakness is wearing too much leopard print."

Jackie's relationships, including marital, have been fewer and less publicized than Joan's. Ex-husband Anthony Newley publicly declared, during *Dynasty*, "Joan

Collins is a commodity who would sell her own bowel movement." A subsequent husband, said Joan, became fat and lethargic and received a reported $1 million divorce settlement, which was echoed in the aftermath of Joan's 1983 marriage to blond Peter Holm, twenty years her junior. Joan wrote in her book *Second Act*, "I suppose I should have smelled a very large rodent when our wedding pho-

Joan Collins (*right*) with sister Jackie

tographs taken during the ceremony by Peter's best friend, Hassa Olafson, appeared in a supermarket tabloid. I was furious . . . . Peter pretended shock, horror, and outrage. But as the two Swedes were joined at the hip, always closeted away together in Peter's office jabbering away in their mother tongue, I became suspicious."

In 1986 Joan decided to divorce the man who'd become a sort of business manager to her. The proceedings made international headlines, with Holm comparing Collins to Alexis in *Dynasty*, seeking a huge settlement, and picketing Joan's house with signs reading "Joan, you now earn over $100,000 a week, because Peter negotiated, supported, and assisted you for two and a half years. Please give him a decent home" and "Joan, you have our $2.5 million, 13,000 sq. ft. home which we bought for cash during our marriage. I am now homeless. Help!"

His 1987 settlement was much less than expected. The relieved Joan, who has not since wed, was gifted by friends with a T-shirt reading "Holmless." She was later quoted, "I never speak of them [her ex-husbands], except under hypnosis."

It was literary superagent "Swifty" Lazar who got Joan into publishing: "It doesn't last forever for actresses . . . I urged her to forget that crap and write the great books instead of looking for the great roles . . . . Will this hurt her relationship with her sister? Why should it? Joan's a star; you can expect her to do anything. She's great!"

Early on, Joan's fame was a great barrier to Jackie's emerging identity in England. At one point, the struggling actress was billed as "Jackie Collins, younger sister of film star Joan" (who was partly named after Joan Crawford, her mother's favorite star). In frustration, she temporarily changed her name to Jackie Curtis, after her favorite star Tony Curtis (born Bernard Schwartz). She then switched to Lynn Curtis and did some film and television but would obviously never be a challenge to Joan Collins, so—as many younger siblings do—Jackie flew the coop and started over again, far away in California.

Joan admitted in her book *Past Imperfect* that she was spoiled: "I was so overprotected that my mother even put ice cream in the oven for a few minutes before I ate it so the chill should be off!" Not that unusual for the first baby born into an affluent household. The eldest of three, including a much younger brother named

Bill, Joan was the apple of her father's eye. Joe Collins, a successful Jewish theatrical agent, had married a Gentile, and intended to call their firstborn Joe Jr. Instead, the baby was called Joan, who later reminisced, "I can't pinpoint exactly when I stopped being Daddy's little darling. It could have been when little baby Jackie arrived to take some of the attention away from me."

In the mid-1970s, after her film career seemed largely spent, Joan helped send a little attention Jackie's way when she decided to make a comeback in a movie of Jackie's novel *The Stud*. However, not one studio would back a picture starring a woman past forty, and Joan spent years raising the financing after Jackie wrote a sexy screenplay. But come back she did, and *The Stud* (1978) was a solid hit, particularly in Britain. The following year saw Joan starring in a sequel, *The Bitch*, a precursor of sorts to her bitchy *Dynasty* character, which she accepted after Sophia Loren declined to play Alexis because "I'm too good."

In the 1980s the sisters' fortunes soared: Jackie's novels became best-sellers and TV mini-series and she herself achieved celebrity status; Joan was an international star due to *Dynasty* and other media ventures. At last, Jackie, beautiful and self-confident, had in her own way caught up with big sister Joan. Yet their relationship became touchier, as Jackie no longer automatically accepted the less-successful, kid-sister label. "The ideal would have been if Jackie had kept writing the stories that Joan could star in. Period," said actor-producer Derek Nimmo. "What complicated things was when Joan got into the writing game. Not kosher, one might say, to invade your sister's turf . . . . Things are sometimes pretty chilly between them. They definitely are solo acts. Neither appreciates being linked with the other, except in passing . . . . Still, they always kiss and make up.

"I think being foreigners [in America], and as they age, there's far more they have in common than not. And I don't think the rivalry's quite as great now as it used to be. Although every time Joan has a new novel out, it's not exactly a marvelous time for Jackie."

It used to be that Jackie didn't like for Joan to talk about her too much in public, which Joan wasn't much inclined to do, being herself a natural center of attention. However in *Second Act*, her 1996 memoirs, Joan did state that Jackie lost her virginity to Marlon Brando. As Jackie became a frequent and popular TV talk show guest, she began speaking out about Joan, which has caused a few rifts, for example in 1998, when Joan flew back to L.A. from Europe to throw herself a star-studded sixty-fifth birthday party on May 23. Guests included Robert Wagner and Jill St. John, producer Allan Carr, George Hamilton, Stefanie Powers, and *Dynasty* costar Diahann Carroll. But not Joan's L.A.-based sister.

Columnist Arlene Walsh reported in *Beverly Hills (213)*, "The big gossip of the evening was that Joan had not invited her sister Jackie and her fiancé Frank Calcagnini. Apparently, Jackie has been saying some naughty things about her sis on British TV that she didn't think would travel (Joan also resides in France). But bad news travels fast, and Joan's putting her on the bench for a while." Proving once again that celebrity and one of its main offshoots, public curiosity about private lives, can stymie any two sisters' relationship.

SUCH UNDEVOTED SISTERS:
Joan Fontaine and
Olivia de Havilland

"Sisters often don't get along. But they also have their good times . . . . The feud between Olivia de Havilland and Joan Fontaine is long-running and it is real. It's not for show. It's for getting the upper hand . . . . I think each wants to live just as long as she can, to out-live the other one."—columnist Dorothy Manners

"Everyone wants to know about the feud between my sister and myself, and why shouldn't I admit that I haven't been able to forgive her for not inviting me to our mother's funeral service . . . and for other cruelties. I married first, won the Oscar before Olivia did, and if I die first she'll undoubtedly be livid because I beat her to it."—Joan Fontaine

In the 1940s Warner Bros. was already using the supposedly wholesome rivalry between actresses Olivia de Havilland and Joan Fontaine for publicity and promotion. Officially, the competition began in 1941, when both sisters were nominated for the Academy Award for best actress. The winner was Joan (born 1917), a year younger than the lady-like but steel-willed Olivia, who kept their father's surname for herself alone (Joan and Olivia's British cousins were the de Havilland Aircraft Co.). Fontaine won for her role in *Suspicion* (she'd been nominated the previous year for the classic *Rebecca*). Decades after, she remembered when her name was called:

"I froze. I stared across the table, where Olivia was sitting directly opposite me. 'Get up there, get up there,' she whispered commandingly. Now what had I done! The animus we'd felt toward each other as children, the hair-pulling, the savage wrestling matches, the time Olivia fractured my collarbone, all came rushing back in kaleidoscopic imagery. My paralysis was total. I felt Olivia would spring across the table and grab me by the hair. I felt age four, being confronted by my older sister. Damn it, I'd incurred her wrath again!"

In time, de Havilland won two Oscars, outdoing her younger sister. But from

Joan Fontaine (*left*) with sister Olivia de Havilland

the start, she and their mother, Lilian Fontaine, expected more from the elder child. George Cukor, who directed both actresses, believed, "It really started with the mother. She was a hard, domineering autocrat, a dictator in petticoats. She gave her daughters precious little love and set them against each other." Some felt Lilian was jealous of her daughters' success. In her memoirs *No Bed of Roses*, Joan admitted:

"Never, ever, did Mother acknowledge that she had seen me on the screen during my entire Hollywood career. She never admitted viewing any of Olivia's films either. At least, not to me."

Joan also revealed that her father, divorced from her mother, made sexual advances toward her. When she rejected them, he banished her from his life and home. At seventeen, Joan was also unwelcome in the home of her stepfather and his wife, her mother. Dr. Roni Cohen-Sandler, a clinical psychologist and the author of *I'm Not Mad, I Just Hate You!—A New Understanding of Mother-Daughter Conflict*, believes that because anger in women and girls is taboo in our patriarchal society, daughters often vent their pent-up feelings against their mothers. And sometimes against the older sister, who can be a surrogate mother or at least has many of her prerogatives.

"Joan has often felt that her mother and Olivia were united against her," said George Cukor. "Olivia became a star first, and Lilian did ignore Joan in her favor . . . . Lilian was counting on Olivia to support her in her old age."

Although in the end Joan forgave her mother's slights and dedicated her book to her, she has always resented Olivia's superior attitude, which began as a child and intensified once they entered the same school and then the same profession. "Olivia forbade me to speak to her in front of her friends during school recess." Once Olivia became contracted to Warner Bros., said Joan, "I did all the errands, most of the cooking.

"Mother answered Olivia's mail and remained in readiness should her position as hostess and chaperone be called upon. As for Olivia's and my relationship, she was the star and I was the servitor on probation . . . . I was ruled by Mother and Olivia with an iron hand."

Joan's husband, actor Brian Aherne—who remarked that their marriage coincided with World War II—later informed publicist-turned-author Richard Condon (*Prizzi's Honor, The Manchurian Candidate*), "The mother was ruthless. I think because she had daughters, not sons. Yet she wanted to reap the same benefits as if she'd had two successful, achieving sons. So she planted the seeds of competition in both girls from day one. Which has made for difficult relationships all around!"

There may have been jealousy on the elder's part about her rival's looks. George Cukor observed, "Very often, the younger girl is prettier, or the younger boy handsomer. Now, Olivia has always been confident of her talent, and more critics would call her the better actress. But Joan was truly beautiful, even ethereal. Olivia was often attractive, but anybody would admit that Joan was more so." It was Cukor who gave Joan her big break, in the 1939 hit and classic *The Women*, which he got as a consolation prize for being fired (due to Clark Gable's homophobia) well into production from *Gone With the Wind*—of which Olivia is the sole surviving star.

Like a parent, Olivia felt entitled to a certain measure of, if not respect, then ascendancy. Of the two, she has been the more publicly reticent and old school about airing the family laundry; she has yet to publish any memoirs or even the long-awaited book of *Gone With the Wind* memories. But she admitted, "Joan deserved to win [the Oscar] and did. But Joan is fifteen months younger than I, and I knew I would lose prestige with her if I lost—I have always been a heroine in her eyes—and I did! The goddess had feet of clay, and she let me know it too!"

Lilian shared the goddess' opinion of Joan's screen work, but in her unique, unmaternal way: when Louella Parsons gushed that *Rebecca* had made Joan a star, Lilian answered, "Joan has always seemed rather phony to me in real life, but she's quite believable on the screen."

Alan Napier, who was best man at Joan and Brian Aherne's 1939 wedding (and played the butler on TV's *Batman*), explained, "Miss Fontaine had a lot to complain about in regards to her mother. But she hasn't. It isn't done. Not by a lady, and these two are English roses, ladies . . . . Lilian Fontaine reared them to be ladies and yet to be at each other's throats."

Dr. Cohen-Sandler points out, "If there is one thing your daughter knows, it is that expressing strong feelings is tantamount to social suicide [professional too, in those days] . . . . The fear of being called a bitch may motivate [a female] to hide her anger . . . even to let it fester." Napier said, "No matter what her mother did or said, Miss Fontaine tried not to react.

Olivia de Havilland

In public, at any rate. She felt freer to go after her sister . . . she felt it was more acceptable. Despite her screen image of smiling patience, Miss de Havilland can be quite the heavy-handed high-hat."

Finally, Joan publicly stated, "I wish I *had* a sister. I've always been the intruder in her life, the interloper. As my older sibling, Olivia could have looked after me. *Au contraire*, her desire my whole life has been to get me off-balance. We've not spoken since Mother's death in 1975, and that's it, kid. Never again."

Before Joan married Brian Aherne, the sisters clashed over Howard Hughes, whom Olivia had been dating. When he made a pass at the younger, prettier Joan, she was surprised but agreed to meet him—"seething inside at his disloyalty to Olivia." She determined that the pass was for real, then returned home to show Olivia the piece of paper with Hughes's private phone number in his handwriting, and told her of the "encounter. I gently tried to explain that her heart belonged to a heel . . . . Sparks flew. Hell hath no fury like a woman scorned—especially in favor of her sister. This, plus my engagement to Brian, was very hard for her to take."

By 1946, when de Havilland won her first Academy Award for *To Each His Own*, things had badly deteriorated between the sisters. Joan was at the ceremonies, and after Olivia gave her acceptance speech and "entered the wings, I, standing close by, went over to congratulate her as I would have done to any winner. She took one look at me, ignored my outstretched hand, clutched her Oscar to her bosom, and wheeled away" just as a photographer captured the unfamilial moment for posterity.

In the 1950s they were still keeping up appearances, only. When Fontaine took over the female lead in the Broadway hit *Tea and Sympathy*, de Havilland, who lived in Paris, was in New York and attended the play. Afterward, the entire cast assembled in Joan's dressing room, eager to meet the double-Oscar-winning actress (she also won for *The Heiress*) and hear her verdict. Joan later reminisced unfondly:

"Miss de Havilland was ushered in as we all stood as though for military inspection. 'Well! Isn't it something!' volunteered the Hollywood superstar as she shook hands with the group. Then she quickly turned and left the cast gaping. Isn't it something? Something is what? We all put our heads together, pondering Olivia's enigmatic statement, giving it every inflection, every intonation, accenting first one word, then another. Finally we decided it was like gazing at someone's newborn child in its crib and, wanting to be polite, cooing, 'What a beautiful bassinet!'"

The final straw was their mother's terminal cancer. Olivia took over her care while Joan was touring in a play. (Insiders have said the sisters' versions of the events differ considerably; only Joan has published hers and Olivia eschews biographers.) From long-distance, Joan accepted the doctors' verdict, and said she had spoken with Lilian at length and that they agreed they didn't want her lingering "in pain or indignity." Apparently Olivia didn't accept the diagnosis and wanted her mother to undergo exploratory surgery. Joan was horrified and later wrote, "Olivia, who had not been in touch with Mother for many, many months . . . was now taking charge of the life and death of our eighty-eight-year-old mother."

There was no operation. While Joan was away—she stated she had pneumonia at the time—Lilian died. Joan was glad for her. The last time she'd seen her, "She could no longer hear, see, or enjoy her food; she was no longer interested in life." Then Joan got a letter from a female friend of Lilian's who had been appointed executor. It declared that she had been cremated and there would be a memorial service in two weeks, with Olivia and two of Joan's ex-husbands set to deliver eulogies. "There was no suggestion that [Joan's daughter and ex-husband] be present—and certainly not me.

"It was obvious that Olivia and the executor had taken full charge, making all arrangements, disposing of Mother's effects as well as her body

Joan Fontaine

without bothering to consult me." Joan telephoned the executor and threatened to give the press "the whole story" unless the service were delayed a few days for Joan's hiatus from her play.

Joan's ex, producer William Dozier, father of Deborah, remembered that after the service, "We went up a hillside [in northern California] near the place where Lilian taught drama to the local young people. Olivia and Joan and [a male friend of Lilian's] scattered Lilian's ashes in three installments. Olivia gave a very dramatic, theatrical, deep-chested sigh as she threw the ashes. Joan, very characteristically, just tossed them away!"

Said Joan, "Thus I said goodbye forever to my mother. As for Olivia, I had no words at all." The two hadn't spoken at all during the proceedings, and reportedly never have since, both now in their eighties. The chance for any possibility of reconciliation was severed with the 1978 publication of *No Bed of Roses*, which Fontaine wrote to "straighten out misconceptions, erroneous conclusions, ill-considered judgments concerning my relationship to my family."

The following year, both sisters attended the fiftieth anniversary of the Academy Awards. According to biographer Charles Higham, "They had to be placed at opposite ends of the stage; and when they ran into each other in the corridor of the Beverly Hills Hotel, they marched past each other without a word."

Joan, who reportedly became estranged from Deborah and from her Peruvian-born adopted daughter, settled in Manhattan as her acting career wound down. Olivia remained based in Europe, reportedly close to her daughter and son. Neither sister had experienced a lasting marriage; Joan wed four times and Olivia twice.

De Havilland's friend and frequent costar Bette Davis offered, "They have vastly different personalities, and different ideas of happiness . . . . Olivia is almost like a younger sister to me."

After publication of *No Bed of Roses*, Bette was asked if she'd read her friend's sister's book? "Not yet . . . I will read the reviews . . . . Olivia has at least one book in her . . . . She *may* be waiting to write it until Joan dies! So she can have the last word." As she'd had, as the elder sibling, the first word.

Such Undevoted Brothers

Most show biz brothers seem to get along. Some even become acts, like the Marxes or the Ritzes (most sister acts have been singers). A number of acting brothers have separate surnames, like Charlie Sheen and Emilio Estevez, Peter Graves and James Arness of *Gunsmoke*, and George Sanders—who won an Oscar for *All About Eve*—and Tom Conway.

Some brothers are quite different from each other, like John and Lionel Barrymore or Dennis and Randy Quaid, but most are in competition for similar roles, like Ralph and Frank Morgan (the Wizard in *The Wizard of Oz*; true, he was more dithery than Ralph), Beau and Jeff Bridges, Darryl and Dwayne Hickman (*Dobie Gillis*), not to mention the brigade of Baldwin brothers. Stephen Baldwin admits:

"I get mistaken for my brothers all the time. I have a lot of fun with it. They say, 'You were great in *Sliver*, can I have your autograph?' And I say, 'Go to hell, you bastard.' Then they walk away going, 'That Billy Baldwin, he's a prick.' He does it to Alec too."

If brothers seem less competitive than sisters do, it's partly because there are considerably more roles available to males, especially starring ones, and at all age levels. Actors are also less valued and judged by their looks, so that physical comparisons between brothers are less frequent and less crucial. In short, there are more slices to go around.

When show biz brothers don't get along, it usually has more to do with their personalities—or one's brother's, at any rate—than with the business. Sometimes a younger brother is extremely competitive, and over-sensitive to his elder's achievements, as was the case with silent movie director William Demille and his younger brother Cecil, who would re-spell the family name as DeMille—"two capital letters, because twice as important," he explained to assistant and former actor Henry Wilcoxon.

Cecil Blount's elder brother by three years was the more easygoing William Churchill, who preceded him as a successful motion picture director. "C. B. had an almost pathological dislike for his brother, not so much as a person as an *older* brother, and then for the things he accomplished," said Charles Bickford, whose first movie was DeMille's *Dynamite* in 1929. The actor, best known as the studio head in *A Star Is Born* (1954), believed, "Despite his box office hits, C. B. always felt he had to keep proving himself. It started with the brother, but then he had to try and top every other director in town, and then himself." It didn't end until C. B.'s final movie, the 1956 remake of his own *The Ten Commandments*, which he vaingloriously proclaimed "the greatest film and visual experience of all time!!!"

"C. B. wasn't happy unless he had everyone's attention, and he didn't care how he got it," offered Edward G. Robinson. The younger director made his name with epics, particularly historical or biblical tales. The bigger the cast and budget, the better. Brother William quipped, "The trouble with Cecil is that he always bites off more than he can chew—and then chews it." DeMille's spectaculars were known for taking extreme liberties with historical fact and for rather hypocritically presenting cinema-filling scenes of sex and "sin" which were eschewed and excused by the repentance-laden finale.

Yul Brynner, who starred in *The Ten Commandments*, declared, "Cecil B. DeMille was De phony and De hypocrite of all time. He liked being the biggest fly on the Hollywood shit-hill." Publicly arch-conservative, C. B. had a foot fetish; Paulette Goddard was one of many female stars who got cast in a DeMille film due to her toes and arches, but one of very few to publicly admit it. William Demille allowed, "Cecil was never very close to anyone . . . . His nature is basically suspicious." When the witch-hunts began in the late 1940s, C. B. joined in and helped lead the gang of self-righteous bigots and publicity-seekers.

"DeMille was the sort," explained two-time Oscar-winner Melvyn Douglas, whose wife was a Congresswoman, "who pushed himself higher by keeping others down . . . . Not a nice man. And not a nice brother—he once boasted, in front of a bunch of us, that someday no one would ever mention his brother without saying he was C. B. DeMille's relation." He more than succeeded, for William Demille is scarcely mentioned or remembered at all (he became a drama professor at USC).

DIVA DEAREST:
Maria Callas

ontrary to what one might think," wrote her cousin, "it was not always very pleasant to be related to Maria Callas." Steven Linakis wrote a biography of his late cousin, ironically dedicated "To Litza and Jackie," Maria's unloved—by her—mother and sister, both of whom survived the diva who died at fifty-three, basically from a lack of will to go on.

Earlier, Maria had been closer to her mother than her father, by all accounts a domineering, tight-fisted, and suspicious man with little love for his wife—or his mistress. Maria was born Kalogeropoulos in Manhattan in 1923, and may not have learned until much later that for her mother, her birth was anticlimactic. Litza had lost her beloved son in a typhoid epidemic in Greece only months before. She wanted another son, to replace Vacily. Reportedly, Litza had little or no interest in naming her new daughter, so an arbitrary name was chosen for the infant's hospital bracelet.

Sophia Cecilia Anna Maria, usually called Mary by relatives, was nearly killed at age five. She'd seen her older sister Jackie waiting to cross a street, and left her mother's side to join her. A car dragged her twenty feet before halting, and Maria was in a coma nearly three weeks.

Litza and her husband George argued often. Litza was attractive, as was Jackie, who also became an opera singer. Maria grew up overweight, and didn't become svelte until some time into her career (for inspiration, she affixed photos of Audrey Hepburn to her refrigerator). George became enraged whenever his wife spoke to another man, even the mailman. Litza matched yell for yell, noting that he could act lecherously toward women in front of their children but she wasn't allowed to say good morning to a man. Eventually, Maria joined in such arguments, siding with her mother.

When a friend asked Litza why she put up with George, she wearily answered, "My children."

Another major irritant was George's unwillingness to pay for piano lessons for their daughters. True, it was the Depression; many people were selling apples on the street to survive. But Litza knew that her girls were musical, and finally did get them a piano teacher. Maria in particular learned to play well. Both girls also loved opera recordings, but George put his foot down on voice lessons for the girls. Both loved to sing, especially Maria, who although six years younger, was much more aggressive than the more attractive, slim, and sedate Jackie. The two often fought over access to the piano. Maria usually won; as the baby of the family her behavior was typically considered cute.

Mary's cousin Steven explained, "I seriously doubt Maria knew or sensed that her mother had preferred to have a boy when she was born. She did believe herself to be a fat, ugly duckling, and thought that Jackie was preferred over her, which may have been why she was so assertive, precocious, competitive, and even a bit of a tomboy."

From the first, Maria felt the sort of enti-

Maria Callas

tlement which many youngest children feel. But more so. Her cousin recalled a time when they were about twelve and Mary wanted a turn at the roller skates. Steven said it was his turn. Mary knocked him down and tore the skates off his feet. Even though the corner of his mouth had ripped open and he had to have three stitches, Maria "wasn't in the least sorry." She believed it was his fault, since it was her turn. "Another time, I had fallen off the backyard fence. She let me lay there and wouldn't do anything, although I knew my arm was broken. I had to promise not to say it was her fault. I . . . had to swear it before she went to get her mother."

As an adult and an international celebrity, Maria continued to use and abuse people. Her wants and goals were her own justification. "So much was tolerated from her," said columnist Dorothy Manners. "Because of who she was . . . and her exquisite talent, and the fact that she was a lady. Except that she was no lady."

Early on, Jackie's voice was deemed superior to Maria's, and in 1937 when she was nineteen, Jackie went to Greece. George had continued to refuse his daughters vocal lessons; Litza hoped that her family in Athens would help pay for Maria and Jackie's vocal training. Months later, Litza took Maria too, leaving George at home with, eventually, a housekeeper cum mistress on whose head Maria later smashed a large spaghetti platter. Her provocation? The servant would often make faces while Maria sang at the piano. When the police arrived, Maria told them the bloodied servant girl was "a lunatic" who kept bashing her own head against the wall.

When World War II broke out and the Germans occupied Greece, Litza and her daughters suffered privations which eased once Maria started her fabled career, charming all music-loving nationalities with her increasingly superb voice, if not her heft. After the war, Maria and her mother returned to New York, where George was ensconced with his "housekeeper." He told friends that Litza was back living with him, but "as a sister." She didn't mind her husband's live-in, clean-up mistress, but Maria did. She informed her mother, "If ever I was married to such a man, treating me as he does you, I would take a hammer and break everything he owned with it."

Meanwhile, Jackie stayed in Athens, less than wholeheartedly pursuing her career, since she was torn between it and her boyfriend. Said cousin Steven, "I would never mention her sister Jackie because the mere mention would upset Maria . . . . Recent pictures of her proved her to be stunning. She had grown into quite a beautiful woman in Athens." Litza was also still attractive, and "I could imagine her mother in Maria's stateroom, the purser eyeing Litza and not her daughter, and Maria getting angry, as she always would."

"It's a good thing Maria never had children," stated Pier Paolo Pasolini, who directed her in her only film, the non-singing *Medea* (released in the United States in 1973), about an ancient Greek who murders her children to get back at her philandering husband. "I doubt she has much maternal feeling, but I know she would have been too demanding with children, too harsh."

If Maria's anger and resentments were large, so was her ambition, and unlike Jackie she didn't envision romance or "settling down." One of Maria's biggest breaks was meeting what she called a "pipsqueak" Italian millionaire named Giovanni Battista Meneghini. He was a secretly gay man, overweight, socially and culturally ambitious, an older man who loved music and going out, and being seen with important or beautiful women. Meneghini married Callas and helped subsidize her career, using his contacts to push her along, and he became her manager. Her turning point was performing in Italy, the home of opera (which means: a piece of work).

A second great influence on Maria as an artist, and perhaps the motivator of her weight loss, was another wealthy gay Italian, the aristocrat and director of operas and films, Luchino Visconti, whom Maria strove mightily to please. In the 1950s Maria Callas was a household name, unusual for an opera star. Unlike many opera singers, she *acted* while singing and eventually *looked* like a romantic leading lady. She had slimmed down and become an elegant dresser, and her temperament was becoming widely known as she feuded with rivals like Renata Tebaldi and theater managements—like La Scala in Milan and the Met in Manhattan—and sometimes walked out before or even during engagements. It was said there were fewer and fewer places where Maria could sing, as she had alienated so many managers and impresarios.

★ ★ ★

Meanwhile, Maria had met one of the world's richest men, Aristotle Onassis, a collector of famous women. He enticed Maria—at first with her contractual husband along—into his stellar orbit, for instance frequently yachting on the Mediterranean with guests like Sir Winston Churchill. In time, Maria left Meneghini for Onassis, who also craved her reflected fame and glamour but who unlike her husband had little or no interest in opera. Onassis fancied Maria sexually, though he was married and a father, and he liked that they were both Greek; on his yacht he informed her, "Now the two most famous Greeks in the world are in one place."

Onassis, whom Maria publicly claimed as a platonic friend, would later dump her for a more famous woman, Jacqueline Kennedy, whom he did marry. Maria gave up some of her career to be with Onassis. As with Truman Capote, once she joined the jet set, her career suffered. Additionally, her voice was faltering, and she finally wound up teaching singing for a time. Did she regret having neglected her career, having made quite so many enemies, or having had but

Callas, just after her American debut

two major relationships with men, one of them presumably asexual and both with older, unattractive males? If so, Maria didn't let on. In interviews she put on a smiling, strained mask, striving for genteel conformity while sometimes barely suppressing her anger.

Although Maria had often accused her father of being a cheapskate, once she was a highly paid diva and consorting with megamillionaire Onassis she still didn't give her mother money. When Litza, who'd moved back to Greece to be with Jackie, asked for a possible allowance, Maria responded by letter: "I had to work for my money, and you are young enough to work too. If you can't make money to live on, you can jump out of the window or drown yourself." After the letter, Litza often referred to her daughter as "the animal." Jackie would later receive the same advice and similar wording. Litza's situation was desperate, since George was sending her no money despite a court order. At about this time, Maria began describing him as "a wonderful father" to the press, while publicly ignoring Litza and Jackie and privately warning her cousin—with whom she later broke—"I never want to hear their names again. As far as I'm concerned, they are finished. They are dead." What had Litza done wrong? "My God, don't you understand what she's done to me?"

"What? What has she done to you?"

"Think!"

Maria's reputation suffered when she made the cover of *Time* magazine and her mother, who was interviewed for it, produced part of Maria's callous letter. Whatever hurt Litza had or hadn't done to Maria went undisclosed. But from then on, Maria would have nothing to do with "that lunatic," her mother. Publicly, Maria claimed the letter wasn't from her, saying, "This had to be a crackpot who dreamed that up." Litza returned to New York, while in Athens Maria made a triumphant return in 1957 after an eleven-year absence. But her sister Jackie wasn't even invited to the concert. Jackie chose not to talk to the press about her amazing kid sister.

Litza, however, was preparing to march into a welfare office back in the United States, taking with her a phalanx of journalists and photographers. She intended the world to know that Maria's mother was reduced to welfare. When word of the plan reached Maria and Onassis, who were visiting New York in his yacht, a hasty meeting was arranged with a family representative. "Ari" agreed to $1,000 a month and a villa for Madame Callas. But she received nothing, and in bitter despair tried to commit suicide via aspirins and barbiturates. Eventually she managed to pry a reported $250 a month from her daughter, about as much as she would have gotten on welfare (Callas received a reported $100,000 a year for royalties from her recordings alone).

Maria began to recast her youth, painting herself as the neglected child and her mother as favoring Jackie and working Maria relentlessly: "I was nothing more than a goddamned singing machine making money."

"She bore tremendous resentment after the fact," offered Luchino Visconti. "She did learn to hate her mother. It was a very private matter. She did not discuss this." It was also said that Maria resented her voice, which eventually betrayed her. She would bitterly recall, "I had to keep shoveling it out, screaming my guts out . . . . Well, nobody lasts in this business. Nobody." She, however, lasted less than many.

In the late 1950s George illegally divorced Litza in Florida without serving her with the required papers or informing her of his action. Some time after, he did mail her a newspaper item about their divorce. When family friends tried to effect a reconciliation of mother and daughter, Maria yelled over the phone that she would never talk with Litza again. "No, never! She is ill, mentally ill. My God! Don't you know that?" Then she hung up. Luchino Visconti noted in *OGGI* magazine, "Maria, when she dislikes how somebody acts, she will often call him crazy or insane."

To make ends meet, Litza had to work in Jolie Gabor's pearl shop on Madison Avenue—the famous mother once boasted that she sold "only *cultured* pearls, darling!" Litza's take-home pay was $41.50 a week. In her $10-a-week room, she wasn't allowed to smoke, use an electric iron, have visitors, or turn the light on after 11:00 P.M. "To ensure this," wrote Litza's nephew, "[the landlord] even had a peephole in the wall to look in on her. His wife, an arthritic cripple, made Litza's life even more miserable."

Litza thought she might escape her humiliating poverty by writing a memoir that would of course include her diva daughter. But she was so afraid of possible lawsuits from Maria and/or Onassis that the book was more complimentary to Maria than biographies already on the market. It didn't do very well. Despite its tameness, Maria was outraged, pointing to the book as further proof of her mother's insanity. Litza sometimes regretted the fact that her other singing daughter had not attained the heights, though many felt she could have. At one point, Jackie could have received top vocal training in New York City, with a debut recital at Carnegie Hall. Rather, she passed up the opportunity to be with her fiancé, who was dying of cancer.

One biographer wrote, "The world was deprived of a truly great voice. Perhaps Jackie couldn't bring herself to trade in on Maria's name. Or it might have been that she didn't want to become like Maria. That would have been too high a price to pay."

Many insiders believed that Maria chose to die after losing her career, her friends, and Onassis to Jackie (Kennedy). She became a recluse and died in her Paris apartment in 1977. Dorio Soria, the former head of Angel Records, stated, "Without being able to perform, she apparently had nothing left to live for." Maria's estate was valued at between $10 and $15 million, but her mother and sister had to sue to get their portion—they were upheld by the Greek courts and then the French courts (Meneghini, still alive then, sued as Maria's former manager; after meeting Onassis, Maria had traded in her American citizenship for Greek citizenship, which meant her marriage to the Italian had no validity or even a prior existence under Greek law and would leave her maritally available to Onassis; their nine years together did not lead to marriage—the less self-destructive Jackie Kennedy would not have befriended the short, manipulative Ari without marriage and legal agreements toward her financial future).

"The rich always impressed Maria," explained Pier Paolo Pasolini. "She loves money." Publicly, she professed to love art, though few divas would dream of taking three years off from singing. She proclaimed, "Of course we who are so successful as singers can live in the best houses and drive the best cars, travel to the most exciting places in the world. But none of that is what we're trying to achieve. What we real artists are trying to achieve is honesty in our work and music."

"Unfortunately it sometimes seemed as if Maria Callas cared more about rich admirers, or even her enemies, than family or those close to her," said Leonard Bernstein. As Maria proudly declared more than once, "When my enemies stop hissing, I shall know I'm slipping."

THE MICHAEL JACKSON FAMILY?

A lot of the stuff the public thinks they know about Michael Jackson isn't true," said Michael Peters, who choreographed his *Thriller* video. "Like, they think Michael's so tight with Diana Ross, or those 'dates' with Brooke Shields and Tatum O'Neal. Or he's so tight with his sisters . . . and most people don't know that the real root of a lot of what he's about is how he feels about his dad. He won't go public on Joseph, but he's got stronger feelings on him than anyone or anything else in his life."

Many people imagine that the major Jackson family feud is between Michael and his outspoken sister La Toya, who penned a not-quite-tell-all book in 1991 called *La Toya: Growing Up in the Jackson Family.* Readers expecting the inside dish on possibly the world's weirdest and most controversial entertainer would be disappointed. Rather, La Toya is quite sisterly toward tabloid favorite "Wacko Jacko." The book's central villain is the Jackson patriarch, Joseph, a man with an "inability to express any emotion but anger," and to a lesser but allegedly enabling extent, his wife Katherine. Apparently the rest of the Jackson clan disowned the book and denied its contents. Michael threatened legal action *before* it was published, and ironically La Toya's comments about him during and after the book's promotion were far stronger than those in the book. Columnist Jack Martin quoted her, "As far as his sexual preference, he has never had a girlfriend, ever!"

As to Jackson's sexual orientation, nor does he seem, as choreographer Gregg Burge put it, "a normal, healthy gay male who is capable of initiating or sustaining a mutual relationship with another consenting adult male." Whatever his sexual identity, if any, Jackson has been desperate to seem average—despite being dubbed the Wizard of Odd in every other way—and was the first person in entertainment history to call a press conference, in the early 1980s (he was born in 1958), to announce that he *wasn't* gay!

Arranged marriages and artificially induced pregnancies are options available to men who don't have sex with women but who wish to seem to. However, now that Michael Jackson has two contractual marriages and two offspring in his dossier, he seems more bizarre and reclusive than ever. Eight-years-younger sister

Janet stated before the birth of the second child, "It's embarrassing that wherever I go I am asked, 'How is your nephew?' And I can't answer them because I have never seen him." She sent word to Michael that she'd like to visit him, but to no avail. By then she had become a prime competitor to the Jackson family's most ambitious member—the only one able to challenge him on the charts.

In his self-mythologizing book *Moonwalk*, Michael had noted, "It was great being with Janet because . . . we liked the same things . . . . She was like my twin . . . . When Janet was around and I wasn't working or something, we'd be inseparable." He contrasted this rather patronizing attachment with "La Toya and I are very different . . . . She won't even feed the animals . . . . And forget going to the movies . . . our tastes in films are miles apart." Michael has not addressed the

La Toya and Michael Jackson

fate of his once much-publicized pet chimpanzee, Bubbles. As Jay Leno explained, once the animal grew older and less "cute," it was consigned to a minimal care facility, out of the lap of luxury and out of the limelight.

When Janet told her family that she and her music would someday be as or more popular than her brother's, La Toya reported this to Michael, who wondered in hurt, "How can she be that way?" even though he'd often made similar comments about being number one in the musical family. Former friend and business partner Bob Michaelson declared, "He thought she stole his moves, his sound, his look—right down to the nose." Others have said Michael doted on Janet when she was a cute little girl (she'd had a recurring role on the TV sitcom *Good Times*), but became threatened by the successful, ambitious young woman who became a huge success in her own right.

As for plastic surgery, rumor at first had it that Michael was trying to look like his idol, Diana Ross. A limo chauffeur was quoted in the book *Call Her Miss Ross*, "I said, 'Mr. Jackson, would you like—' and he cut me off. He said, 'Please, call me Miss Ross.' So I did!" Another time, Diana found Michael backstage at one of her concerts, applying her makeup. She turned to an associate and exclaimed, "My God, that boy has got to stop fooling with his face! What is he doing?"

"Trying to look like you," she was told.

"I look like *that?*"

In 1982 Jackson wrote "Muscles" for Diana's latest record, about "the joys of a man's muscles 'all over your body,'" as she said. She teased one of her Los Angeles audiences, "'Muscles' was written for me by Michael Jackson. But I don't know whether it's supposed to be *his* fantasy or mine . . . ." She told associate John

Whyman, "I just wish he would be himself. I wish he would stop worrying about what people will think of him if he just got real." In Diana's movie musical *The Wiz*, Michael played the Scarecrow. But their professional and personal relationships never recovered from Diana's 1985 marriage to Norwegian shipping tycoon Arne Naess. Although invited to the wedding, Michael refused to go, no doubt aware that the diva would no longer be within his circle of influence.

Most insiders believe that Jackson's surgery began in an effort to erase any resemblance to his father Joe. The two have reportedly been estranged since 1981, after the last of their management contracts expired. In early 1983 Michael and his brothers officially fired Joseph, who was furious at no longer receiving a percentage of their earnings or calling the shots. For the time being, he still managed Janet and La Toya. (Michael is one of Joe's nine children by Katherine; according to La Toya he has two others, out of wedlock; and though the Jackson parents often make "moral" pronouncements in public, their first child, daughter Rebbie, was born in 1950, seven months after the marriage took place.)

Joe is said to have blamed Michael for breaking up the family act, the Jackson Five. Michael was quoted saying, "I'd do anything so as not to end up looking like him. I couldn't bear to look at myself in the mirror if I had to have my father staring back at me."

"Joe routinely and savagely punished his children for minor infractions, real or imagined," wrote Christopher Andersen in his unauthorized *Michael Jackson* biography. "Beatings were administered with razor straps, belts, wire coat hangers, rulers, switches, and fists. Bloody noses were not uncommon, and more than once one of the boys was knocked senseless."

The daughters were allegedly part of this abuse: "When he was four, Michael went into the bathroom to discover six-year-old La Toya sprawled on the cold tile floor, sobbing and bloody. Joe had beaten her because she had received a bad report card. Michael merely stepped over her body and, without saying a word for fear of incurring his father's wrath, stood on tiptoe to reach the faucet and wash his hands for dinner."

La Toya's book included charges of sexual abuse of herself and some of her sisters by Joe Jackson, as well as spousal battery. Michael was quoted in 1988, "I'll never forget the times he hit Mother, and I hate him for it!" Through it all, Katherine praised her children but allegedly did little else to shield them. Katherine had vowed not to rear her kids in a broken home, such as she had experienced, and didn't let Joe's frequent infidelities sway her either. Rather, she slid into a mini-world of apparently consoling religious fanaticism, which cut off Michael and La Toya—fellow believers at the time—from any outside friends of dissimilar beliefs. The Jackson parents were known to control their children from early on by making the family circle their friends and boundary. La Toya lost her best friend to the sect, which also sternly forbade homosexuality and premarital sex, etc. In her book, La Toya characterized her parents as extreme anti-Semites.

Michael's megalomaniacal mid-nineties album *HIStory* was notoriously anti-Semitic. Columnist James Bacon suggested it might have been deliberately so, garnering despicable publicity for its bigotry and then more, supposedly positive, publicity for erasing the hate-lyrics. It also sold far short of expectations, marking the beginning of the commercial decline of Michael Jackson. Although he too left his mother's faith, the Jehovah's Witnesses, which had publicly denounced him, he has continued to hold extreme religious views that may have shaped his fears, reactions, and how he molded, or tried to, his public image. A noted control freak, he tries to explain away every irregularity, from his skin tone on. As Boy George wondered:

"Now Michael Jackson says his skin turned white by itself. What about his nose, his lips, and his hair? Did they also decide to turn Caucasian by themselves?"

It's been noted that several of the Jacksons look more and more alike. La Toya has been called "a female version of Michael Jackson, if that isn't redundant," and Janet resembles a better-fed version of Michael. La Toya's book claimed that various family members have followed Michael's esthetic lead, including—most ironically—Joseph Jackson!

★ ★ ★

Michael Jackson was said to resent Elvis Presley's title as "the king of rock and roll," so he labeled himself "the king of pop" and briefly married Elvis's oddly willing daughter. The second wife, Debbie Rowe, was an employee of Jackson's plastic surgeon, who after she became pregnant, by whatever means, allegedly demanded, "Marry me—or you can't see your baby!" The two reportedly live apart (Michael is said to be estranged from his entire family, possibly excepting his mother), and wags have dubbed their possible future divorce Rowe vs. Weird.

The "king" chose to call his son "Prince." Quipped columnist Jack Martin, "The daddy in the widely publicized photos looks like the mother, the mother looks like the grandmother, and the baby . . . Prince, which makes him sound like an Alsatian, looks a damned sight smarter than the pair of them put together." Nonetheless, other than his freakish appearance—the poor black boy who grew up to become a rich white woman, as comedian Red Buttons put it—the most enduring factoid about Michael Jackson is the reported $26 million settlement (which he tried to have his insurance company pay for!) made to the boy whom Jackson was alleged to have sexually molested. Elton John told Barbara Walters that had he been in Jackson's shoes and innocent, he wouldn't have paid the boy and his father a penny. New York attorney Raoul Felder, who commented on the settlement on TV's *Nightline*, declared, "If people believe that Michael Jackson paid millions of dollars and didn't get a promise that the boy wouldn't testify, then they also believe in the tooth fairy."

By then, most of Michael's diva friends, from Diana to Katharine Hepburn to Sophia Loren, had deserted him. Elizabeth Taylor kept protesting his "purity" and "innocence," and in 1999 admitted to the ever-ready-with-a-sympathetic-ear-and-camera Barbara Walters that one of her and Michael's strongest bonds was that both had been abused as children by their fathers. Roseanne, who alleged child abuse via both her parents—they deny it—was one of very few celebrities who spoke out against the controversial singer. She told *Vanity Fair*:

"He is the perfect picture of a child molester. He had the perfect circumstances. Everything. But you know what? People don't know anything, so [they] go, 'Well, we let our kids sleep with him and share his bed 'cause he took 'em to Toys 'R' Us. He's a nice, nice boy . . . .' He's thirty-five fucking years old, and I think he got all this facial surgery done to obscure his age . . . . Yeah: 'He's Peter Pan, so we can let our little boys sleep with him!' But there are a lot of people—most people, according to those awful polls—who don't believe the kid accusing him. Nobody believes any kid . . . ."

La Toya said that she had seen purported pay-off checks that her angry mother had shown her years before. "I don't know if those children were apparently bought through the parents by Michael or not, but I have seen these checks . . . the sums are very, very large amounts." She later said she went public about her brother—though not in her book—because of her own alleged experiences with sexual child abuse.

La Toya was quoted in 1993 in *Beverly Hills (213)*, "There were little boys around the house all the time." Biographer Christopher Andersen chronicled a list of boy companions of Michael's, including then-child star Emmanuel Lewis, who when older remained friends with Michael, and when interviewed by *People* magazine would not discuss the subject of girlfriends. Despite his girlish demeanor, Michael, according to associates and La Toya, had a will of iron, and of all the Jackson children was the most prone to stand up to his father. "Whenever Joseph raised a hand in anger, everyone else stood still and braced for the blow. Michael raced off . . . [and] was so fast, he could pause to fling a shoe at Joseph, and still elude him." La Toya noted, "As always, his victim was someone smaller," and claimed her father "kept a cache of loaded weapons under his bed and in closets." Her mother strongly but ineffectively objected, as "he'd once accidentally shot out her brother-in-law's eye during a hunting trip."

Michael would ask their mother, "How could you marry him?" La Toya theorized, "Maybe because of her [having had] polio she felt lucky to have a husband at all." The Jacksons called their mom Mother and their dad Joe; "Mama" and "Papa" were their maternal grandparents.

One additional resentment was that the young boys—the Jackson Five—had had to "hone their act in sleazy strip joints," said one biographer. Of course when La Toya posed for *Playboy* magazine, Joe was furious. Said singer Charles Brown, "I'm not proud of the whole Jackson phenomenon, as I am of several other black entertainers. I'm a bluesman, but I got a university education. I wanted something to fall back on, something to make a permanent part of *me* . . . . With the Jacksons, it's all about making money, keeping the act together, anything at any cost."

"And nothing is like it seems. When Michael married the Presley girl, right after the ceremony [in the Dominican Republic], he and she were chauffeured to where they were going to stay—in separate cottages five miles apart. All publicity . . . . Then that 'Jackson Family Honors' TV special—that was an embarrassment, and not just to them. In fact, I doubt they felt any embarrassment. Some people are just takers." The 1994 NBC special was taped at the Las Vegas MGM Grand Hotel, having been postponed from Atlantic City in 1993 due to the Michael

Jackson scandal. The big question was, would La Toya show up and disrupt the proceedings? She had booked a hotel suite nearby, but Jackson security forces were instructed to bar her from entering if she did try to join the family.

In her book, La Toya alleged that her parents tried twice to have her kidnapped, and that she only wed her personal manager as a legal precaution against possible parental custody. She and Michael had left home in 1988, within days of each other. "The only thing that had held us there, I now see, was each other." When La Toya, far less independently successful than her brother, tried to go her own way professionally, her father allegedly phoned her new manager to shout, "I own her! She's mine, and that's how it's always going

Michael Jackson

to be! I will never let her go!" La Toya says Joseph threatened her, "Before I let go of you, I will sit on you for five years, and you'll go nowhere. I'll call every radio station in the country and tell them not to play your records! . . . If you don't want me to manage you, *nobody* will know about you, you're history.

"You're the last Jackson, and I'm not letting you go!"

So La Toya made her manager Jack Gordon her husband and her legal guardian, bitterly noting, "How ironic that my mother and father's detesting Jack had resulted in his becoming their son-in-law! . . . Their interference forced me to do something I wouldn't have done under any other circumstances. All my life I'd hoped I'd marry once and forever. Now, of course, that's impossible."

When she called her mother at the MGM Grand and pleaded to be part of the family festivities, Katherine said only if La Toya signed a gag order. Meanwhile, 11,000 fans were waiting, and the entire family was ninety minutes late. NBC had paid $3.5 million in broadcast fees on the understanding that Michael would participate, but when he arrived, he refused to go on. According to biographers, he booked a suite at another hotel, "wishing to avoid contact with his family as much as possible." Janet did likewise, staying at a hotel separate from Michael. Janet did open the show, but "then stormed out, refusing to participate in a family sing-along finale."

The show partly took the form of a pretentious awards ceremony, with awards bestowed upon Elizabeth Taylor, gushing about Michael as "the brightest star in the universe," and Berry Gordy, whom Michael hugged warmly. It was noted that at no time that evening did Michael make eye contact with, much less hug, Joseph Jackson. When he referred to "my recent trials and tribulations," insisting that "in the end, truth always triumphs," an audience member yelled, "So why did you pay the kid money, Michael?" The question was edited out of the videotape.

Biographer Christopher Andersen pointed out, "Michael discovered that his dangerous fascination with young boys had cost him dearly. Between the settlement, including legal fees and case-related costs, and the gifts lavished on his 'special friends' and their parents, Michael had spent over $40 million. Factor in the cost of canceling the *Dangerous* tour, as well as the lost future endorsements, and that price tag easily topped $100 million."

At the "Jackson Family Honors," Michael was urged by the crowd to sing. Most had come to hear him. Originally, tickets had been priced at $1,000, but were offered for $50 just before the show. Michael, though, wasn't in a singing mood. He did later join the clan in singing "If You Only Believe," greatly disappointing the throng. Nicknamed the "Jackson Family Fiasco," the event resulted in a lawsuit contending that Joseph, Michael, and eight other family members had not paid the producer and some 200 cast and crew members the $2.2 million due them. The suit also asserted that the Jacksons had advertised the special as a charity event but "kept $300,000 in cash from a loan to finance the show, spent $39,000 on room service—including $250 bottles of Dom Perignon—bought $30,000 worth of clothes for themselves, and spent $7,500 to have a fleet of limousines sit unused at the curbside for four days."

The family claimed that the "Jackson Family Honors" cost $5.7 million to put on and grossed only $4.5 million. Although millions were spent, only $100,000 was earmarked for charities. "What's really frustrating is how arrogant the Jacksons are," said veteran musical producer Gary Smith. "Now they have the nerve to say, 'We won't pay you.' Where's the *honor* in that?" Not all in the family, anyway.

Deadly Rivals

MADONNA VS. SANDRA BERNHARD

"I'll flirt with anyone from garbagemen to grandmothers."—Madonna, on The Tonight Show

"It went highly out of control. Everybody picked up on it, and the question was, 'Are we sleeping together?' It's not really important."—Madonna, on her "surprise" at public perceptions of her flirting with non-grandmother and non-heterosexual Sandra Bernhard

"I felt used," said Sandra Bernhard *after* l'affaire *Madonna. "There is such a thing as loyalty."*

There's also such a thing as a certain blonde's ambition and her reputation for using almost everyone who has crossed her path. Shock has been Madonna's stock in trade, and metamorphosis—who's that girl *now?*—her methodology. Would-be diva Bernhard became Madonna's best known and longest-running critic after the bumpy end of their relationship (1988–1992). Madonna's mistake was taking on a celebrity, one with considerable mouth and chutzpah. And one with a similar penchant for baring nearly all in public.

"I dream about Madonna more than anyone I know or don't know; somehow she is indelibly written into my subconscious," wrote Bernhard in her sarcastically titled 1988 book *Confessions of a Pretty Lady.* In her dreams, Sandra tried mightily to impress Ms. Ciccone, who is typically "too preoccupied to notice me."

Madonna met Sandra during a date with Sean Penn at a party given by Warren Beatty. "It was an auspicious evening," Madonna reminisced for *Vanity Fair.* "I met my friends Sandra Bernhard and Warren Beatty on my first date with Sean." Rumor would have it that she slept with all three (separately). Madonna later wed Penn; it was a stormy union that ended after he allegedly physically abused her and left her tied to a chair; a police report was filed. Madonna later worked with and for Beatty in the movie *Dick Tracy.* Some said that she used him for publicity, others said vice versa. Economically, he used her: producer-director Beatty earned $9 million and 10 percent of the profits while Madonna got scale, $1,440.00 a week.

In her stand-up act, Sandra would plead with her absent gal-pal, "Be my friend, come live with me, Madonna. Push me over the borderline, Madonna. Fuck up my head, Madonna." Obviously, Bernhard derived her share of publicity from the friendship. The daughter of a proctologist and an abstract artist ("That's how I see the world . . . . My family wasn't the 'Brady Bunch.' They were the Broody Bunch"), the actress-comic-singer was strongly ambitious. For a time, it looked as if she would become a real star, via movies. Her characterization of the demented fan Masha in *The King of Comedy* (designed for

Madonna in a brunette mode

Johnny Carson but starring Jerry Lewis as a top TV talk show host) was widely acclaimed. Her offbeat looks and personality, and her abrasiveness, were a breath of fresh air, for a while.

"She is not someone the general public can take much of for very long," said Howard Brookner, who directed Madonna in the musical film *Bloodhounds of Broadway*. He correctly predicted, "Sandy will never be a mainstream star."

She then appeared in the megaflop *Hudson Hawk* (1991), which, however, didn't hurt Bruce Willis's career. "Sandy wants so much to be a leading lady . . . she has diva written all over her attitude," offered Brookner. Instead, Bernhard appeared mostly in other people's projects, like her recurring gay role on *Roseanne*. She sometimes got publicity out of Madonna *and* Sean Penn. "A third wheel," some of the press called her, and reported Penn's (characteristic) ire when Madonna showed up late for the opening of his play *Hurly Burly*—with Sandra in tow.

"You cunt, how could you do this to me?" he hissed at her later at a party. Whether he was more upset about Madonna's tardiness or her tomboy guest was anyone's guess.

Intriguingly, Madonna's core audience comprises teenage girls and gay men, two groups that would seem to be immune to her sexual appeal. But as the big blonde has said, she is all things to all people, and loves "to push people's buttons." Which she and Sandra definitely did in 1989 at a *Bungle the Jungle* concert benefit where the two sang a suggestive version of Sonny & Cher's "I Got You, Babe." Dressed alike in graffiti jeans and sequined bras, the twosome rubbed against each other and made sexual moves. Madonna told the audience, "Don't believe those stories!" about the rumors that she and Sandra were lovers.

Sandra countered with, "Believe those stories!"

Madonna later explained, "I think in the very beginning there was a flirtation, but I realized I could have a really good friend in Sandra, and I wanted to maintain the friendship."

Not that Madonna claimed to be 100 percent heterosexual, as nearly all stars do. She admitted, "All of my sexual experiences when I was younger were with girls. I mean, we didn't have those sleepover parties for nothing."

Then, on David Letterman's show, Madonna and Sandra added fuel to the rumors by carrying on like sweethearts. Madonna recalled, "It wasn't exactly clear how things were going to go. But Sandy started playing up that we were girlfriends, and I thought, Great, okay, let me go for it."

The tabloids had a field day, and suddenly the big media question was, incorrectly, "Is Madonna a lesbian?" rather than, "Is she bisexual?" Eventually she advised, "I've certainly had fantasies of fucking women, but I'm not a lesbian . . . . After they give me head I want them to stick it inside me." She also declared that with men she did *not* give oral sex, for reasons of comfort and sexual politics: "I contend that that's part of the whole humiliation thing of men with women. Women cannot choke a guy . . . ."

Initially, Madonna seemed to relish the role of sexpert, trying to expand sexual boundaries for the masses (and/or remain in the limelight?). When writer Don Shewey asked if she was kinky, she teased, "I am aroused by two men kissing. Is that kinky? I am aroused by the idea of a woman making love to me while either a man or another woman watches. Is that kinky?" The tabloid press thought it was worse. The *New York Post* shrilled, "What a Tramp! Vulgar Madonna is the degenerate Queen of Sleaze."

Madonna must have realized that those outraged by her frankness were not among those likely to buy her music anyway. She did appear to be trying to raise public consciousness with her comments and output. "Just as people have preconceived notions about gay men, they certainly do about gay women. So if I could be some sort of a detonator to that bomb, then I was willing to do that."

She continued in a highly erotic mode with her docu-film *Truth or Dare* (titled *In Bed With Madonna* in Europe) and photo book *Sex*. She outed her brother Christopher in the gay magazine *The Advocate*, at first angering him because now his father officially knew, but retaining their close relationship—she later tried to fix him up with gay British actor Rupert Everett (*My Best Friend's Wedding*). And she publicly admitted that she was drawn to lesbian singer k. d. lang, who reminded her of "a female Sean Penn" (minus the violence).

When MTV banned the video of her song "Justify My Love" in 1990, Madonna went on ABC-TV's *Nightline* to defend her vision and to accuse MTV of hypocrisy and a double standard. She asked, "Why is it okay for ten-year-olds to see someone's body being ripped to shreds or Sam Kinison spitting on Jessica Hahn? Why are we [dealing] with these issues? Why is that okay? . . . We already have these videos that display degradation to women and violence that are played twenty-four hours a day.

"Why do parents [or MTV] not have a problem with that, but why do they have a problem with two adults—you know, two consenting adults—displaying affection for each other, regardless of their sex?" Critics of MTV charged that the censorship boiled down to two men kissing on American TV.

As for the Madonna-and-Sandra "controversy," she wondered, "The rain forest is dying. What do you care more about, the rain forest or our sexuality?" She bravely noted that whether or not the two had slept together, she was willing for people to think they had. But eventually she and Bernhard were media-paired *too* often, and the publicity was no longer under the blonde's control. Mr. Blackwell named the pair to his annual worst-dressed list as a unit: "The Mutt & Jeff of MTV," adding that Madonna's "gal-pal clung to her legendary side like a buck-toothed Eve Harrington."

The friendship that had begun in 1988 was becoming too high profile for the solo act's taste. And it was labeling and marginalizing the pop diva. "Madonna cringes at the word *lesbian*," explained friend and artist Keith Haring before the Hype Priestess let Sandra Bernhard expand

Sandra Bernhard

her sexual image but constrict her mainstream appeal. "Madonna would rather not have the labels . . . . She's basically straight, but also likes women sometimes."

The key seemed to be Madonna's degree of control. *Truth or Dare* (1991) briefly included Sandra. But the same-sex lovers referred to in their snippet of chat were Sandra's, with Madonna guiding the conversation. The megastar also reunited with a housewife she'd known as a teen way back when, and told the camera that she had "finger-fucked" Madonna. As has often been said, Madonna talks to shock. But pictures are far more potent, and cut from *Truth or Dare* was footage—not from the distant past—of Madonna passionately kissing her female backup singer Niki Harris.

With her 1992 book *Sex*, Madonna appeared to have gone as far as she publicly dared. Her ever-mutating persona began shifting toward movie star as stateswoman (*Evita*) and motherhood sans contractual mate. By the time of Madonna's very (hetero)sexual flop movie *Body of Evidence* (1992), she and Sandy were on the outs, no pun intended. At a screening for *Body*, Bernhard was reprimanded for talking too loud. She yelled back, "This is not a serious film!" and walked out.

What forced the break wasn't just the sapphic media connotation of chumming with Sandra, but the fact that Madonna took over Bernhard's friend Ingrid Casares—a model turned nightclub impresaria—to whom Sandy had introduced her. Post-Sandra, Madonna's friendships—whatever their private extent—with gay women like Ingrid, k. d. lang, and model-actress Jenny Shimizu have been relatively non-public. It's unlikely Madonna will ever be "exploited" for publicity by a woman, or man, again. (Madonna's friendship with non-performer Ingrid is still going strong.)

Since she did the dumping, Madonna made scarcely any public reference to Sandra Bernhard. When stars aren't evenly matched, it doesn't behoove the bigger one to discuss the other—words validate, and they publicize. A royal silence on the person or subject allows the diva to save her words for her latest project. Rather, she did speak out on another megastar at about that time: Michael Jackson. She admitted she wanted to do a duet with him but not "some stupid ballad or love song—no one's going to buy it."

She told *The Advocate* that her gay male dancers would "pull him out of the shoe box he's living in," and opined that Jackson was "a space-alien drag queen and should come out of the closet."

Post-Bernhard, Madonna kept talking about homosexuality, usually male, but downplayed her own bisexuality. Even so, she couldn't repress media fascination with her private life. In 1994 *Esquire* polled 1,000 "young American women" on whether they'd rather sleep with Madonna or Jodie Foster. Madonna got 34 percent of the vote, Jodie got only 17.7 percent (other celebs were included). In July 1995, *Movieline* magazine's cover featured Drew Barrymore's frankly bisexual interview and, inside, a photo of Madonna and Ingrid kissing on the lips.

By 1995 Madonna had claimed, "I'm not a lesbian. I love men," which is technically correct and inspired *The Advocate* to select the blonde man-trap (as well) as its Sissy of the Year, a non-award given to homophobic celebrities like, say, Mel Gibson.

Madonna moved on to single motherhood—for that matter, so did Bernhard—but the ex-manicurist kept up her stream of Madonna quotes (as of mid-1999, she's reportedly still dissing her in her one-woman show *I'm Still Here . . . Damn It!*). Said Sandra:

"I feel sorry for Madonna, because she doesn't know who she is. That's why she dyes her hair so much. She tries to steal other people's identities."

"I can hear Dietrich screaming from her grave, 'Kill that trash!'" back when Madonna appropriated Marlene's Look.

"You can be a celebrity and not get too noticed. Unless you're out with a publicity hog like Madonna."

"She's a lonely bitch . . . . Did I tell you about my nightmare? I dreamt I was Madonna, shopping at Tiffany's, where I was trying to buy some class."

"I don't think I'd want Madonna's fame. You have no time, you have no opportunity, to be yourself. It's next to impossible, and I think it really limits your ability to be creative."

After Madonna wrote a tribute to designer Gianni Versace for *Time* magazine, Bernhard described it as another example of her insincerity, alleging that Madonna had made fun of the gay designer while he was alive. Model Jenny Shimizu, who met Madonna while making her video *Rain*, was later asked why they were no longer friends. "I don't think we were ever friends," she replied; Madonna "reneged on the whole homosexual thing . . . . Homosexuality is a business. It makes money.

"[But] if you go home and call everyone a bunch of fags and butt-fuckers, you're just using homosexuality for your own benefit. It's like, 'Homos like me. Buy my records.'"

Charges of being the ultimate user, and turning away from most everyone in her life (including the father of her daughter), have followed Madonna her entire career. It has not stopped her ascent, though it may have curbed it; for example, her non-nomination for the Oscar for *Evita*. Alienating too many people catches up with one to some extent. As can alienating heterosexual *and* homosexual audiences (bisexual ones officially don't exist).

Madonna has proudly allowed, "I am a sexual threat." However, when sex began threatening her career—or at any rate her mainstream image—she drew back and changed course. After all, she hadn't fully consolidated her iconic status with movie stardom—hit movies—and was thus still vulnerable. Now, as an entertainer and sex symbol past forty, Madonna will have to rely on more than looks, eroticism, or shock value to propel her career forward or even keep it at or near the same level as before. Her liaison with Sandra Bernhard constitutes a colorful chapter in her story, one that certainly didn't hurt her career or pocketbook. But one that has since gained her, apparently, an irksome gadfly, a mouthy dissenter, and a quotable enemy for life.

P*ri*M*adonna*
THE WOMAN YOU LOVE TO HATE

Some of Madonna's remarks and confessions sound awful. For instance: "I have a streak of tyranny in me that runs very deep. I can be a bitch and overbearing and demanding, and I can act like a child." The comment is true of dozens of male and female superstars, but most wouldn't have the nerve or honesty to admit it. Let alone exult. Some people applaud Our Lady of Perpetual Promotion while others wonder if her 15 million minutes of fame will *ever* be up.

"Everyone's entitled to my opinion."—Madonna, to her employees

"I can throw a fit, I'm master at it."

"I'm tough, ambitious, and I know exactly what I want. If that makes me a bitch, okay."

"I saw losing my virginity as a career move."

"I am ambitious, but if I weren't as talented as I am ambitious, I would be a gross monstrosity."

"All those men I stepped all over to get to the top—every one of them would take me back because they still love me."

"So I'm not the world's greatest actress."

"My movie company is Siren Films. You know what a siren is, don't you? A woman who leads men to their deaths."

"It's a great feeling to be powerful. I've been striving for it all my life. I think that's just the quest of every human being: power."

"Power is a great aphrodisiac, and I'm a very powerful person . . . ."

"Really overweight girls or guys with lots of acne follow me around and pester me. It's frightening because, not only are they bothering me, but they're horrible to look at too."—Madonna, on some of her fans

"Every time they jump out to take pictures, it's like they're raping me . . . . They might just as well take a gun and shoot me."

"[Antonio Banderas] probably has a really small penis."—Madonna, after Banderas's then-wife scared her off a potential affair with him

"[La Toya Jackson] had a tit job for sure. This [posing nude] is desperation. Well, maybe she'll get a job out of it."

"[Mariah Carey] needs to get a life."

"She's a *cochon* [*pig* in French]."— Madonna, on Zsa Zsa Gabor

"Warren [Beatty] is a pussy . . . . He's a wimp . . . . I know I have a much bigger following than Warren does, and a lot of my audience isn't even aware of who he is."

"Kevin Costner has personality-minus."

"I'm everything."

Pop Tart
THE STARS VS. MADONNA

"Like a virgin, indeed! . . . She is a woman who pulled herself up by the bra straps, and who has been known to let them down occasionally."—Bette Midler

"You know Madonna just bought a home . . . with nine bedrooms. You know what that means? No waiting!"—Jay Leno

Madonna posing as Jayne Mansfield

"Who is this Miss Madonna? The idea that she would make a film from my *Blue Angel* is outrageous! She's no angel—on the contrary!"—Marlene Dietrich, who died in 1992

"The first time I heard of Madonna, I thought she was a nun. Nowadays, people wonder: What has Madonna got? Has she got beauty, talent, charisma? The correct answer is: Nun of the Above."—Joan Rivers

"Madonna, Madonna, Madonna. I'm sick of hearing about Madonna."—Whoopi Goldberg

"I'm sick of her because I have no respect for the way she utilizes her talent. She could do so many things that are more constructive."—Jennifer Jason Leigh

"There's a central dumbness to her."—Mick Jagger

"Madonna is a no-talent. She slept with everybody on the way up. That's how she made it to the top."—La Toya Jackson

"She is the worst possible Italian-American role model. At least since Al Capone and that ilk."—Don Ameche

"Madonna said I looked like I had a run-in with a lawnmower and that I was about as sexy as a Venetian blind. Now there's a woman that America looks up to as being a campaigner for women, slagging off another woman for not being sexy."—Sinéad O'Connor

"She wants it both ways. To be a feminist and strong role model, and to be a sex symbol and slut. Sorry, Madonna. No can do."—former talk host Virginia Graham

"I think it's about feeling desperate. Some people don't exist unless someone [else] is looking."—feminist comedienne Elayne Boosler, on why Madonna shares so many intimacies with the public

". . . a crass social-climber and a tramp."—Jackie Onassis's assessment of Madonna after her son brought her home; Jackie warned him to stop seeing the married woman

"As easy as it would be for me to nail a custard pie to the wall."—Shirley MacLaine in 1991, when asked how easily she could deal with having Madonna for a sister-in-law

"She's an off-her-beam sleaze."—Zsa Zsa Gabor

"I could rip her throat out. I can sing better than she can, if that counts for anything."—Meryl Streep, after a year of preparing for the musical film *Evita*

"What I like is her variety, her changing and challenging . . . it's also what I dislike. She has little integrity. She'll espouse something, not out of sincerity, but for publicity. She's not two-faced, she's multi-faced, if not exactly multi-talented."—novelist Harold Robbins

"Ah, Madonna. The bland leading the blind."—writer Anthony Burgess

"Madonna is like a McDonald's hamburger. When you ask for a Big Mac, you know exactly what you're getting. It's enjoyable, but it satisfies only for the moment."—Sadé

"Even her becoming a mother looks like a calculated career move. She went as far as she could with sex, including flirting with bisexuality . . . . But she's smart. As she passes forty, she'll have to rely on something other than sex to shock people or attract attention."—director Alan J. Pakula

"It seems to me that when you reach the kind of acclaim that she's reached and can do whatever you want to do, you should be a little more magnanimous and a little less of a cunt."—Cher

SUICIDE AS REVENGE:
Rachel Roberts vs. Rex Harrison

"I don't think Ray killed herself because of Rex Harrison. She was much stronger than Carole Landis . . . . Rachel would have killed herself anyway. In Los Angeles she kept saying that she'd lost her will to live. But she did orchestrate it with an eye toward getting back at Rex, oh, yes."—comedian Kenneth Williams

Rex Harrison is a dirty so-and-so, and you can quote me on that!" said Patsy Kelly. The late comic actress specialized in playing maids on screen, then in life became a glorified maid to bosom buddy Tallulah Bankhead. She once cracked, "Estelle Winwood is not Tallulah's best friend! I am! And I've got the scars to prove it!"

One of Patsy's Hollywood friends was film star Carole Landis, who killed herself in 1948 when her affair with Rex Harrison (married to actress Lilli Palmer) went nowhere. "He'd led her on," explained Patsy. "The guy's a crumb, a user. He's led more pretty girls on than anyone but Bert Parks," the Miss America emcee. Landis's suicide finished "sexy Rexy" in Hollywood. For a while. A cold, arrogant Englishman, Harrison was never much liked in the movie capital. It was mutual. Late in life, he admitted:

"I was ambitious. That meant the far larger American market. But my lifestyle and outlook are more European . . . . In Europe people may pry into the lives of royalty and leaders . . . there isn't that obsession Americans have with film personalities." More than once he said that had he been homosexual—as many at first thought he was—his private life would have remained private. As a flamboyantly heterosexual figure, his personal life was open season for tinseltown columnists.

Lilli Palmer admitted, "He made it hard on himself by being a Latin lover with an English accent . . . . He expected his good little German wife to stay at home, but for himself Rex made no such limitations." During his marriage to Palmer, Harrison fell in love with another blonde beauty, Englishwoman Kay Kendall, a model turned actress. When he discovered that she had fatal leukemia—she didn't know it, apparently—he arranged with Lilli to get a divorce so he could wed Kay in 1957. After her death (in 1959), Harrison planned to remarry Palmer.

But by 1959 Lilli had fallen in love with Argentinian-born actor Carlos Thompson, and married him instead. "I'm afraid Rex didn't understand how I could do such a thing to him." In 1962 he married Welsh-born actress Rachel Roberts, his fourth of six wives (like lady-killer Henry VIII). They were a legal couple until 1971, at which time Rachel, the nineteen-years-younger star of British classics like *Saturday Night and Sunday Morning* and *This Sporting Life* began telling the press about her ex:

"What *made* him, originally, was starring in gossip. Wives, lovers, the Carole Landis suicide . . . . He genuinely hated all that scandalous publicity. On the other hand, he was privately grateful to finally become a star."

"Rex cannot be pleased. Servants have got slapped with his tongue or hand. Eventually, his servants and wives leave him. Rex is one of those what thinks living well is the best revenge. It may be, but the revenge is taken out on his nearest and dearest."

Harrison did live like a king and was known for his sometimes unrealistic standards. "In his own home," said Roberts, "he would send back a wine because it wasn't good enough! I half-expected him to tell the waiter he would never patronize this establishment again!" But Rachel could be difficult too. At a film premiere party, she became annoyed at the attention being lavished upon Elizabeth Taylor, Richard Burton, and Rex. She tried to attract the photographers' eyes by climbing on a table and hiking up her dress. When her husband began to scold, she snarled, "Don't you talk to me! You can't get it up, you old fart!"

Douglas Fairbanks Jr. was quoted, "Rachel was, let's say, neurotic. But then, we have a lot of people like that in the acting profession" (his first wife was Joan Crawford). Harrison quipped, "Pure and simple, Rachel was an absolute bitch and pure hell to live with."

After six years away from the screen, she returned in 1968 to costar with Harrison in the flop *A Flea in Her Ear*. She found he was as difficult to make a movie with as to live with: "Rex was nicer to his leading ladies than to his wives. They got the pleasant public face. Wives get the cold reality. If we hadn't been shackled together, he'd have flirted with me on the set, just for appearances, for his credentials—those get more important as a man gets older. Rex was always afraid of being past it."

Rex was Rachel's second and final husband. The last nine years of her life, she took assorted lovers, including younger costars, a Mexican businessman, and a black hustler. She declared, "I'm a clean, middle-class slut." On screen she played a variety of parts, including a sapphic German ladies' maid to a princess in *Murder On the Orient Express* (1974).

Increasingly, she was prone to deep depressions. Friend Pamela Mason felt, "Ray is an excellent actress, but she's not the only one who thinks she hasn't achieved her potential," and far from the London stage would be unlikely to. "She hates aging," added Mason, for Roberts remained a vibrant and sexual woman whose roles, however, became tougher and bitchier as she matured.

Said Rachel, "My idea of heaven is to be surrounded by pussycats, a glass of wine in my hand, someone playing piano, and me singing." Her depressions were made worse by her drinking problem, and her fantasies—chronicled in her personal journals, which also abounded with imaginary sexcapades—turned more frequently toward suicide. Exacerbating her depression was Rex Harrison's comeback in *My Fair Lady*, touring in the musical whose 1964 film version had won him an

Rex Harrison

Academy Award. Pamela Mason was quoted in the book *No Bells on Sunday—The Rachel Roberts Journals*:

"I think [the suicide] was related to a deeper disturbance . . . . Hate was part of it too. A mixture . . . . What Rachel could not endure was the apparently effortless success that Rex was rightfully enjoying—and without her." Somehow, Rachel fantasized that Rex returning to *My Fair Lady* meant he might return to *her* (he'd finished with his latest wife, the daughter of a baron). Possibly she believed she could turn back the clock by reclaiming Harrison, with whom she re-established contact.

Friend and director Lindsay Anderson (*This Sporting Life*, 1962) stated, "She wanted Rex back. Desperately. She pointed out to him that she'd never remarried . . . . When he made clear that that was an impossibility, she was devastated . . . then came the thoughts of reprisal, of hurting him, hurting herself, hurting him through hurting herself."

A school chum was quoted in *No Bells on Sunday*, "I can understand her end very well. She'd put on weight, had a drinking/love problem, work problems. Oh, yes, I think I'd have taken that way out too."

Despite quality films like the Australian *Picnic at Hanging Rock* and small roles in Hollywood hits like *Foul Play*, Roberts felt her career, like her chance for a lasting relationship, was over. Her pill intake had also escalated, and while in London to visit Lindsay Anderson she collapsed and was hospitalized. In Rachel's mind, Rex Harrison was her only salvation. Friend and actor Kenneth Williams noted, "She loved remembering the good times in Portofino, Italy. Their gorgeous villa with the gorgeous view . . . one got the impression she longed for that place and for that former glory as much as, or more than Rex, who was merely a symbol of how much better it had all been."

Rachel Roberts

But the past was unrepeatable, and Rachel, who'd tried suicide before, made new plans: this time she was determined it would work. The time was November 26, 1980. Rachel, fifty-three, would use pills *and* lye, in case the pills again failed to work. She also remembered to eat a crumpet, or English muffin, so she wouldn't vomit up the pills. Those in the know—she had several transplanted British friends in L.A.—said she planned the event to coincide with the Los Angeles opening of Harrison's *My Fair Lady* tour, so as to steal his headlines and dampen the publicity for the seventy-two-year-old's triumphant return to the town that had shunned him thirty-two years before, after Carole Landis's suicide over him.

Lilli Palmer later explained, "Rachel probably wanted to prove she could still compete with Rex . . . . But I believe the Central American gardener came a day later than intended (and found the body), and so she didn't make the headlines on the day she wanted. The local coroner didn't disclose or know that it was a suicide until days later . . . . In a way, it was a Britannic version of *A Star Is Born*, only much more complex."

Afterwards, scores of friends and associates made comment on Roberts's life and death, but Harrison was unsurprisingly reticent. Pamela Mason (ex of James Mason) wrote:

"I do believe that the fact she took her own life almost on the eve of his opening night in *My Fair Lady* is not coincidental. The lye was the extra pain she believed she could cause him. I don't think she even remotely remembered what grief and professional harm had been caused to Rex . . . when his girlfriend Carole Landis had committed suicide in Hollywood." Nor the grief and harm it had caused Landis.

"There's always something unreal about suicide," said friend and author Gavin Lambert, "except of course for the person who commits it. Rachel . . . openly wished to be a movie star." Kenneth Williams: "She was an all or nothing personality. Her friend in Los Angeles Sybil Christopher [whom Richard Burton had divorced to wed Elizabeth Taylor] was working at the ICM talent agency. When Ray felt that her acting career was at a standstill, she seriously considered giving it all up to become a secretary at the agency!"

Lindsay Anderson, who took charge of her ashes, felt, "She lived a dramatic life . . . and she even loved the dramas of Rex Harrison's moodiness and occasional cruelties. What she hated was blandness . . . boredom." Of her dramatic end, friend Sybil Christopher said, "When she died, I felt she had got what she wanted at last—peace. Every time I hear John Lennon's song *Woman*, I am weeping for *her*."

Burt Reynolds vs. Loni Anderson

"She's vain, she's a rotten mother, she slept around, she spent all my money."—Burt Reynolds, on divorcing Loni Anderson

Burt Reynolds went over two decades between marriages. His first wife was Britisher Judy Carne, who became briefly famous as TV's Sock It To Me girl on *Rowan & Martin's Laugh-In*. The union lasted from 1963 to 1966. Carne revealed, "I left him the day he threw me against our fireplace and cracked my skull." There followed relationships with Dinah Shore and Sally Field, whose Oscars seemed to come between them. Although Reynolds has often noted his desire for an Academy Award, he has—too concerned with box office and the sure thing—shunned a roster of roles such as those that brought Oscars to Jon Voight in *Coming Home* and Jack Nicholson in *Terms of Endearment*.

Then came Loni Anderson, best known pre-Burt as the blonde from *WKRP in Cincinnati*. She and Reynolds were together eleven years, five as husband and wife. In 1993 the public suddenly found out that it was over when he served her with divorce papers and a one-way plane ticket away from their waterfront Florida mansion. Burt claimed it had ended two years before, when he allegedly caught her "in a romantic clench" (sic) with a young man. Reynolds said there was "none of the intimacy of a married couple" thereafter. He investigat-

ed "her actions." And though for some time he was the number one box office movie star, he complained that she spent "money as though it was as plentiful as sand in the Saudi desert."

The likable but fading superstar (born in 1936) stated in his 1994 memoirs that he believed the divorce would be quick, quiet, and painless, especially as he offered her a settlement of $10 million. Rather, the prolonged and very publicized action "turned out to be a doorway leading straight to hell. It created more problems than it solved" and tarnished his image, partly because he kept flinging accusations at an actress who remained cool and collected. While Reynolds ranted and raved on national TV, she said nothing—until her 1995 memoirs, titled *My Life in High Heels* (his were *My Life* and did not list a cowriter).

Pre-Burt, Loni had twice been married and divorced and had reared a daughter (Loni was born in 1946 or '45, a few other sources offering 1947 and 1950). "I wouldn't have married [Burt]—or adopted a son with him—if I hadn't expected us to be together the rest of our lives," she wrote. Anderson found out the hard way that regardless of blame—and not *everything* is revealed, even in the messiest of stellar divorce wars—a mate who is a superstar may have the money, power, and quirks to make breaking up an ordeal and a national humiliation. Eighteen months after declaring for a divorce, Reynolds whispered to her in court,

"Honey, please make them stop this now. Don't let them humiliate me anymore." Then he walked past her.

Loni claimed to be dumbfounded: "I sat back in my chair, stunned. Excuse me? *Honey*? Don't *let* them? Hey, this divorce was never *my* idea." She recalled some of his humiliating actions, like granting an interview to the *National Enquirer* accusing her of "sleeping around," and posing for the tabloid in a hot tub with another woman, "a woman, it turned out, who had been in the background for years, a woman who'd been waiting for my husband in a hotel room a few blocks from where I sat beaming with pride the night Burt won his Emmy for *Evening Shade*."

Burt and Loni met in 1978 on Merv Griffin's talk show. He inquired how her husband was handling her success on *WKRP*. He knew firsthand, via Judy Carne, how difficult it could be for an actor when his actress wife became more celebrated than he. In 1980 Loni played Jayne Mansfield in a TV movie, with Arnold Schwarzenegger as her husband Mickey Hargitay. Loni felt an affinity with Jayne; both had become successful after switching from brunette to blonde, and both became mothers early via teen marriages that didn't end well. Contrarily, Loni had had breast reduction surgery, while Jayne's overendowment became the mainstay of her short-lived career.

"I think one reason Burt and Loni were so attracted," says a longtime gay actor friend of Reynolds, "is that the public liked them as a couple. The dark action hero and the non-challenging blonde heroine . . . . Both have a great sense of humor. Both are realistic about their level of talent. When Burt was with Sally Field, her talent intimidated him, especially after it was publicly honored

like that . . . . I think Burt and Loni were in love with the reflections and complements of themselves, and later when they found that wasn't enough, they decided to adopt. I know Burt has always wanted to be a father."

Anderson admitted that part of the problem was Reynolds's moody reliance on prescription drugs for assorted injuries and ailments. To some degree, the two had separate lives and friends, and rarely worked together. Well into their relationship, Loni discovered that Burt was ready to go back to Sally Field, who he said—according to Loni—"loves me more than you ever will." Anderson wondered whether "it had been going on for months. Or maybe he had been juggling us both all along." They hadn't yet legally wed, though Loni said Burt had proposed. Burt eventually disclosed his hurt and disappointment with Field for not having disputed the false AIDS rumors (he had a serious but non-fatal problem that caused his alarming weight drop). Loni did marry him, despite doubts expressed in her book, if not to the actor himself at the time.

Stars get their way, more than most husbands. Anderson recounted the time in their Venice hotel room when Burt objected to her nudity—she was wearing only a towel, having emerged from the bathroom. "He said I was immodest, disgusting, that I had deliberately walked in front of the window, and that someone might have seen me." He said that he "couldn't" talk to her about it, and "didn't say another word to me for two hours." That night he informed her, "If you're completely naked, it's not mysterious, it's not sexy. I don't ever want to see you naked again."

Loni claimed that his fading movie

career made Burt more difficult. The publicity from their 1988 wedding returned him to the limelight, but he still had to turn to television, doing *B. L. Stryker* and later *Evening Shade*, where occasional reports filtered through of tantrums and chair-hurling. Adopting Quinton seemed to help Burt's mood. According to Loni, she offered

Loni Anderson and Burt Reynolds in *Stroker Ace*

to become artificially inseminated by Reynolds, so as to have another child, but he declined. Later, when they were on the verge of adopting a daughter, he allegedly switched tracks, explaining, "There's too much going on right now."

Loni wrote, "Four years later I discovered that at the same time Burt turned down the second baby, Pam Seals [his subsequent companion] had begun appearing as an extra on the *B. L. Stryker* set." The beautiful Anderson didn't imagine "the possibility of another woman," more so since "he never was sexually voracious, not even in our earliest, most passionate days." Yet according to Anderson, her husband was jealous of actors she'd merely costarred with. When he informed her that the *National Enquirer* would run an article about her supposedly having had plastic surgery unless he gave them an interview, Loni

said she didn't care. Then he said that if he didn't cooperate, the tabloid would reveal the identity of Quinton's birth parents. Loni then agreed he should cooperate "with them on some bogus story about his ongoing business difficulties." The real story the *Enquirer* had, and withheld, was the Pam Seals affair.

Reynolds's mood swings, pill problems, and on-set tribulations continued. Then, said Loni, out of the blue she was warned that two sheriffs were waiting outside the mansion's gate to serve her with papers. Why hadn't Burt told her he wanted a divorce? she wondered. She was to vacate immediately, and not take their son out of the state, though she was directed to go to California. She suddenly realized that Burt's and her attorney was now Burt's attorney. Then Reynolds "waived this, waived that, saying that yes, I could leave with Quinton. They wanted me out of here, they wanted us all gone."

A friend admitted to Loni that he and others had known about Burt's steady girlfriend from the first year of the couple's marriage. "I heard that Burt was telling our mutual friends they weren't allowed to speak to me anymore." Also, the cars that were "theirs" were "disappearing," plus art and antiques they'd collected when living in Bel-Air while he filmed in L.A.. Loni declared that she then received an envelope containing sixteen handwritten pages from Burt done "with a black marker, full of exclamation marks and underlined words . . . . It was the most vicious, vindictive, threatening object I had ever seen—if it had been alive, it would have been festering." The letter, "in obscene and abusive language," allegedly threatened "a plan of attack—on me—that would go into effect unless I appeared with him at a press conference, 'full of laughs and holding our precious Quinton,' ready to back his story that the divorce was a mutually agreed-upon decision."

Reynolds had supposedly "eavesdropped" on some of Anderson's phone calls and claimed to know "deep dark secrets" about a female friend of hers. The letter added, "If you ever doubt I'm too much of a nice 'gentleman' to destroy you, and *everything, every person*, that respects you, you're wrong." Weeks later, he made his notorious appearance on *Good Morning, America*, flinging accusations that to most people put him in a worse light than his eventually-to-be ex. Loni's girlfriend referred to it as "the Barney episode," due to the purple suit Burt wore on TV. Next, an *Enquirer* piece came out, alleging that Loni had been sexually involved with a man, *after* which Reynolds became involved with Seals. Loni's daughter Deidra stated that she knew the man in question and it was entirely platonic. She advised a reporter, "Everyone in Burt's personal life is on his payroll, because that's the way he can feel he has control." She said the man in question was actually "a protégé of Burt's, hired to keep my mother out of Burt's way.

"There were countless times when we would all go out to dinner, but instead of Burt joining us, Terry would come."

Loni later explained, "For years I had heard . . . about Burt's fear of confrontation with the women in his life. Oh, he wasn't reluctant to mix it up with a director or a stagehand or writer, but he was legendary for not being able to end a relationship with a woman in a straightforward fashion. I knew this because many of the women themselves told me their end-of-Burt stories." Contrary to myth, said Anderson, she and Reynolds maintained separate finances, including the cost of her lavish wardrobe. "He never gave me any spending money, although the court records state that Pam Seals regularly received an allowance. I paid the nannies, I paid for all Quinton's clothes, I paid for the adoption, I paid for the moves, I pay for Quinton's and my travel.

"Not until the last four months we were together did I ever have an allowance or credit card from Burt."

Loni noted that during the five years of their marriage he had earned $38 million, and that she could have also requested a portion of the estimated $50 million he earned during the six and a half years they lived together before marriage. "According to his accountants, all of it—and more—had somehow disappeared." When asked what she wanted for a settlement, Anderson reportedly said a home: "I *had* a home once, and I sold it, because he asked me to. I want Quinton well provided for, and I want a home for us." The money from the sale of her home, she wrote, had gone into three of Reynolds's houses and their remodeling. "Before we were together, his houses were just places on the map that he collected. And then threw stuff into."

She claimed to have waived alimony after the first eight months they were separated. "And so the house I live in now is my settlement." She gets child support for Quinton, but noted, "He's occasionally late with the payments. And he says he cannot find some of my things—furniture, paintings, some jewelry—that were in the Florida house. They belonged to me before I met him, so he doesn't think they're important."

Loni concluded that an unexpected gift derived from the demise of her marriage was "the end of my lifelong belief in the Prince Charming myth. And about

time too . . . . I learned the hard way that just as I no longer have to save anyone, neither do I have to *be* saved." Reynolds looked back and wrote that despite his sagging big-screen career, "with Loni beside me, it didn't matter. We formed a double-bill everybody wanted to catch. *People* magazine described us as the quintessential blend of beefcake and cheesecake . . . . The non-stop publicity also enabled me to make believe that nothing had changed in my career."

"When a man trades in one younger woman for another," says Burt's platonic pal, "it usually means he's seeking youth. But not so much hers as his own."

JOHNNY CARSON VS. JOAN RIVERS

"Men who claw their way to the top don't get chastised for it. But look at all the grief they gave Joan Rivers for clawing her way to the middle."—TV reporter Ruth Batchelor

Even after my husband Edgar died, *nothing*. I figured the rift was over now, or there would be some communication at least. But *nothing*... not a phone call, not a note, not a condolence card."

Johnny Carson's break with aspiring talk show host Joan Rivers had been very public and well-publicized—despite, or because of, his Great Silence. Nearly all *The Tonight Show* put-downs of Rivers were indirect quotes from staffers, with Carson—the then-king of late-night TV—acting as though she'd never existed. Famous for his inaccessibility, his actions spoke louder than his unspoken—public—words—even after the crushing blow of the suicide of her longtime husband and manager Edgar Rosenberg, which followed on the heels of the cancellation of Rivers's nighttime talk show that banished her to temporary unemployment and then daytime TV.

Yet what did she do to merit such hard feelings? Not only from the cool-as-a-cucumber Carson, but also from much of the male-dominated media who judged Joan more harshly than if she'd been an ambitious man. After a long and slow start as one of only a few working female stand-up comics, Joan Rivers (nee Molinsky) broke through in 1965 via Carson's *Tonight Show*. Rivers always admitted that Carson had made her a star—"overnight," she wryly added.

What she didn't often say is that before that, his show—renowned for its sexism—had rejected her seven times. She was too abrasive a woman for *The Tonight Show*. In the 1980s, butch stand-up comic Paula Poundstone of San Francisco was rejected by the same show for not being "feminine enough."

It was also in 1965 that Joan, who'd had a prior six-month marriage, wed producer Edgar Rosenberg. It was Carson who'd recommended her to Edgar for a job, and thus the future pair met. After the 1987 suicide, she wrote, "I was amazed that I never heard a syllable from Johnny Carson .... I thought he would have, for a moment, remembered that he had known Edgar even before I did, and let bygones be bygones."

In 1971 Rivers became a guest host on Carson's show. In 1983 she became the permanent guest host, a significant break-through for a woman on TV. She knew it was a matter of time until Carson retired, and had hopes of possibly inheriting his throne some-day—until she saw an NBC memo listing proposed Carson replacements. All ten names were male. Clearly, she'd hit the glass ceiling. Virginia Graham, one of the first women to have a talk show, explained, "In the daytime, in the early evening maybe, women are toler-ated. But come nighttime and those pricey prime-time hours, with the hubby half-asleep and a beer in his hairy little hand, the powers that be relegate us to sitcoms and the com-mercials.

Johnny Carson

"Television does not do well by the female gender. If you landed here from Mars and judged by what you saw on the boob tube—which is the wrong nickname for it, in my humble opinion—you'd think women were a fourth of the population, not half, and you'd think we all dropped dead around age fifty!"

Naturally, Joan Rivers began evaluating her future. Once Carson retired and she was off the show, she'd be off late-night TV altogether. But in the mid 1980s, Twentieth Century-Fox was forming a fourth TV network and creating a compet-ing talk show against Carson. Joan, known as the Queen of Comedy, was approached about hosting such a show. She and Edgar agreed, and did not inform Carson. Such a tactic is debatable, though anything but rare in show business. Had she informed Carson, she would have been off his show immediately.

The Late Show Starring Joan Rivers began in 1986 and did well at first, attract-ing an audience riveted by Rivers's livelier, sometimes brazen, ask-anything style. It also drew a commercially more desirable younger crowd. But as ratings failed to meet expectations, her Fox bosses turned against her and particularly Edgar. As her manager, he had significant input into the show but clashed with Joan's boss Barry Diller, who eventually informed her, "You can stay, but he can't." She chose her husband, a loyalty that received scant press coverage, and in 1987 Fox fired her, and not long after, Edgar ended his life with an overdose of pills.

As a new widow, Joan was advised that her career as a funny woman was dead too. "Who wants to hear jokes from a widow? No one will laugh." She was dropped all around, and for a time was unemployable. Compounding the situation was her daughter, Melissa, blaming her for Edgar's death; they've long since reconciled—as Rivers put it, "I gave birth to my own best friend . . . a best friend for life." There was also Joan's private guilt, which she later made public, over the fact that shortly before he unexpectedly died, she'd decided to divorce Edgar, whose pride and health problems had become injurious to her career.

In 1989 Rivers came back with her own daytime TV show, then worked her way into all media except music. But she never got over her amazement at Carson's magnified sense of betrayal. When she'd called him to explain her decision to do her own show on another, new network, he'd hung up on her. "Nobody wants to admit these great icons are killers. When I dared cross Johnny Carson to go to Fox, he came on like a gutter fighter—and let his representatives do the talking. Bob Hope could not even say my name. To succeed in this rough business, we all have to be killers, myself included.

"God knows what any of those people came out of and how hard they had to fight, what humiliations they suffered. Johnny Carson once said, 'I started in Bakersfield doing magic off the back of a truck to guys standing in cornfields.'"

Competition and grabbing center-stage were the name of the game for Carson, who at different times had wanted to be an actor or singer. "Some men without obvious talent get shunted off into hosting game shows," observes a former *Jeopardy!* staffer. "They do it for the money . . . it's a steady gig. But all too soon they find they're trapped and typed as hosts, and no one will hire them as actors" —which happened to Johnny Carson, who by the time of *The Tonight Show* was considered a non-actor.

Neighbor Truman Capote felt, "He was frustrated. He learned to love his success hosting on TV. Yet he also knew that was *it*. Nothing else. And," he added à propos of nothing, "Johnny admits that when he does get drunk, he's a very mean drunk." In the book *Conversations With Capote*, he said:

". . . his second wife, Joanne. She was very good to him. She did a tremendous amount for Johnny. I don't think Johnny would have survived or have had remotely the career he's had if it hadn't been for her. But he was mean as hell to her. And they lived right next door [in the UN Plaza building]. He would holler and get terribly angry, and she would take refuge in my apartment. She would hide, and Johnny would come pounding on my door, shouting, 'I know she's there.' And I would just maintain a dead silence."

A former *Tonight Show* staffer opines, "The thing with Joan Rivers comes essentially from his attitude about women. He thinks they're in his control, like the wives or whatever . . . . His first three wives were called Joanne or Joanna, like that, and Joan [Rivers], professionally, became his TV wife, in a way. When she, as it were, divorced him for another, newer network, he was devastated.

"He also hated it that he'd been bested by a woman. From men he expects maneuvering and the usual, but from women he only expects loyalty and obedience. He's of the old school."

Said Joan, "Johnny pretended that he never watched my shows. But [the producer] would say, 'Of course Johnny never watches, but he wanted to know if that joke was from us or you?'" Rivers allowed, "In Johnny's shoes I would have felt just as competitive. I've yet to meet one person who got to the top with generosity."

It was easy to get on the wrong side of Carson, as Rivers found out. When she became temporarily acclaimed for the freshness of her probing questions, Carson's people winced—never mind the star himself. Small talk, inoffensive and bland, was

Johnny's forte. He habitually shied away from possible controversy and pressing issues. Author Jeff Rovin noted, "Celebrities like Milton Berle, Elliott Gould, and Nipsey Russell are shunned—people who surprise Carson by discussing topics for which he isn't prepared or are looking to plug causes. Even Robert Kennedy was unwelcome on the show because he wanted to discuss poverty."

Joan revealed that when she'd often guested on Johnny's show, despite their on-air camaraderie, during the commercial breaks, "We found we had nothing to say to each other beyond, 'How's Edgar?' and 'Gee, the band sounds good.' Even those banalities lapsed after thirty seconds when Johnny would fall silent, drumming his pencil on the desk."

Joan Rivers

Truman Capote believed, "Nobody knows Johnny. He has no friends. Just the people of his staff . . . . The only time he comes alive is on camera. The moment the camera goes, so does he."

The fact that, before she defected to Fox-TV, Rivers had been offered her own talk show by the likes of Viacom, ABC, and Orion went largely unreported in the media. Most reporters weren't interested in the story's background, just in getting more juicy quotes. All Carson himself uttered was, "I think she was less than smart and didn't show much style." Joan more or less followed his lead in not fanning the flames. Until her book *Still Talking*, an extension of her earlier memoirs.

She then admitted, "Nobody from Carson's staff ever walked into the dressing room and said, 'God, the ratings were terrific this week.' They always found the one failure . . . 'You lost Detroit.' And [Edgar and I] would think, Oh, my God. We lost Detroit. That kept us off-balance, and for a long time I was quiet, not wanting to cause any trouble."

Key ratings were also kept from Rivers. And not just from Joan. Eventually, she recalled, NBC vice-president Jay Michelis "told me that, in fact, my ratings were higher than Johnny's. This information, Jay said, was kept from Carson for fear of upsetting him. *People* magazine confirmed this in a story, quoting the Nielsen company that in my three years as a permanent guest host, Carson averaged 6.5 in the week before my guest-host shots, and I averaged 6.9 [million households].

"Because advertising revenues are based on ratings, I was far more successful than I had been allowed to know."

Nonetheless, Carson's staff increasingly controlled Joan's choice of guests and even comedy material. Then she saw the top-secret list—whose existence was later denied by NBC's president—of Johnny's potential male-only successors. It had been smuggled to her by Jay Michelis. Joan felt incredulous and betrayed, and began with husband Edgar the negotiations with Fox that would lead to her own short-lived show that so outraged late-night TV's king. By the time Rivers had seen the list, her access to Carson had already been cut off:

"Never were we allowed to speak directly with Johnny Carson. That was forbidden. He was kept under a bell jar. Everybody had to deal with Henry Bushkin, his personal lawyer and mouthpiece in all business dealings." Virginia Graham had found, "Johnny is not terribly articulate. He's better off using a spokesman than trying to get across his own message"—which he continued to do, once the Johnny vs. Joan battle was on. Said Rivers, "Johnny himself maintained the dignified silence of an abused innocent. But Carson's hired mouths were out in force, assuming a moral tone as though I had committed some kind of sin . . . . Johnny is very shrewd. I admire anybody with such longevity. Staying at the top required what he did to me, it takes saying, 'This girl is going up against me. Let's kill her.'"

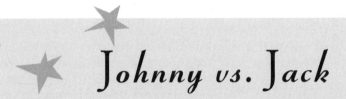

Johnny vs. Jack

*B*efore Johnny Carson, there was Jack Paar. His version of *The Tonight Show* was viewed by many as wittier, more topical, and sophisticated. Eventually he clashed with NBC once too often, and quit. "He was a man ahead of his time," felt talk host Virginia Graham. "Carson was more to the taste of a network, more bland, less provocative."

"His show is only a third of what I did," Paar said in the sixties of his successor, a former game show host.

Carson occasionally poked fun at Paar's loner image, for instance chortling that Jack was in Maine "communing with a moose." The perhaps overly sensitive Paar fired back, "If Johnny needs a feud to help his ratings, he'll find [it's] like tickling. He can't do it to himself."

Carson, who disliked small talk in real life, defended his small-talk format by saying that he avoided topical subjects and issues because he wasn't well enough informed. "Neither was Paar," he added. To which Jack replied, "It's the first opinion I've known Carson to have."

Where Paar had enjoyed scintillating guests and encouraged spontaneity, Carson was known for pre-written or staged "ad libs." A guest who'd been on *The Tonight Show* informed (writer turned director) Nora Ephron, "Merv Griffin isn't out to top you. You say a funny line on his show, and he laughs. Carson repeats it, scavenging, hunting all over for the last vestiges of the joke, trying desperately to pull a laugh of his *own* out of it."

DAVID LETTERMAN VS. JAY LENO

"I don't get his clothes. I just don't get it. I don't get the pushed-up sleeves, the luminescent ties."—David Letterman, on Jay Leno's wardrobe

In show business, as in life, there are always more contenders than prizes. When friends or peers compete for the same plum, one wins and the others more or less sour. David Letterman said he didn't "get" Jay Leno's clothes, but more to the point, he didn't get *The Tonight Show*, the crown jewel of late-night TV, when Johnny Carson vacated the throne after thirty years. To make matters worse for Dave's ego, he had once been top dog when Leno was an eager pup.

"At some point, people started recognizing me," wrote Leno in his 1996 memoirs *Leading With My Chin*. "It began happening more and more sometime during 1982, the year *Late Night With David Letterman* debuted on NBC. Over the next several years, Dave would have me on his show once every six weeks or so." Leno has always credited Letterman with his big break (as Joan Rivers did Johnny Carson). Jay's approach was to try and entertain Dave, his peer. "Those shots were the most fun that I'd ever had on television. Having grown up in New England, I felt that doing the other talk shows required a certain sense of decorum.

"Whether it was Johnny or Merv or Mike, these were all *adult* men, all my elders . . . . For the longest time, I didn't know whether to address Johnny as Mr. Carson or sir. But Dave's was the first show on which I felt that I could really just be me." He added that everyone working for Letterman was their age or younger, "Plus, I always knew how to make Dave laugh."

It didn't occur to Letterman to consider Leno a real rival. Leno wasn't widely considered a comic with a big future. In fact, many insiders felt his big face, or jaw, was a hindrance to his ever hitting the big time, especially as an actor. Leno recalls playing umpteen "goofy guy" roles on other people's shows, and being told by TV decision-makers that he had "a face that can frighten children." Which, he says, must come as news to the nieces and nephews he's close to.

Jay's longtime manager, the bombastic Helen Kushnick, felt that Letterman may initially have been good for Leno, but wasn't good to him. "Dave has more than an edge. He has a grudge . . . there's a sarcasm. He was always patronizing towards Jay." Leno innocently noted that "[Dave] knew when I pulled out old material that he'd heard me do years earlier at The Comedy Store. He'd laugh less at the joke than at the idea that I was desperately reaching so far back."

What it boiled down to was Letterman's abiding goal of succeeding Carson on *The Tonight Show*, after years of following him at 12:30 A.M. with his own show. It was by no means a foregone conclusion that Carson's permanent guest host, Jay Leno, would succeed him. In fact Carson was known to be cool toward Jay, and when he did finally step down in 1992, never acknowledged his successor. Thanks to his talent, affability, and Kushnick's maneuvering, Leno landed the coveted title of *Tonight Show* host. Which astounded Letterman, who felt it was rightly his. Dave called NBC's executives "pinheads" and "weasels."

Some NBC execs felt that Letterman was fine after midnight, attracting a hipper, younger crowd. But he might be "too much" for Johnny's crowd. Although both hailed from the Midwest, the younger, more abrasive Dave was a spiritual New Yorker. "His humor is more pointed, more insulting, and almost always more ironic than Leno's," opined National Public Radio commentator Steven D. Stark. "If Letterman is far more cynical than a Carson or a Leno, it's because world-weary New Yorkers aren't the optimists westerners are. If they were, they would have gotten in the wagon—covered or station—and left for greener pastures too."

In 1992 Leno debuted as host, while Letterman was still—contractually—doing his later show (owned by Carson's company). NBC did not get fully behind Leno, whose ratings were lower than Carson's, and at one point went behind Jay's back to offer the show to Letterman. With provisos, including a significant time delay until Leno's NBC contract expired, and apparently for not enough money to suit Dave's taste. Delighted *and* indignant about the offer, Letterman telephoned his mentor for advice. Carson said that if it were him, he would walk out on NBC.

So in 1993 Dave's anti-*Tonight Show* debuted: *The Late Show With David Letterman*. CBS was paying him a reported $14 million annually, plus ownership of his show and a percentage of the profits from the show following his, *The Late Late Show*. Letterman's company, Worldwide Pants, also owns the sitcom *Everybody Loves Raymond*.

Jay Leno readily admits that he earns well less than his East Coast counterpart, but makes extra millions via personal appearances and his nightclub act. Nor, say insiders, is he as competitive or validation-needy as Letterman. Leno breezily explains, "This is actually a very simple job—write joke, tell joke, get check." Letterman isn't as basic about his work, and his angst has ramifications. One NBC executive said of the CBS host in *Vanity Fair's* October 1996 issue:

"Dave isn't happy, and it shows. Physically he doesn't look well. He oftentimes looks like he's in pain—which isn't real entertaining." There are some guests who shy away from Dave's more demanding, potentially uncomfortable manner. Author and wit Quentin Crisp found that "Mr. Letterman is rather difficult to work for because he expects you to be funny, and frequently, but not quite as funny as he is." Some guests are blunt: Cher told Dave, "You look like shit," and confessed she'd avoided his show because she thought he was "an asshole." Later, Shirley MacLaine apprised her host, "I guess Cher was right."

On occasion, Letterman has gone too far, prompting lawsuits that had to be settled out of court by the network's legal staff. For instance, when he parodied Martha Raye's ads for denture powder and had her selling condoms; the ex-comic sued him for $10 million and defamation of her condom-less character. Or when he facetiously "explained" that a particular Stupid Pet Trick was due to the owner having performed "unethical and intricate spinal surgery on the dog."

David Letterman at a press conference about his move to CBS

Unlike Jay, who courts and cooperates with the media, Dave is often known to cancel interviews at the last minute, and shuns seeking out celebrity guests himself. He also insists that he's never viewed any of Jay's shows; Jay says he watches Dave several nights a week and has stated he wishes Letterman would return the compliment. "That kind of hurts Jay's feelings," admits Leno's wife Mavis.

Letterman and his staff—some of whose members nickname Jay "The Jaw"— have derided Leno's accessibility and upbeat attitude. Jerry Seinfeld once called Jay "Robocomic" because he would do at least 250 appearances around the country each year, sometimes in remote locations like a North Carolina island club where the audience had to be rowed in. "[You] go where the people are," explained Jay.

★ ★ ★

"I have an expression," Jay is quoted saying in the book *The Leno Wit.* "Think like a man; smile like a woman. And that's how I get through life. Most people don't know how I feel on most subjects. I don't have a temper. I don't get depressed." And he only needs four hours' sleep a night!

Leno even apologizes for Letterman, having offered, "I don't think Dave has a mean streak in him. I've never seen him do anything mean. He's just honest. I've just seen him speak his mind. He'll say to a guest, 'Well, that's completely stupid, and you're an idiot.' But he believes that! I believe it too, but I probably wouldn't *say* it."

One former Carson staffer believes, "Jay is a better actor than Dave. He can camouflage . . . he gives the audience what it wants," pointing out that between 1975 and 1984 Leno appeared on several TV sitcoms as a guest actor. The more conventional-looking Letterman had more opportunities to become a successful actor, and was a regular on Mary Tyler Moore's post-*Mary Tyler Moore Show* non-sitcom series, which flopped. Virginia Graham, once TV's leading female talk host, clarified, "Some of us don't relish being actors in the sense of reading other characters' lines . . . . We're *all* actors. But some of us like to be in control . . . the same way that one exerts a gracious control when hosting a party." The former Carson staffer notes:

"Dave is an in-charge guy . . . . He's shy about pushing himself. You can imagine how much he liked to do auditions to get jobs—*not*. He's found his niche, hosting. This is it. When he stops, he'll be like Johnny: vanished."

Until the 1991 announcement of Carson's retirement and Leno's succession, Jay didn't know that, according to *USA Today*, David Letterman would be "fit to be tied when told of Leno's appointment." Said Jay, "I must admit I did not have a clue till it hit the papers that Dave had designs on the job." Either Letterman was, until then, a very good actor, or Leno was a bit disingenuous about the job that every comedian craved. "Jay's been completely tuned in to California and the whole Carson tone and style since he moved to L.A. in '74," said Helen Kushnick, who in 1992 became Leno's executive producer on *The Tonight Show*.

She correctly predicted, "Now everyone's gonna hate him, but who cares? He's got the throne." Letterman's friendship with Leno ceased abruptly.

Leno had indeed earned his top spot, but found that it entailed unprovoked hostility from other quarters and did not guarantee top ratings. Letterman's staff declared war on Leno, and until July 1995, Dave's show posted the better ratings. If Dave didn't publicly gloat, his staff did. The media tried to analyze what Jay was doing "wrong," despite the fact that if two shows compete, one is bound to outperform the other, if not necessarily by much. The comparisons between Dave and Jay were constant, and pitted the former friends against each other as if in a death match.

"The thing that's hard to figure out is, there's no bad guy here," Leno repeatedly said. "This is not a situation where one is evil and one is good . . . . It's only television. What are we talking about here? . . . It doesn't have to be a war mentality." But it is, and more than ever the media thrive on manufactured controversies and adversarial pairings. Much was made of Letterman bowing as a CBS host at $14 million a year while Leno had bowed as *The Tonight Show*'s host at a mere $3 million a year. Jay refused to hang his head in shame. Wife Mavis revealed, "I've never met anybody who's better at living in the moment."

The first two years or so—ninety weeks—of head-to-head competition with Letterman, Leno remained unflustered. Jay edged away from the controlling and sometimes underhanded Kushnick, at least after NBC fired her, and forged his own post-Carson identity and set. The turnaround occurred when English film star Hugh Grant, after his arrest for soliciting oral sex from a prostitute in Hollywood, made his first post-arrest talk show appearance with Leno. (He had been booked to appear before the incident.) Grant's contrite and articulate guest spot, tremendously hyped beforehand, boosted his new movie *Nine Months* as well as *The Tonight Show*, which finally surpassed Letterman—and thereafter retained its ratings lead.

Hollywood historian and author William K. Everson wrote, "Many who watched Jay Leno after Johnny's departure were comparing him, and unfavorably. Jay is not Johnny. Johnny is not Jay . . . no one is someone else . . . . With the Hugh

Grant show, people watched Jay on his own terms and thought he was good . . . . He's more entertaining and uplifting, if you will, than Letterman, who is too acerbic for many." During the 1999 Clinton impeachment proceedings, some critics felt that where Leno often ribbed the president, Letterman was gratuitously vicious, even desperate.

Before that, Leno had informed the NBC brass that he would not accede to their request that he have John Wayne Bobbitt do a walk-on that might boost the night's ratings. He explained, "To me, Bobbitt is a wife-beater. Why reward somebody like that by putting him on TV? That's not entertainment, that's sensationalism."

Jay Leno

Although he can afford to maintain a loftier standard of friendship than have several of his competitors, it is the defections of former friends that hurt Jay the most. "If I can't take it when [critics] are making fun of me," he figures, "I wouldn't be a very good sport." But a lack of gratitude, though unsurprising in show business, invariably stings. For example, comedian Dennis Miller blamed Leno himself for the guest-star booking wars that Helen Kushnick had waged—wanting and demanding first crack at any desirable celebrity. Kushnick had deliberately kept Jay out of the arena: "Just do your jokes, I'll get you the guests."

Leno had invited Miller onto *The Tonight Show*, but the following day Miller denied being invited and called him a liar. Jay, in *The Leno Wit*, affirmed, "Of course I said it. Do I think he is talented? Yes. [But] I do find it odd that people seem to forget who got him his apartment when he came out here . . . who lent money to his brother to buy a car." *C'est la guerre!*—or, that's show biz!

In 1994 Bill Carter published a book about the struggle for Carson's throne, titled *The Late Shift*. It was a success, but elicited a lawsuit from Helen Kushnick, who felt she'd been misrepresented and vilified. The suit was settled out of court (Kushnick died the next year). In 1996, HBO premiered a made-for-cable-TV movie from the book, starring two unknown but relatively look-alike actors as Dave and Jay. Leno was good-humored about the depictions. Letterman—who was reportedly still smarting from Jay's 1995 Emmy award for best variety program—called the telefilm "moronic . . . the biggest waste of film since my wedding photos." He criticized the depiction of himself, then added that at least his character was more visually pleasing than the Leno look-alike, whom Dave described as "Elephant Man."

As he himself noted in his list of "Top Ten Insults for Dave Letterman," "Letterman, let's face it—you put the 'suck' in success."

One of the secrets of his success, says Leno, is that where many entertainers have "one car and several women, I have one woman and several cars." His work, his wife, and his cars, usually in that order, are his life. If he's learned that being top dog has its price, he also still loves what he does:

"This is the discussion Jerry Seinfeld and I used to have all the time—why would you go to Europe on vacation when you could do your act? I mean, people are applauding and laughing. What else can you want? I mean, sex is okay, but it doesn't last as long as your act."

WILD, WILD MAE WEST

Mae vs. Jayne

ae West was reputed to be the most jealous woman in show business. She believed herself to be in a class all by herself—a legend in her own time, and in her own mind. She had a particular aversion to other sexy blondes, and only acknowledged the late Marilyn Monroe as *close* to her class. Never mind that Mae was older than any of them, born in 1892 or '93 depending on the source.

Because she lived in a cocoon of constant praise and protection, West rarely got the chance to encounter younger women, let alone famous blondes—except for Jayne Mansfield, whom Mae thereafter hated with a passion. Years after the car accident that ended Mansfield's life in her mid-thirties, West was still writing and saying things like, "She was so full of evil that one day her head just popped off and exploded."

What had prompted such vitriol? The top muscleman in Mae's famous nightclub act fell in love with the voluptuous blonde who was born in 1932. Hollywood columnist Joyce Haber later recalled, "Mae was furious . . . . It was one of the few times that reality had intervened and pointed up her real lack of youth. Presenting an image of youth and sexuality was her whole career." In her semi-fictitious memoirs, West offered an imaginative retelling of the story. She said two men were fighting over her—never mind that their combined ages were probably less than hers—and she never mentioned Mansfield by name. "I wouldn't give her all that free publicity," she eventually explained.

A few years prior to Mansfield, Mae had taken a nameless dig at Marilyn Monroe and her new husband Joe DiMaggio by referring to her bevy of musclemen, "Why marry a ballplayer when you can have the whole team?"

Mae's muscleman act was a big hit across America in the 1950s. Her last movie, in 1943, had been a flop, but she drew audiences eager to see a bona fide movie star—even a former one—in the flesh. Mae also pioneered the spectacle of on-stage beefcake, which specifically attracted female and gay male audiences. In 1956 she presented a new edition of her act, replacing her Mr. America with a Mr. Universe—"He's Bigger! He's Better!"—in the impressive person of Hungarian-born Miklosi "Mickey" Hargitay.

Among the flock of celebrities who came to view Mae and her men were

Jayne Mansfield

Liberace and Truman Capote. Also the First Lady of the American Stage Katharine Cornell. In her autobiography, Cornell wrote that she complimented West upon her performance, only to be told, "Thanks, honey, hope I can say the same about you sometime."

In his column, Walter Winchell intimated that Mae and Mickey Hargitay were more than just employer and employee. West, now sixty-three or sixty-four, was always partial to gossip items linking her with younger men. This at a time when such a combination was widely considered "unnatural." Mae, however, believed herself ageless and universally appealing. Part of her tremendous belief in herself was rooted in her blondeness. For her, as for Hollywood, a blonde was a special, and an especially sexual and sexually alluring, being. Mae was ever jealous of her blondeness. Even with males; her light-haired musclemen were told to darken their hair for her act. She also refused to autograph prescreen photographs in which she was a brunette. Usually she tried to buy such photos, in order to destroy them, and became incensed if a fan refused to sell.

All was well in West's world until another celebrity came to see her act: Jayne Mansfield, who was starring in the Broadway play *Will Success Spoil Rock Hunter?* (which she subsequently filmed; its British title was *Oh! For a Man*). Jayne fell for Mickey, the jewel in Mae's crown of Adonises. The busty young blonde pursued him, and soon they were being photographed all over town and featured in the columns. One typical caption of the pair read "Hello Jayne, Goodbye Mae." Needless to say, Mae was beside herself, even though the publicity was good for business, and her receipts jumped at the Latin Quarter, owned by Lou Walters (Barbara's father).

Mae demanded that Hargitay dump that "phony Hollywood blonde." He replied that Mae was no natural blonde herself. An already married but ambitious man—he later wed Mansfield—Hargitay advised the press that Mae had offered to double his $300 a week salary if he'd give up Jayne. When reporters asked how he had come to choose Jayne over Mae, he ungallantly wondered why he shouldn't prefer a twenty-two-year-old to a woman "of about seventy."

Mae then got hold of the press and let it be known she would soon be trading Hargitay in for the new Mr. Universe who was about to be crowned. "Oh, he can stay around," she drawled, "but he'll have to go back to the line. That's where all last year's models go."

"That's funny," Mickey told reporters. "If I'm zee old model, then vat is she?"

Hollywood or Bust:
JAYNE MANSFIELD

"I'm not the first star to be well equipped, though I daresay I'm more munificent than most!" enthused Jayne Mansfield, who was born Vera Jane Palmer and became a blonde sex symbol via a bottle and an extra-large bust. Unlike the egocentric Mae West, Jayne molded herself into the very epitome of a dumb blonde. She explained, "Someone asked Marie McDonald if she minded being nicknamed the Body, and she said that in Hollywood a girl doesn't get very far being known as the Brain . . . ."

"Nothing risqué, nothing gained!"

"Publicity can be terrible. But only if you don't have any."

"I think reviews are terribly, terribly unfair, and I can explain that. Reviews are terrible because they hurt actors, and reviews are also terrible because trees have to die to make that paper. You see?"

"The longer I'm around a man, the more likely he is to try something funny. Like they always say, familiarity breeds attempt."

"Mamie—what's her last name? It begins with V. D. . . . I don't see her as a rival, no. Of course, she's blonde. So many are. But—if you know what I mean—she does seem rather small for her size . . . ."—Mansfield, on her busty rival Mamie Van Doren

"I don't know anything about her except the common gossip I heard. When it comes to men, I heard she never turns anything down except the bedcovers." —Mae West in the mid-1960s on Mansfield

"I won't say she was dumb, but one time Jayne squealed out loud on the set [of *Will Success Spoil Rock Hunter?*] and said she had a terrific idea. The director stared at her, then said, 'Treat it gently, dear. It's in a strange place.'"—costar Tony Randall

Jayne got into the act by publicly stating, "If I look that good at sixty-four, I'll have no problems."

When Mae referred to Jayne as "a cheap blonde," Mansfield asked in print, "I wonder when was the last time anybody took a picture of her in a bikini?" (The answer: never.) Later she added, "I think most of Miss West's curves now are from overeating . . . and I always thought her famous walk was more funny than sexy—it looks like she has sore feet."

The savvy West soon realized that it was no use batting barbs back and forth. "Without my name, no one's going to print this trash," she fumed. The press feud may have been good for business, but was bane to Mae's ego and ageless, unassailable image. The press had also tried, unsuccessfully, to involve *the* Hollywood blonde, reporting that Marilyn Monroe had engaged an ex-tutor of Mae's—whoever that would be—to coach her on "replacing" Mae West. Mae curtly responded, "I don't need any replacing just yet," and arranged to hold a press conference at her next stop, Washington, D.C.

Her favorite muscleman, Chuck Krauser (aka Chester Ribonsky and later renamed Paul Novak), and Mae would field questions. Ostensibly, the press conference was to end speculation that Mickey Hargitay was leaving Mae's show because of his infatuation with Jayne Mansfield. In fact, Mae would have fired him in a moment, except her contract stipulated she must have the current Mr. Universe in her show, and so she couldn't shed Mickey until the 1957 Mr. Universe was crowned.

The publicity event would have come and gone quicker if Hargitay hadn't decided to crash it. He later explained, "She was going to spread lies about me, and lies about Jayne . . . . Before I met Jayne, Miss West made it clear she desired my company. She was always feeling my muscles. But after Jayne, she was lying and saying she never found me attractive . . . also making remarks about how Jayne had an ugly mouth or her breasts were too big and not real—all lies!"

When the excited Hungarian began gesturing with his hands, Chuck Krauser stepped toward him and socked him in the lower face. Hargitay, taken unawares, fell backward over a chair, causing Mae West to topple to the floor with a thud. "You can't do this to me!" she screamed. "I'm an American institution!"

The matter went to court when Hargitay charged assault. Krauser pleaded self-defense, and Mae played the courtroom for all it was worth. "Men have fought over me before," she purred, "but never in public, like this. I prefer doin' such things behind closed doors. Know what I mean?"

Behind the scenes, she obtained affidavits from her musclemen—what could they do, refuse?—stating that she'd never shown anything but professional interest in Hargitay. She wasn't about to concede that any man had ever turned her down or dumped her. On the stand, she refused to utter Jayne Mansfield's name, scarcely acknowledging her existence, and only once telling reporters, "She's a dangerous publicity seeker. Maybe if she went to school and learned how to act she wouldn't have to do that."

Newspapers referred to the "Defense of the West," but Mae only became agitated if reference was made to "The Old West." Marjorie Main, best known as the movies' Ma Kettle, had been a colleague of West's and a friend since the 1920s. She later reminisced, "Mae turned that whole episode around. It started with the couple [Mansfield and Hargitay] scoring points off her, but it ended up looking like Mae was so modest and dignified, all those strapping young fellows fighting over her!" As for the three-day trial, it was dismissed by the judge. Jayne went on to temporary movie stardom and matrimony, while Mae waited until 1970 to make a movie comeback in the flop *Myra Breckinridge*, and remained single. Earlier, she'd claimed, "I'm single because I was born that way," until a husband from her distant past surfaced in the media.

In 1967 Jayne Mansfield was killed in a hugely publicized auto accident that also took the life of two men and her inseparable Chihuahua. The episode, in which she was decapitated, became much more legendary than her career, which had finished with topless appearances in seedy nightclubs. Tommy Noonan was the only actor to have costarred with the Big Three Hollywood blondes: Jayne, Mamie Van Doren, and Marilyn (he was Monroe's bespectacled suitor in *Gentlemen Prefer Blondes*). Noonan offered, "I once asked Jayne about the whole Mae West thing.

"She giggled. She didn't think there was a lot to it, just three people doing a publicity stunt for their own purposes . . . . She didn't seem very antagonistic about Mae West, just said she was a feisty old gal who always had to have her way."

If Jayne didn't continue the feud, Mae did, at least in private. "She shot up to the top of Mae's hate list," explained Marjorie Main. "It was a sore topic guaranteed to rile her . . . . When the poor soul died, I don't think Mae went into mourning or anything like." Years after Mansfield's death, West—according to biographer Maurice Leonard—suggested that a writer friend might do a story based on the affidavits she'd collected. He declined, saying the subject was of no interest, as Jayne was dead. Mae retorted, "That's where you're not thinkin' clear. It's when [Mickey Hargitay] gets desperate that he'll try to peddle a story, 'I Was the One Man Mae West Wanted But Couldn't Get.'"

Rather, when she updated her memoirs to coincide with *Myra Breckinridge's* release, Mae included a new chapter—ghost written for her—titled "*My Full Story* by George Eiferman," one of her 1950s musclemen. Though by then Jayne Mansfield was dead, the unflattering long-ago incident still bothered her, and this was Mae's way of presenting her side without possibility of reply from Jayne, and seemingly via a third party, the better to illustrate West's supposed aloofness to the whole matter.

Unfairly, the chapter alleged that Hargitay had told Eiferman that Jayne's mouth was "ugly"—physically, or what came out of it?—and when Eiferman purportedly asked Hargitay if he liked Jayne Mansfield (the pair were later played on TV by Loni Anderson and Arnold Schwarzenegger)—his future wife and the mother of their children—Mickey supposedly said, "Not much."

In one of her 1930s movies, Mae had called her male lead a "fascinatin' monster," a phrase which seems perfectly apt for the real-life Mae West.

Mae vs. Raquel

When Mae West returned to the silver screen in *Myra Breckinridge* (1970), she hadn't appeared in a movie since 1943. This time, she wasn't starring, although she demanded and got top billing. The title role, a transsexual, was played by Raquel Welch and critic-turned-one-time-actor Rex Reed, who upon *Myra's* release placed it on his list of ten worst films of the year. Mae was enacting an oversexed talent agent named Letitia Van Allen; she had the spelling changed to "Leticia" to obviate crude jokes.

However, Mae West was seventy-six at the time. Which in her mind made no difference at all, though her character used her office cum boudoir as a casting couch for the sexy young men who came to audition. In any case, *Myra's* producers hoped their two leading ladies would get along, as they had various scenes together and West could easily hold up production if so inclined. It was decided they should meet before the movie began shooting. Welch, twenty-nine, agreed to meet her at Mae's fabled suite at the Ravenswood apartments.

Both women behaved like pros. Raquel presented Mae with a large bouquet of roses and said, "I've admired you for a long time" (no doubt without stressing the adjective). Mae smiled and purred, "Pleased ta meetcha, honey," then used the bouquet during the ensuing photo session to hide the fact that while Welch had a small waist, she had none.

Victor Davis, show biz editor for London's *Mail on Sunday*, interviewed Mae at that time. At her white-and-gold apartment, he was asked, "Tell me, honey. What's this Rock Walsh like?"

"You mean Raquel Welch, Miss West?"

"If you say so, honey."

This was Mae West's first color motion picture, but her wardrobe color scheme was black-and-white to flatter her mature figure. She decided to make it hers exclusively, and Raquel Welch was informed no black-and-white for her. The result? She showed up one day in a black outfit with a ruffled trim that was the lightest shade of blue possible—which photographed white. The rest of the stars were costumed by Theadora Van Runkle, but Mae was gowned by Edith Head ("Edith Head gives good wardrobe," according to graffiti).

Mae also informed her director that her character was never to be referred to or asked to behave as any older than twenty-six years old. Mae believed devoutly in her sex appeal. One morning, stepping out of her trailer at Fox, she smiled at producer Robert Fryer, "Tell everyone to relax because when I come on they'll all get sexy." Mae's dressing room had been further upgraded after she threw a minor tantrum in front of reporters when one of them mentioned that she'd been put into Barbra Streisand's "old room" from *Hello, Dolly!* West shrilled:

"I'd like to see someone break records like me, and then I'll respect them as a star. Till someone can do that, I feel I'm in a class by myself . . . . So don't say they put me in someone else's room!"

Before long, Fox president Richard Zanuck was quoted, "I've never seen so many personality conflicts on one picture." Rumor had it that everyone was feuding with everyone. Designer Edith Head had no feud going, but declared that she'd gladly return one of her eight Academy Awards just to be released from *Myra*. The studio finally took a full-page ad in *Variety* comprising an ensemble photo of the principal cast and crew and the caption "Togetherness."

Though *Myra* was given an unfair, in retrospect, X-rating and would later go down to box office failure, the New York premiere was a media event, and the movie initially broke records in Los Angeles and Manhattan. The *L.A. Times* reported:

"The principals were topping themselves for sheer venom. For example, when star Mae West said she was going to the East Coast for the premiere, star Raquel Welch decided, at the very last minute, that she'd go too. When the two arrived at Times Square, Raquel got a 'moderate' welcome from fans, but Mae was mobbed by 10,000. Mae West, nevertheless, refused to sign autographs or to pose with Raquel Welch for pictures. In turn, Raquel Welch refused an invite to the party *Time* magazine gave in her honor."

Understandably, West got the bigger welcome, having been away from movies for over a quarter-century, while Raquel was making a few a year. West's refusal to pose with Welch wasn't due to arrogance, but anxiety over photographic comparisons of the two actresses.

Mae West at age seventy-six in *Myra Breckenridge*

Though Welch made no public cracks about the "Old West," the day after the premiere, at a press conference held in her suite at the Sherry Netherland, Mae stated, "I wonder how any actress, with any following, could have played Myra . . . . They only signed her because they couldn't get anyone of stature to play the lead," a grave slip, for West had insisted that *she* was the lead.

Child star turned diplomat Shirley Temple threatened to sue Fox over use of a clip from one of her movies in *Myra Breckinridge*, and the often reactionary *Time* branded *Myra* as being "about as funny as a child-molester." Many reviews zeroed in on Mae's age-defying act and how she managed to get away with what she did and said. One noted encounter was a scene between her and a cowboy whom she asks how tall he is. "I'm six feet, seven inches, ma'am." To which Leticia/Mae lustily coos, "Never mind the six feet. Let's discuss the seven inches."

In the 1930s, William Randolph Hearst had branded Mae West "a monster of lubricity." The old hypocrite—his mistress was actress Marion Davies—was said to be jealous that the next highest-paid person in the United States after him was the fascinatin' Mae, a female. Some of *Myra*'s reviewers felt that West had by now become rather quaint, and that the offense, if any, lay with the other stars and/or the transsexual theme, or Farrah Fawcett's topless scene in bed with a clothed Raquel Welch (once Fawcett became a star, the scene was cut from some or all videocassette copies of *Myra*, which subsequently got an R-rating). A few critics cruelly derided Mae's "mummified" looks—the same critics who don't look askance at the habitual sexual pairing of, say, a male star in his sixties and an actress in her thirties or even twenties.

Raquel Welch in *Myra Breckenridge*

It was just as well that West was kept from reading such reviews. (She seldom read at all, and when decorating her Santa Monica beach house had ordered "books by the yard" for show.) Months after *Myra* had come and gone, Mae was still telling the press that *Myra* had been a personal triumph and that she planned to do three more movies in the near future (she did one more big-screen sexpot turn, at age eighty-four). In the fall of 1970, the *L.A. Times* published a dissenter's opinion:

"Mae West has become a tiresome old bore forever talking about how wonderful she was and thinks she still is . . . . She needs to be straightened out that she was, or is, a sex symbol. She was never anything of the sort. She was a comedienne . . . . No man in real life ever gave much thought to Mae West being the girl of his dreams . . . . An old lady who thinks of herself as a sex symbol is sad and somewhat revolting."

In 1985, in a preface to a reissue of his novel *Myra Breckinridge*, Gore Vidal wrote, "Twentieth Century-Fox bought the film rights as a vehicle or, to be more precise, a hearse for Raquel Welch, John Huston, Mae West, and an assortment of other exciting non-actors . . . . For the first time in the history of paperback publishing, the film of a book had proved to be so bad that the sale of the book stopped." Vidal claimed never to have seen the movie, which, like Mae's later *Sextette*, is nowhere as horrific as reported, and has become a cult film over the years.

Among the "other exciting non-actors" in *Myra* were newcomers Tom Selleck (as "Stud") and Farrah Fawcett as a more prominent stud's girlfriend, who is enticed into bed by Myra. There were on-set rumblings at the time of bad feeling between Raquel Welch and Fawcett. But as it wasn't a clash of two stars, then, it went unreported. In interviews ever since, however, Farrah has refused to discuss Welch, only admitting in a 1998 *TV Guide* that Raquel treated her very badly.

The moral, or lesson, from all this: with most stars, the longer they've been a star, the worse they treat a younger star or a newcomer. It's sometimes said that in Hollywood it's dog eat dog—or occasionally diva eat diva. For, as former studio head David Begelman put it, "The gut feeling in this business is annihilate or be annihilated."

BIRDS OF A FEATHER FEUD TOGETHER:
Cecil Beaton vs. George Cukor

eorge Cukor directed perhaps more Hollywood classics than any other director. But because he was neither publicity-prone, unlike C. B. DeMille or
Alfred Hitchcock, and didn't stick primarily to one genre, unlike John Ford or
Hitchcock, he wasn't as famous or celebrated. Part of the reason Cukor was
publicity-shy was his homosexuality, also his self-consciousness about his bespectacled plainness and initial overweight. Unlike the gay or bisexual and very plain
Vincente Minnelli, he never took a wife or used women as "beards."

Although he worked in Hollywood, an industry much beholden to Jews and
gays, Cukor, a gay Jew, venerated outward conformity, or "passing." When asked
his religion, Cukor replied that he was an American. For, in that "golden" age, to
be different in any way was thought bad or risky. So Cukor downplayed his sexuality and religion, even in Hollywood, though eventually he did come out of the
closet.

I interviewed George Cukor and Cecil Beaton, each more than once, both on
tape, eventually including part of the sessions in my book *Conversations With My
Elders*—interviews with six men of cinema. In their distinct ways, both men were
charming and articulate; each had enjoyed a magnificent career and worked with a
galaxy of the century's luminaries. But both became defensive and feisty when the
other was mentioned.

Cecil Beaton began as a photographer and worked his way to the top of that
profession (which Gore Vidal has adjudged the most overrated art). The
Englishman also became an expert in historical recreations for stage and screen, a
master of art direction and costume design. His first Oscar was earned for the costumes for *Gigi* (1958), a film on which he worked with Minnelli. Beaton would
win two more Academy Awards for *My Fair Lady* (1964), for art direction (with
Gene Allen) and costume design, to George Cukor's belated first and only Oscar
(contrasted with the multiple Oscars given such heterosexual directors as Ford,
John Huston, or Billy Wilder).

Cukor, who had a lengthy tenure at MGM, generally got along with everyone.
But Cecil Beaton was, or had been, anti-Semitic—alas not unusual in a nation

which at the time had an empire, or dictatorship, over hundreds of millions of people of varied colors, races, and religions. In a 1938 *Vogue* illustration, Beaton had inserted semi-hidden slurs against prominent Hollywood Jews. After the ensuing scandal, he claimed that his drawing hadn't meant to defame anyone. He "explained" privately that he believed Jews had less artistic taste than Gentiles did!

A terrific snob, Beaton had worked his way up through England's fossilized class system to consort with the rich, the famous, and the royal (he'd begun by photographing society ladies). In time, he would claim more than friendship with Greta Garbo, his friend and photographic subject. Cukor found such a fiction appalling. He'd directed the sapphic or bisexual Swede in the classic *Camille* and her final movie, *Two-Faced Woman* (1941).

Cukor and Beaton had met during preproduction of *Gone With the Wind,* which Cukor was hired (later fired) to direct. While in Los Angeles, Cecil attended some of Cukor's renowned parties but disliked the "crude" Hollywood talk. For his part, Cukor had a "love-hate relationship with Britain," according to Beaton's biographer Hugo Vickers. He was well pleased when producer Jack Warner decided that the expensive screen version of the megahit musical play *My Fair Lady* would *not* be made in England.

Beaton was irked by Cukor's delight; the director hated the idea of "all those tea breaks they're always stopping for over there." Cukor was irked that Beaton had been hired before he was (Vincente Minnelli had been approached to direct, but wanted a percentage of the profits; Cukor earned $300,000 for *MFL*). Much of the press was annoyed that Eliza Dolittle would be played by superstar Audrey Hepburn, not Julie Andrews, the Broadway Eliza. Hepburn was the second actress, after Elizabeth Taylor, to earn $1 million for a movie (Rex Harrison, not the first choice to play Henry Higgins, whom he'd done on Broadway, was finally signed at $200,000; wife Rachel Roberts stated, "Despite his aloofness, Rex would have jumped through hoops to get the assignment" which landed him an Oscar).

MFL went on to win the Best Picture Academy Award and become a musical classic. However, a number of people in it had clashes or initial differences. For instance, lyricist and screenwriter Alan Jay Lerner objected to the choice of Hepburn and rarely visited the Warners lot in Burbank. Rex Harrison was at first cool toward the first-billed, younger, and more highly-paid Hepburn. And Beaton disdained art director Gene Allen; in his diary he described him as "a former policeman, stocky and apple-faced, with a bullet head and a child's starry eyes of wonderment." It was established by Beaton before filming began that he, not Allen, was the designer and had been hired as such—and was to be deferred to.

Cukor, who dressed plainly, found Beaton's dandyism amusing and was sometimes derogatory about it. Cecil often affected Edwardian suits and almost invariably wore a hat to camouflage the sparsity of his hair (which Cukor did not conceal; born in 1899, he was five years older than Beaton was). Truman Capote, a friend of Beaton and Hepburn, was assigned to do a magazine piece on the making of *My Fair Lady*. He later remarked, "George was a dog type and Cecil was a cat type. That's it in a nutshell." From the start, there was a tug of war between them over the leading lady. Cukor, as director, was the boss; despite his reputation as a "woman's director," he guided several *actors* to their Oscars—among them James Stewart, Ronald Colman, and Harrison.

"Audrey won her Academy Award, bang, in her very first [starring] role," in *Roman Holiday* (1953), said Capote. She may have correctly assumed that she would not even be nominated this time out, and in her mid-thirties a primary concern was looking her best—she knew it was Beaton who would make her look beautiful, especially after Eliza's transformation from cockney to lady. Cukor had been hired to guide Hepburn's performance; designer Beaton was hired to do the look of *MFL*. Cecil was also an incorrigible shutterbug and diarist who frequently published books of photography and/or his journals. Carlos Clarens, who authored a book on Cukor, felt, "Beaton

Cecil Beaton

was a greedy-guts. He wanted glory from this film, and he wanted a higher profile than ever before.

"He also knew going in that he had to get a book out of it." The eventual book was titled, to Cukor's chagrin, *Cecil Beaton's Fair Lady*, an illustrated—with Cecil's drawings and stunning photos of Audrey as Eliza—diary of the making of the film. It soft-pedaled the feud with Cukor and painted not just a rosy but an ecstatic picture, opening with the sentence: "To work on a project such as *My Fair Lady* is to have the greatest creative experience that anyone working in the theatre can enjoy."

The book was dedicated to Jack Warner, Beaton's ally when he clashed with Cukor. "As an imported and internationally recognized commodity," wrote Clarens, "Beaton was a prize. His work was visual, and movies are nothing if not visual . . . . Cukor began directing in the early 1930s and was a known commodity in Hollywood—highly rated but for a number of reasons not overly esteemed." For one thing, Cukor didn't trumpet his own horn as often or loudly as Beaton.

Cecil was proud of his relative autonomy and at first enjoyed his sojourn in Los Angeles. Particularly the weather—until he was "forced" to spend most of a year in season-less California—and the camaraderie of the English group, including actors Wilfrid Hyde-White (as Colonel Pickering) and Mona Washbourne (as Prof. Higgins's housekeeper). Washbourne later offered, "I don't think Mr. Cukor and Cecil ever actually blew up at one another. But their relationship did grow more and more gelid . . . . Cecil once passed a remark that Mr. Cukor was inappropriately named, as his name meant, in Hungarian, I believe, *sugar*. To be fair, Cecil could be quite lemon-ish now and then!"

Beaton often blanched at Cukor's foul language when issuing orders on the set. Rex Harrison was quoted in the biography *George Cukor, Master of Elegance*: "Cecil was too fussy. George was modest and down to earth." One of Cukor's favorite put-downs was "pretentious," which he used repeatedly about Beaton, whose office was festooned with photos of himself with Jackie Kennedy, Garbo, etc. Beaton also disliked Cukor's habit of beginning to speak before entering a room, and often not completing a sentence. He wrote, "It surprises me to feel so much more foreign than during any previous visit. Never before have I realized quite so definitely the schism between certain English and Americans."

Said Harrison, "At first Cukor failed to realize that Cecil was selling himself. But soon he began to resent the publicity Cecil was getting just for himself." Besides selling articles and photos to *Vogue* and *Ladies' Home Journal*, Beaton was designing textiles and wallpapers and doing drawings for galleries while toiling on *MFL*.

★ ★ ★

Cukor later complained that Beaton had no team spirit, and after all film is a collaborative medium. Beaton had little sense of working under anyone, including Cukor. He was beholden to producer Warner. Also to powerful CBS chief (for Columbia Records had an important stake in *MFL*) William S. Paley, who'd asked Warner to hire Beaton. (Cukor had wanted to work with his frequent artistic collaborator George Hoyningen-Huene.) Significantly, Babe Paley, wife of the closetedly Jewish TV tycoon, was best friends with Cecil's pal Truman Capote, who would incorrectly boast that it was he who'd gotten Beaton the plum assignment:

"I told Babe to tell Bill that for *My Fair Lady's* production design, he really had to get Cecil Beaton if he wanted a top-drawer production and lots and lots of Oscars . . . . After I told Babe that Cecil was the official photographer to the royal family, she set to work on Bill."

Of course, most of Beaton's work was done by the time production commenced. But he was needed for his expertise, especially where Hepburn was concerned. He helped with her hair and costumes and took the obligatory film stills. Because Audrey also desired the sort of authenticity that Hollywood could usually take or leave, she legitimized his orders, selections, and changes. Wrote Cecil, "The books in the top of [Henry Higgins's] library are too brightly coloured. Audrey has too prettified hair with unsuitable *chic* side curls, and Mona Washbourne's wig has completely lost its style. By now the hairdressers are really doing what they like. A halt must be called. I wonder if it is my own fault that it all falls so far short of fun?"

Under Beaton's careful direction—or rather, scrutiny—detailed tests were made of all the principals' costumes and key scenes, particularly Hepburn's. The essence of *MFL*, based on Shaw's non-musical play *Pygmalion*, was Eliza's aural and visual transformation from guttersnipe (the part that challenged Audrey, whose mother was a Dutch baroness) to elegant lady. The star sat for hours with Beaton, the makeup and hair people, and often gave up her lunch hours to work on the cockney accent or pose for Cecil. The competition between Cukor and Beaton over the beautiful and prestigious Hepburn only deepened their rift.

The lengthy production schedule and hot Los Angeles summer—worse in the San Fernando Valley, where Warners was located—made disagreements more intense. Ironically, when the two men's tempers flared at each other, the film's mostly heterosexual crew derisively—according to one Cukor biographer—labeled both of them "these queens" or "these fags."

Beaton wrote, "I am looked upon as something as curious and unaccountable as the unicorn," and told friends that Cukor fit into the Hollywood establishment much

George Cukor with Candice Bergen and Jacqueline Bisset, stars of his final movie

more comfortably than he ever could have. Besides, "In the States, the intolerance for anyone different—more individual or intellectual or simply *different*—is far more pronounced than at home."

Englishman Jeremy Brett enacted the small role of Eliza's suitor, the one who sings "On the Street Where You Live." He informed *Entertainment Monthly*, "Mr. Cukor knew which side his bread was buttered on. He did not know that *My Fair Lady* would be his last major success . . . . He kept a distance from Cecil Beaton partly because he was a foreigner and a noticeable homosexual. Mr. Cukor put the work first; he didn't want distractions or controversies.

"In the play, there was something of a homosexual undercurrent between Henry Higgins, a 'confirmed old bachelor,' and his chum Col. Pickering. In the film, Mr. Cukor did away with that entirely . . . . I think he went to great lengths to avoid homophobia." Despite the great lengths, he was surrounded by it, hence his never having received an Academy Award for such films as *Dinner at Eight*, *Camille*, *The Women*, *The Philadelphia Story*, *Gaslight*, *Adam's Rib*, *Born Yesterday*, *A Star Is Born*, etc.

Rex Harrison explained, "George was very anxious about the look of the film, but at the end he let Cecil have his way. Otherwise there would have been one constant clash of two very strong personalities." Before long, the two men weren't speaking. Messages were delivered by intermediaries. The final straw was Beaton continuing to take posed portraits of Audrey Hepburn, who looked more lovely and regal than she ever had or would. Beaton "borrowed" her when she wasn't before the camera, but Cukor felt that when Audrey wasn't working, she should be resting.

In October 1963 the last break took place. According to Gene Allen, "There are all kinds of ways and times to do publicity shots. But you don't interrupt the director's day to do them. That's never taken place in the history of the business. It may be with some lesser directors, but you don't take Audrey Hepburn away from George Cukor . . . . But Cecil saw no reason why he couldn't take Audrey off the set." Cukor resented Beaton's taking liberties, also Hepburn's growing dependence on Beaton and their friendly conversations and common interests and background (Audrey's father was British).

Via an assistant, Cukor ordered Beaton to stay away from Hepburn while she was on the set. Beaton was appalled. He already felt that the director treated him "like an IBM machine." He would go on to write, "I have come to feel that to snap the camera on the set is in the nature of an indecency. In fact, it has given me quite a complex . . . . It is only natural that I should wish to record, in my own way, the work that I have done, particularly upon the exquisite leading lady for every infinitesimal detail of whose appearance I am responsible." As for Cukor's laying down the law, "I was later told that it took George Cukor two hours to recover from his displeasure with me enough to continue."

Weeks later, before filming was completed, Beaton decamped and returned to England. He continued to speak for publication about the making of *MFL* and the difficulties involved, usually without naming Cukor. The media impression was that he was crucial to the film, which Cukor would resent the rest of his life. Beaton did eventually seem sorry for the men's inability to get along, and later made light of their feud. He explained to me: "[Cukor] was angry and won the show of strength. Miss Hepburn had to defer to her director.

"But I had the photographs . . . and [the resulting book was] well worth it. Miss Hepburn was an ideal subject. I coaxed the heavy eye makeup off her, and we developed what she called her Flemish look. Interesting, because she was born in Belgium, you know."

Meanwhile, back in Burbank, Cukor was free of Beaton but the year-long production wore on. Everybody was tiring, especially the overworked leading lady, whose marriage was dissolving due to her being a bigger star than Mel Ferrer. On November 22, when President Kennedy was assassinated, she and Cukor wept openly, and Hepburn called an early end to the day's work. After *MFL* wrapped, she checked into a hospital to recuperate.

Most everyone involved agreed that the finished product was a triumph and a high point of all their careers. Once rested, Cukor advised friends, "We were happy making it, with one minor but very irritating exception. The initials are C. B., and it's not DeMille." Alan Jay Lerner urged Cukor not to make public comments against Beaton, but Cukor kept sniping long after Beaton did. Jeremy Brett stated, "I think George Cukor had a male version of the queen bee syndrome. He is said to have been jealous of other homosexual gentlemen who were talented . . . he wanted to be the token gay, as it were, although not acknowledged as such."

Both men, especially Cukor, suffered from the homophobic propaganda they'd grown up with and internalized over the many decades. In years to come, according to biographer Emanuel Levy, Cukor referred to Beaton as CCC, "Classed as Cunt by Cukor." Cecil, however, did not go public with his conviction that the director had been wrong not to inform Hepburn that nearly all her singing in *My Fair Lady* would be dubbed (by Marni Nixon, who'd done the same for Deborah Kerr in *The King and I* and Natalie Wood in *West Side Story*). Jack Warner had made the decision, and he and the director allowed Audrey to believe that she would do her own singing and to rehearse rigorously for it.

When Nixon's husband created a minor media stir by claiming Marni wasn't getting enough credit, Cukor was furious. He told the press, "[Marni Nixon] is where she belongs, appearing with Liberace."

Come Oscar-time, Audrey Hepburn was not nominated, but nearly everyone else was. *My Fair Lady* swept the Academy Awards and got Cukor his belated Oscar. And two—two more—for Cecil Beaton, which irked Cukor, who fumed, "He's always grabbing for more, and damn if he doesn't get it!" *MFL* was the final true peak for both Beaton and Cukor. Each went on to prestigious projects which didn't attain the same success—e.g., Beaton worked with Barbra Streisand in *On a Clear Day You Can See Forever* and Cukor with Maggie Smith in *Travels With My Aunt*.

Their amazing careers wound down, and neither man was as busy as he would have liked to be. But each remained top-echelon. Before his death in 1980 Beaton was knighted by the queen, whom he'd photographed as a little girl. With the 1981 MGM flop *Rich and Famous* (starring Jacqueline Bisset and Candice Bergen), Cukor, who died in 1983, became the oldest-ever director of a major studio motion picture.

George to George

"It's so silly. Everyone knows which singers give good throat, not necessarily in front of a mike . . . . If the public knew the half of it, there wouldn't be all this prejudice and jumping to conclusions about what one is because of the way one acts or dresses. I'm waiting for someone to do a study on the cause of heterosexuality. Seems only fair . . . ."—Boy George

"I got a message from Aretha Franklin saying she'd love to do a song with me. Later, after she'd done the [duet]

with George Michael, the *London Evening Standard* asked me if I thought she'd called the wrong George. I said, 'I think she banged on the wrong closet.'"—Boy George

"Sleeping with George Michael would be like having sex with a groundhog." —Boy George, on his hairier rival

"I've always kind of liked him. I've always admired his strength of character. But I don't really call what he's been doing 'strength of character.'"—George Michael, on Boy George's comments

"I suppose he thinks there's a lot of character in lying to the public . . . or trying to confuse it, or pretending he's this *and* that but not really *that*. It's called selling out, sweet-ie."—Boy George

"If you go around covering up your tail so heavily, people are going to start wondering . . .what it is you've got to hide. That girl Pat Hernandez whom he's with was my fag hag for three years, and when I read the newspaper story 'How Pat Broke My Heart,' I was tempted to write one called 'How Pat Broke My Hoover' [vacuum cleaner]. Because the idea of her and George having a relationship is about as likely as my having sex with a door."—Boy George

"He's been looking for love in all the wrong public places."—Boy George, after George Michael's arrest in a Beverly Hills restroom in 1998

"Boy George, since Wham!, has been trying to out me. He knew I had boyfriends. I refused to rise to the bait with him . . . . He's never said anything that really bothered me until . . . in that article he said that I thought I was too good for the gay community. I felt like

Boy George

that was really over the top. He did an article directly after I was arrested—interestingly enough, he writes a column for one of the tabloids, which is exactly where I think he belongs. It's an English tabloid called the *Daily Mail*. It's also pretty right-wing and homopho-bic.

"I think it's quite interesting that he writes for them, so I guess he'll go for anyone who pays him. For a gay man, his attitude towards me is identical to the paparazzi's. Am I too good for the gay community? No. Am I too good for the likes of Boy George? Yes."—George Michael

"It's justice [the arrest], and while George did nothing wrong, I applaud him for finally coming out . . . . It's long over-due for a man with $50 million in the bank."—Boy George

"You have to hand it to George—he could have denied everything, as most Hollywood celebrities do after they're arrested. Then again, he keeps such a big distance between himself and his sexuali-ty, or bisexuality, or whatever . . . and like he's no activist—as if he did more than his share just by being arrested and finally 'fessing up. Like he's done more than anyone else!"—Boy George

TRU/GORE

"Gore Vidal has never written a remotely imaginative novel. Except one, Myra Breckinridge. *You can sort of thumb your way through that."—Truman Capote*

"Truman Capote has made an art of lying. A minor art."—Gore Vidal

hy would the two most famous gay novelists of their generation hate each other so much? Truman Capote and Gore Vidal had a decades-long feud which eventually devolved into a celebrated, long-running lawsuit. "They entertained us as much with their feud as with their books," felt novelist Bob Randall (*The Fan*). "Truman was the first writer to become a full-fledged celebrity, known to people who never read his books."

Precocious young men and ambitious young writers, Capote and Vidal each wanted to be number one. Tennessee Williams, a friend to both, opined, "Playwrights are not as concerned with the competition as authors are, I think." Truman's early short stories won prestigious awards and acclaim, and in 1948 his debut novel *Other Voices, Other Rooms* made him an overnight celebrity. "Gore has always been jealous that even though I'm one year older than him, I hit it big right away . . . I was what you could only describe as a phenomenon," said Capote (1924-1984).

Truman couldn't help attracting attention, for he was cherubic-looking, child-like yet lethally witty, and possessed a unique, babyish voice. Contributing to the curiosity and indignation about him was the photo on his first novel's dust jacket, with the author reclining on a sofa, gazing seductively into the camera like a male Lolita. Some critics labeled the photo a "perverted Peter Pan." Others nicknamed the book "Other Vices, Other Rooms," as its theme was partly homosexual and the story partly autobiographical. Much of Capote's early fiction was inspired by his Alabama childhood.

In 1948 Gore Vidal published his third novel, his first best-seller. It too had a homosexual, or bisexual, theme. *The City and the Pillar*, based partly on closeted screen star Tyrone Power and his closeted first wife, actress Annabella, got Vidal banned from review in the *New York Times* through most of the 1950s. During that

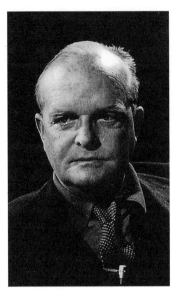

Truman Capote

uptight decade, Vidal had to take a pen name to publish mystery novels, and worked as a screenwriter, contributing to but not credited for *Ben-Hur*.

Originally, Vidal and Capote had often met for friendly lunches in Manhattan's finer haunts, dishing the latest dirt and discussing their plans and ambitions. But by 1950 they were sworn enemies. At first it was attributed to Capote's smaller output bringing him more wealth and celebrity. "Gore believes in quantity. I believe in quality," he said more than once. The trio later admitted that the turning point had occurred during a get-together at Tennessee Williams's home. Vidal aloofly avoided the topic, Capote disingenuously said he couldn't remember *what* had happened, but Williams revealed that Gore accused Truman of lifting his story material from Southern authoresses like Eudora Welty and Carson McCullers, to which Capote charged that Vidal's plots were lifted from the daily newspapers. Whatever else was said, nobody knows. But the friendly alliance was shattered.

Gay playwright William Inge (*Picnic, Bus Stop*) once wrote, "It's the same with any minority—gays, racial, religious—where they start out as friends, or at least allies with a common enemy, the majority. Then when both individuals become national figures, the ranking begins—number one, number two, . . . It's no longer minority vs. majority, it's one celebrity vs. another celebrity."

In public, Capote and Vidal competed to supply quotable put-downs of each other. As Truman changed from literary writer to sometime writer and pal to the rich and famous, Gore noted, "He simply wanted to be famous through writing," adding that Truman's "gift for publicity is the most glittering star in his diadem." Truman noted of the expatriate Vidal, who lived in Italy, "He thinks distance will make the American critics' hearts grow fonder . . . I guess Gore left the country because he felt he was underappreciated here. I have news for him: people who actually read his books will underappreciate him everywhere."

Capote, who composed some of his fiction in Europe too, remembered, "I was visiting Italy some time after Gore moved there, and eventually we connected on the telephone. He called me to say, 'I passed by your hotel yesterday.' I was perfectly candid and said, 'Thank you so much.'"

Over the years, Vidal maintained a steady output, while Capote's decreased as his socializing increased. He became known for the feminine company he kept, usually the swan-like wives—white, angular, and graceful—of rich and powerful men like CBS chief William Paley and FIAT tycoon Gianni Agnelli. The press said nothing at that time about his lifelong relationship with dancer turned writer Jack

Truman in the Valley of the Dolls

Like Capote, novelist Jacqueline Susann was a master of self promotion. She broke records by having three number one best-sellers in a row, starting with *The Valley of the Dolls*. Though not a purveyor of literature, she was often asked her opinion of Truman, whom she ridiculed on TV with homophobic—though herself bisexual!—stereotyping, primarily limp wrists rather than comments. Capote responded in kind, but more articulately; on TV he declared that "Jackie Susann looks like a truck driver in drag."

She decided to sue, though her husband-manager advised against it. Then she demanded a public apology, which Truman declined to give. On Johnny Carson's show she became exasperated because she'd agreed to appear to plug her latest book. The host pressed her—just one question: "What do you really think of Truman?"

She paused, then answered, "I think he was one of our best presidents."

Truman Capote repeated his description of Susann, and she went ahead with her suit. Then suddenly she dropped it. No one knew why, until she died of cancer. Capote reportedly sang, "Ding dong, the witch is dead!"

In the book *Conversations With Capote* he was quoted: "I caused Jacqueline Susann's death! She was lying in bed dying of cancer. I didn't know. I was on television and somebody asked me what did I think of Jacqueline Susann. And I said, 'She looks like a truck driver in drag.' And she was watching the show. She fell out of the bed. (*Laughs.*) Her husband picked her up. She was coughing up blood and never recovered.

"She sued me for a million dollars. (*Laughs.*) She was told she had better drop that lawsuit because all they had to do is bring ten truck drivers into court and put them on the witness stand and you've lost your case."

Dunphy. Ditto Howard Austen, the life partner of Gore Vidal. Each relationship spanned several decades, but as Bob Randall said, "American media prefer to focus on either heterosexual romance or feuds."

In the late 1950s Capote became more prominent via a short novel, *Breakfast at Tiffany's*. It was taken to heart by a wider public because it featured a heroine and was hetero-themed. He then took five years to pen *In Cold Blood*, his best-selling 1965 "non-fiction novel." Vidal felt that Capote had finally found his true voice, that reportage was his forte, not fiction—"the realm of those with creative imagination," of which he felt Tru had none, though critics have often stated that Capote wrote the most beautiful sentences in the English language during this century.

Gore Vidal

However, novelist Mary McCarthy was not alone in rejecting the notion that Capote had invented the non-fiction novel. She thought, "His greatest contribution to literary innovation was to publicize the author first, the book second." Nonetheless, *In Cold Blood* was a sensation, and to celebrate the end of his Herculean labors in and out of Kansas, where the murders had been done, Capote threw the 1960s' most celebrated party, the Black & White Ball. Truman sighed, "It's true that success loses you more friends than failure, you know," but he managed to round up a few hundred rich and famous ones to attend his ball at the Plaza in Manhattan. He explained, "I'm very social. I love being with people . . . . Gore doesn't really like people. He's closer to a recluse."

The success of *In Cold Blood* made Capote an expert of sorts on American crime and criminal law. He was hired to do TV specials on the subject; not all of them aired. And he gave endless interviews, disclosing a sometimes contradictory set of opinions. Though nearly out of the closet and pro-gay on most issues, he was anti-feminist, pro-Reagan (California's homophobic governor) and pro-William F. Buckley, and for the death penalty at a time when most liberals were still against it. Gore Vidal dubbed him "A Republican housewife from Kansas with all the prejudices."

Capote announced several literary projects in the wake of *In Cold Blood*—some fiction, some non-, and some in between. Mary McCarthy declared that writers like him represented "the mirror on the whorehouse ceiling." To which Truman replied, "If there's anyone in American literature who knows what a whore would see when she looks at the ceiling, it's Mary McCarthy." In fact, Capote would never write another full-length work again. His subsequent books were short stories or non-fiction pieces collected together.

★ ★ ★

"Truman does have his share of personal demons," offered friend Leo Lerman, an editor at *Vogue*. "Not his sexuality, which isn't a problem—that problem would be homophobia. Specifically, his appearance. Truman really wanted to be an actor. But a star actor. And his physical type . . . that's impossible. So he became a star as an author and a talk show guest and jet-setter." He also fueled his social pace with alcohol and drugs, and got increasingly little work done.

"He really gave himself to his friends," said Lerman. But Truman also took from his friends in that their lives and personae became grist for his literary mill. He was toiling, he frequently announced, on a Proustian epic called *Answered*

Tru Venom

Truman Capote could have had more feuds going than anybody had the victims of his venom chosen to respond in kind. The "Tiny Terror" was more than outspoken—he was an A-1 interviewee with a knack for making comments that were (usually) just this side of libelous. Competitive and self-praising to the nth degree, he rarely had a good word to say about other writers, particularly living American writers, since he considered himself the greatest in that category.

"I don't think William Burroughs has an ounce of talent."

"I never liked any of [Irwin Shaw's] novels."

"You can't scarcely be as bad a writer as A. E. Hotchner."

"I don't think anything Hemingway did was one of the best of anything. There was a mean man . . . . I disliked him. Everything about him. He was a closet queen and everything else."

"I'm not a great admirer of Faulkner . . . . For the most part, he's a highly confusing, uncontrolled writer . . . . I knew Faulkner very well. He was a great friend of mine. Well, as much as you could be a friend of his, unless you were a fourteen-year-old nymphet."

"I'm one of the few people in the world who has actually read [Thomas Pynchon's] *Gravity's Rainbow* from page one to the last page, since I was a judge on the National Book Awards in which it was being considered. It didn't win because of me."

"Well, Jack Kerouac . . . that's not writing. That's typing."

"I think [Louis Auchincloss] is a second-rate Stephen Birmingham. And Stephen Birmingham is third-rate."

"Tom Wolfe is just not going to last. I love some of the things he's done, they're just terrific . . . but you won't think so in years to come. Because of his style. But if he hadn't used that style, nobody would have paid attention to him, and he wouldn't have had the success that he had."

"[James Michener] has never written anything that would remotely interest me. Why on earth would I be interested in reading a book called *Chesapeake*?"

"I hate [John Updike]. Everything about him bores me . . . . He's so mannered. There's such a thing as style, there's such a thing as a stylist. I consider myself a stylist. I consider him a mannered style, not a stylist, because it isn't even something that's his own . . . . I told him how much I disliked his writing . . . he didn't laugh at all."

"Saul Bellow is a nothing writer. He doesn't exist . . . . He's a dull man and a dull writer. Hello, Saul, how are you?"

Prayers, about the behind the scenes of the rich and famous. Chapter excerpts began appearing in *Esquire* in 1975. The first was a social bombshell, and overnight Truman lost most of his high society friends, who barred their gates to him with an understandable sense of outrage and betrayal.

Capote professed at different times to believe his friends would be flattered by his writing about them so intimately—with pseudonyms of course—or that they wouldn't care. Or perhaps he felt it would be worth the loss to create a "masterpiece, comparable to *In Remembrance of Things Past*, but modern and much more sexually candid." The one novelist Capote consistently admired and sought to parallel was the French homosexual author of the century's most acclaimed, enduring—and possibly longest—novel.

Meanwhile, Vidal, who never believed Tru could finish the work, had made a 1960s comeback with *Julian*, a novel about the Roman emperor who tried to restore polytheism after the official incorporation of Christianity. At decade's end, *Myra Breckinridge* became a runaway best-seller. Twenty-one years before, Gore had daringly tackled homosexuality on the page; now he presented a male cinéaste turned female. Critic Rex Reed and Raquel Welch played the before and after of the transsexual character in the disastrous movie version. Capote crowed, "America fell in love with my Holly Golightly, but they hate his Myra. And *Breakfast at Tiffany's* was a big hit, in spite of what those Hollywood people did to it."

Truman himself tackled the movies when he played mystery novelist Lionel Twain in the comedy hit *Murder By Death* (1975). He proclaimed, "They're [other writers] all jealous, I'm sure. Norman Mailer used his own money to star in three films, but I'm getting paid. And Jimmy Jones and Irwin Shaw told me they were jealous. And Gore Vidal must be dying. But then I always said that Gore was the only person who could possibly have played Myra Breckinridge" (years later, Vidal made appearances in a number of films).

Hollywood Reporter columnist George Christy later recalled, "I was on the set [of *Murder By Death*] one morning when a chandelier fell and crashed a foot away from Truman. He chuckled. He said, 'I guess Gore Vidal must be lurking in the wings!'"

San Francisco Chronicle columnist Herb Caen, who knew both Vidal and Capote, felt, "Truman and Gore are very different beings. Tru tends to exaggerate or even fabricate, and you can't trust him to keep a secret. But honestly, he is more fun. He has a sense of humor. Ask his friends, and he does have several, about how he hangs on to and cherishes friendships . . . . Ever since he lost so many friends to that *roman à clef*, he now values those he still has."

For all their differences, the two had much in common: mothers named Nina with whom they had love-hate relationships, being gay and ahead of their time, being only children and spoiled. Both began writing seriously as teens, and each took his writing reputation very, very seriously. Carson McCullers said of Vidal that because he came from an affluent, politically influential family, he felt entitled to great success. (Gore said of the author of *The Heart Is a Lonely Hunter* that "An hour with a dentist without Novocain was like a minute with Carson McCullers.")

Tru Venom II

*C*apote wasn't any easier on women than men. When he disliked someone, she *stayed* disliked!

"Streisand's great fault as a singer [is] she takes every ballad and turns it into a three-act opera. She simply cannot leave a song alone . . . . I wrote 'A Sleepin' Bee' for my play *House of Flowers*. Streisand recorded it on her first record and in her interviews she always says that's her favorite song, but she certainly doesn't do it very well."

"I wouldn't pay 25¢ to spit on a Georgia O'Keeffe painting. And I think she's a horrible person too. I know her . . . . So arrogant, so sure of herself. I'm sure she's carrying a dildo in her purse."

"I love old Virginia Woolf, fake that she is . . . . But pinned down to it, I can't think of a single thing of Virginia Woolf's that I like. And I've read them all."

"I mean, anybody that could have given the Nobel Prize to Pearl Buck ought to go and be examined by a mental institution."

"[Joyce Carol Oates] is a joke monster who ought to be beheaded in a public auditorium . . . . To me, she's the most loathsome creature in America. I've seen her, and to *see* her is to loathe her. To read her is to absolutely vomit."

"Meryl Streep, I think, is the Creep. Ooh, God, she looks like a chicken and [has] a mouth like a chicken. She's totally untalented as far as I'm concerned."

"Well, Jackie [Kennedy Onassis] better not go on a talk show. She wouldn't know what to say . . . . I hate her. I used to be great friends with her. I hate her. I absolutely despise her . . . . She's insincere. She's a person who basically has nothing but contempt for most everything in the world . . . . She's a very opportunistic, insincere, vain, rather mean person."

"Jackie's younger sister Lee . . . well, the way I feel about Jackie, that goes *triple* for Lee. And then some!"

Eventually Vidal did run for office. More than once. Capote's friend, designer Cecil Beaton, believed, "He hoped to become a Senator and thereby lift himself above the range of other novelists." A relative of Gore's states anonymously, "He rather turned against politics when he saw he would never win, not in the U.S. anyway. It's one of the factors that has embittered him." Likewise Truman grew increasingly bitter that he was never awarded a Pulitzer or Nobel Prize. "A lot of it has to do with plain old jealous, spiteful homophobia." It's also likely that the outsized success and egos of such talented and at times acidic personalities as Capote and

Vidal alienated many of their peers and prize-givers. Each man was far more out-spoken and honest than most writers or celebrities of the day.

When talk show host Phil Donahue asked Truman how he felt when truck dri-vers, for instance, would watch him on television and make fun of him, he cheer-fully replied, "Well, *I'm* the one *they're* watching on TV . . . ."

"Capote and Vidal both have a knack for making enemies," said Leo Lerman. "Particularly each other. You know what they say: familiarity breeds contempt." In George Plimpton's oral history of Capote, writer Dotson Rader describes a 1970s visit to a gay Los Angeles back-room bar:

"To keep the police out, you had to join the club in order to get into the bar: the legal pretense was that it was a private club. Five bucks. Truman was handed a membership card to fill out and he said, 'What if it gets raided and they find out I'm a member? It'll get into the newspapers.' The cashier said, 'Well, we can't do anything about that, Truman.' He'd recognized him. So he said, 'Just put down any name.'

"So Truman put down 'Gore Vidal' and gave his Los Angeles address. Truman debated the next day whether he should secretly call the police and initiate a raid."

★ ★ ★

Capote, who wound up more of a talker than writer, spoke too often and too carelessly about Vidal. He handed Gore the ammunition he needed in a 1975 *Playgirl* interview—Truman was reputedly drunk during the Q/A—when he declared that Vidal had been drunk and bodily thrown out of the White House at Robert Kennedy's behest when JFK was president. Vidal was related to Jackie by marriage. Truman was repeating gossip, and got the story wrong. Vidal may have had no more to drink than the other guests at the social function, and was not thrown out, though there was an altercation with Bobby Kennedy, after which Democrat Gore did turn against the Kennedy clan.

The younger writer sued. "I can't believe it!" wailed Truman. "He's suing me for a million dollars—I've never heard of such a thing!" The case dragged on and on, in the meantime losing Capote two more rich and famous friends: Jackie Onassis and her sister Lee Radziwill. The latter had been a protegée—back when she had acting aspirations—and very close friend of Truman's. But when he requested Lee to make a deposition supporting his version of events at the White House, she refused and cut all communication with him. Finally, Capote got gos-sip columnist Liz Smith to intercede for him, and the ungrateful Lee simply told her, "Who cares? . . . They're just two fags, anyway." Ever after, Truman publicly slammed the Bouvier sisters for all he was worth.

Capote and Vidal both commented on the lawsuit to the media, though Truman not as recklessly as before. Both maintained that they would never give in to the other. Each asserted that the suit was proof of the other's shortcomings. Tru, who seemed more obsessed with Gore than vice versa, said the suit was the latest result of "Gore's complete obsession with me" and advised, "Much as I don't really care about psychoanalysis, I think he ought to go to an analyst and find out what it is that's bothering him so much."

In a deposition, Gore was asked when he'd last seen Truman, and said it was at a party where he'd accidentally sat down on Truman. Why did he do that? "I thought he was a pouf," he said of the short, by then rotund writer. And what was Capote sitting on? Vidal was asked. "I assume a smaller pouf." In one interview, Gore archly offered that while he had been the subject of a book by a Professor Dick, Capote had been written about by a Professor Nance (sissy).

As the suit languished, Truman tried to win sympathy with interviewers by saying it was bankrupting him. But he sold a "non-fiction novella" titled *Handcarved Coffins* for a very impressive sum to a producer, though it was never filmed. He said, "I think Gore bitterly regrets having got into this," lamented the $80,000 in legal fees it had already cost him, yet exulted that "Magazines have devoted whole issues" to the lawsuit, then insisted, "I would never sue anyone over anything they said about me. And I've had everything said about me that you could possibly think of! It just isn't done in civilized company."

Leo Lerman explained, "Vidal made fewer remarks about the case as it dragged out. He saw that nobody's mouth could compete with Truman's, and he knew all he had to do was wait, that he would win." At last, in 1983, the suit was settled, with Capote writing a letter of apology—though claiming he'd been misquoted!— to *Playgirl* which was reproduced in newspapers throughout the land, reimbursing his nemesis for some of the court costs, and agreeing not to discuss the matter further. Said Lerman:

"It should never have happened. It made both look bad. Both have said nasty things about each other and about others . . . . I think Gore sued as a way of getting back at Truman. Up until that time, they had relished their feud. Or at least Truman had, since he seemed always to have the upper hand. I think the final result was that it made Vidal look like an embittered sourpuss and Truman like a careless, messy gossip."

Gore went on to novelistic best-sellers based on American history and non-fiction acclaim for his essays. Even Capote admitted, "His essays are quite good, generally speaking. Especially if he doesn't *hate* somebody too much, then they're really quite good."

When Vidal was contacted in 1998 at his villa in Ravello about the frequent public entwining of his and Truman's names, he wrote back that it baffled him, as he had virtually nothing to do with Capote and hardly ever saw him since the 1940s. Like Davis with Crawford, the more seriously regarded half of a celebrated feud was the one more anxious not to be permanently associated with the other.

Toward the end, Capote sank faster and irrevocably into a morass of drugs, alcohol, and depression. *Answered Prayers*, the masterpiece he kept claiming to have written except for the finishing touches, was, other than those few chapters, mostly in his head. Truman and Jack Dunphy drifted more and more apart—unlike Vidal and Austen, who met in 1950 and are still together. In 1984, aged fifty-nine but disillusioned and lacking hope of ever successfully kicking his habit, Truman flew to Los Angeles on a one-way ticket. He had apparently chosen to die at the hillside home—a womb with a view, he once called it—of his good friend Joanne Carson.

Years later, Ms. Carson called this writer to arrange for actor-activist Edward James Olmos to write a foreword to the book *Hispanic Hollywood*. Olmos, she explained, was her best friend "since Truman . . . although of course nobody is Truman and no one could ever really replace him." Part of Truman's ashes were later co-mingled with those of Jack—over their memorial stone, with a plaque, in Bridgehampton, Long Island—and part were kept by Carson and now reside at the small but chic Westwood Memorial Cemetery where are also found the last remains of Marilyn Monroe, Natalie Wood, Burt Lancaster, Dean Martin, and many other stars.

Gore vs. Chuck & Buckley

"The Marie Antoinette of American politics."—Gore Vidal, on William F. Buckley

"Now, listen, you queer. Stop calling me a crypto-Nazi or I'll sock you in your goddamn face and you'll stay plastered." —conservative William F. Buckley to Vidal, during a live telecast from the 1968 Democratic Convention in Chicago

"Buckley is jealous of Gore Vidal . . . Buckley has never written a book that anyone can name . . . . Years ago, Buckley copied Truman Capote by doing a book à la *In Cold Blood*. He befriended the murderer of a fifteen-year-old girl in Mahwah, New Jersey. The book came out two or three years after Capote's, but I can't remember its name."—columnist Herb Caen

"It was Vidal's idea that Ben-Hur and Messala had become such fierce enemies because they'd once been lovers. And that's the way I played it in my scenes with Chuck [Charlton Heston in *Ben-Hur*]. It's the only way it makes logical or emotional sense . . . . Vidal told the director [William Wyler] about it, but I don't think he told Chuck. Chuck never had much use for anyone but his director."—Steven Boyd

"A celebrity endorsement doesn't change any votes . . . . I don't think that any American much cares to plumb the shallows of Charlton Heston's mind and follow his advice."—Gore Vidal, on nineties gun advocate Heston

"I don't think Heston has ever been afraid of any actor. But now, with this war of words with Gore Vidal, he's more than met his match. I don't think Charlton Heston will be carrying this thing much further—not if he's smart."—Dorothy Manners, former columnist who'd been Louella Parsons's assistant

WOMEN'S WRITES:
Lillian Hellman vs. Mary McCarthy

hen one writer publicly criticizes another, beware! Actors and other show biz types are definitely public figures and as such are legally open to significant criticism, parody, etc. But even a successful and renowned writer like the late Lillian Hellman could be ruled a non-public figure and thus protected from the sweeping calumny of a lesser known and perhaps jealous writer like Mary McCarthy.

A critic, novelist, and social commentator, McCarthy (1912–1989) published over twenty books. She became famous later in life, particularly via her best-selling novel *The Group*, which became a non-successful 1966 film (marking Candice Bergen's screen bow as a lesbian named Lakey). Lillian Hellman (1906–1984) became famous with her first play, *The Children's Hour* (1934), which dealt with lesbianism in a then "daring"—that it mentioned it at all—but reactionary manner. Many years later it was discovered that Hellman's plot about two female school teachers was not entirely original, as she'd allowed others to believe. Rather, it was based on a nineteenth-century Scottish court case which ended the longtime loving relationship of the women who were also professional partners. It did not end, like Hellman's play, with the suicide by hanging of an embarrassed lesbian woman (Martha, played by Shirley MacLaine in the 1961 film version).

Hellman's other plays included *The Little Foxes, Watch On the Rhine, Another Part of the Forest,* and *Toys in the Attic.* She wrote screenplays and then best-selling memoirs like *Scoundrel Time,* about the McCarthy witch-hunts, and *Pentimento,* an episode of which became the 1977 movie *Julia* with Jane Fonda and Vanessa Redgrave.

Although Hellman was Jewish and McCarthy had a Jewish grandparent, and Hellman was very secretly bisexual (as revealed in posthumous biographies), both women advocated communism, an ideology which in the 1930s attracted numerous celebrities and intellectuals. Unbridled capitalism had resulted in the Crash and the Great Depression, and in the fascist-driven thirties, Marxism seemed a potent antidote to Hitler, Mussolini, and company. Both women felt passionately about liberty; the fact that communist governments invariably tend toward dictatorship, anti-Semitism, and homophobia obviously didn't signify.

Ms. McCarthy (no relation to Senator Joseph McCarthy) soon grew disenchanted with hardline communism, while Hellman remained loyal to the USSR and a staunch Stalinist (though Joseph Stalin was one of the century's most murderous dictators). Besides Marxism and writing, the two women had little in common. McCarthy saw Hellman as a professional celebrity and as constantly self-serving, particularly once her series of memoirs began issuing forth. Mary believed that Lillian bent or even bypassed the truth in such writings as *Julia* in order to make herself a dashing heroine. It later appeared, after the matter was thoroughly researched, that there really was no Julia and that "Lilly" never did those brave, daring things which Jane Fonda did in the movie. Hellman also distorted her response—in print, decades after the fact—to the anti-liberal witch-hunters of the McCarthy era. Her reputation for standing up to the goons of HUAC (House Un-American Activities Committee) was based more on what Hellman claimed she did and said than on the facts.

McCarthy apparently resented all this more than anyone guessed, for her reaction was extreme, and she was injudicious enough to air it on national TV, on *The Dick Cavett Show*. Actually, her remarks first appeared in print, in a scholarly periodical, the *Paris Metro*, in 1978. Over a year later, she repeated them on Cavett's show, and weeks after, Lillian Hellman sued her, Cavett, and Channel 13—the Public Broadcasting System's New York affiliate—for $2,250,000—one and three-quarters million for "mental pain and anguish" and for being "injured in her profession," and half a million dollars for punitive damages.

Hellman, who'd met McCarthy but twice—in 1937 and 1948—had probably been aware of the *Paris Metro* remarks but did not sue at the time. How many people, after all, read it? But the wider the medium, the more viewers, listeners, and readers, the greater the likelihood of filing suit. Hellman, a fighter and self-proclaimed "stubborn mule," was prepared to battle McCarthy to the bitter end. No out of court settlement was likely.

McCarthy's bankruptcy, however, was likely: she admitted to $63,000 in savings. By contrast, Hellman was a millionaire, and as somebody rich and famous, was getting her legal services free. (A legal fund to aid Mary McCarthy was started by friends and supporters, and by enemies of "lifelong Stalinist" Hellman.)

It happened like this: in October 1979, McCarthy taped a two-part interview with Dick Cavett, who asked her to name contemporary writers who were overrated. She didn't name any names, so he repeated his question, changing the adjective to overpraised. Then McCarthy answered, "The only one I can think of is a holdover like Lillian Hellman, who I think is tremendously overrated, a bad writer, and a dishonest writer, but she really belongs to the past."

"What is dishonest about [her]?" queried Cavett.

"Everything," replied McCarthy. "I said once in some interview that every word she writes is a lie, including *and* and *the*."

The episodes aired in January 1980 and were viewed by Hellman in her Park Avenue apartment. Afterward, she called several people in a rage, including Cavett, who offered her the chance to appear on his show and make a rebuttal. Lillian refused. Two weeks later she sued; Cavett was eventually dropped from the suit because he hadn't participated in the program's preparation. McCarthy heard about the suit while lecturing in Europe and at first thought little of it. But when she returned to the United States, she found the literary community in an uproar.

Most literati deplored both Mary's gratuitous comments and Lillian's decision to sue a fellow writer. Some felt she had no right to sue, since she was an author and McCarthy a critic. Nearly everyone agreed that McCarthy had crossed the line, but

Mary McCarthy

writers and publishers alike feared the outcome of the suit, which could have inhibited critics from speaking or writing their minds. Hellman charged that her critic's statement was "false, made with ill-will, with malice, with knowledge of its falsity, with careless disregard of its truth, and with the intent to injure the plaintiff personally and professionally."

★ ★ ★

McCarthy claimed not to remember exactly what she'd said on Cavett's show a few months before. Everybody else knew exactly what she said, as the words had been reprinted and repeated over and over, on TV, in print and reprint, and at cocktail parties. McCarthy asserted that her remarks were "literary criticism" and as such protected by the First Amendment. Truman Capote stated, "Mary McCarthy has lost her good sense. Her judgment is clouded by her bitter jealousy, and I think successful writers *should* be defended from those who feel that success, talent, or fame give them the right to say any outrageous or TV-worthy thing that enters their green little heads."

Others, like Norman Mailer, chided McCarthy but feared Hellman's suit more. *Dissent* editor Irving Howe said, "It's not just two old ladies engaged in a cat fight. The question involved—of one's attitude toward communism—is probably the central political-cultural-intellectual problem of the twentieth century." Lillian Hellman put it more basically: "I think she has always disliked me." She was convinced it was a case of "with malice toward one," while most of Manhattan's cultural elite felt it was a political and/or literary rivalry.

Hellman, who declined to appear on Cavett for fear of looking "silly," let it be known she would drop the suit if McCarthy would publicly apologize. The latter refused, insisting that would make her look like a liar, which is what she accused Hellman of being. Her lawyers asked her to list every instance of a written comment about Hellman in her published work. There were only four.

McCarthy's lawyers didn't make an appeal to dismiss the suit on the grounds that her statement wasn't defamatory, because clearly it was. Rather, they defended her on the basis of commenting about a public figure. Hellman held that she was not a public figure, although in 1976 she'd appeared in a Blackglama mink ad under the caption "What Becomes a Legend Most?" (the series never identified its mink-wrapped celebrity subjects). The legal process dragged on—McCarthy, PBS, and Cavett were each represented by different law firms—and McCarthy was put on the spot as to what exactly lay behind her sweeping statement.

She had to retract or explain that of course she didn't mean that every single word was false, but that "Nothing in [Hellman's] writing rings true to me. That does not mean that her writing is made up of literal lies . . . . I mean the general tone of unconvincingness and falseness." Meanwhile, Hellman's autobiographical writings were re-examined for revisions of historical fact, and an elderly Hungarian woman claimed that Lillian had stolen *The Little Foxes* from her late playwright husband, whose agent had submitted a play to Hellman's friend and producer Herman Shumlin.

More damning was the publication of *Code Name Mary*, the memoirs of Dr. Muriel Gardiner Buttinger, whom it gradually became clear was the original for Julia from the eponymous movie. But as Lillian had never met Muriel, the implication was that Hellman's *Julia* was a fiction. Mary McCarthy told her lawyer Benjamin O'Sullivan that though the case was resulting in political lines being drawn throughout the literary world, "In fact my remark on the Cavett show wasn't political, overtly or covertly.

"To me, the woman is false through and through. It's not just the fresh varnish she puts on her seamy old Stalinism. In one of the 'autobiographical' volumes she tells some story about 'Dash' [Lillian's longtime friend, author Dashiell Hammett] and a pond on her property full of turtles; I no more believe that than I do her account of her House un-American [sic] performance. This isn't true of all old Communists and fellow-travelers. I imagine Howard Fast [author of *Spartacus*] is fairly truthful, for instance, and Arthur Miller [playwright and last husband of Marilyn Monroe], in contrast to Hellman, behaved very straightforwardly during the un-American affair . . . . [Hellman] wants it to look as if I'm persecuting her for her 'brave' support of progressive causes."

The lawsuit was no boon for Hellman, and did serve to remind people that McCarthy—who normally got far less publicity and limelight than Lillian—was still around and had been a significant critic for a long time. British writer Anthony Burgess noted, "Even something as daunting and fundamentally grubby as a lawsuit imbues its 'costars' with a certain grim glamour and, necessarily, stature."

Finally, in 1984, in an eighteen-page opinion, Judge Harold Baer Jr. denied McCarthy's motion to dismiss suit on First Amendment grounds. He declared that McCarthy's statement about Hellman "seems to fall on the actionable side of the line—outside what has come to be known as the 'marketplace of ideas.'" Most resoundingly, Judge Baer stated that Lillian Hellman was *not* a public figure, and was thus entitled to greater protections than, say, actors or politicians, whose work for the most part is performed in public.

McCarthy was astounded, and many in the cultural community saw it as a blow to free expression, a possible move toward increased censorship. An appeal was launched by McCarthy and PBS. But before the appeal could be tried, Lillian Hellman died at seventy-eight. According to biographer William Wright, a nurse described her condition during her final days:

Lillian Hellman

"She was blind, half paralyzed, had suffered strokes, had rage attacks, crying fits, couldn't walk, couldn't eat, couldn't sleep or even find a sitting position that wasn't agony." At which point Lillian's friend Peter Feibleman left the nurse and entered her room to gently inquire, "How are you doing, Lillian?"

"Not good, Peter. Not good."

"So what's the matter?" he asked, expecting a long or brief catalogue.

"This is the worst writer's block I've ever had."

Hellman's death obviated the legally key question of whether First Amendment rights extended to television, as McCarthy's defamatory remarks had been made, or repeated, on TV. In June 1984, McCarthy's team had enlisted constitutional lawyer Floyd Abrams, who'd successfully defended the *New York Times* against the U.S. government of Richard Nixon in the *Pentagon Papers* case. In August 1984, Lillian's suit was officially dropped.

McCarthy was of course immensely relieved, but soon cocky: "There's no satisfaction in having an enemy die—you have to beat them." But if Hellman had beaten McCarthy, Mary would have had to sell her home in Maine (in 1980 she'd quickly transferred what assets she could from New York to Maine.) McCarthy's expenses had reached $25,000 before the trial, and though a female sympathizer wrote her a check for that amount, she claimed to be out of pocket "something over $20,000." According to McCarthy, a tycoon friend of Lillian's had offered Hellman an "offense fund" of up to $500,000.

Asked years later if she would have done the same thing again, Mary said, "If someone had told me, don't say anything about Lillian Hellman because she'll sue you, it wouldn't have stopped me. It might have spurred me on. I didn't want her to die. I wanted her to lose in court. I wanted her around for that."

Disingenuously, McCarthy declared there had never been a feud, a sentiment denied by her biographer Carol Brightman. "She's not much present to my consciousness," McCarthy had lied when discussing the Cavett show. "Friends of friends have told me she's been obsessed with Hellman over the last several years," said Truman Capote. But taking Hellman on was foolhardy, for she was powerful and not afraid to prove it. Before the McCarthy lawsuit, Lillian's publishers, Little, Brown, had canceled a book by ultra-right author Diana Trilling which was critical of the memoir *Scoundrel Time*.

McCarthy's lifelong friend Eve Stwertka wondered if Hellman's early success writing plays "may have caused Mary a great deal of bitterness." McCarthy was a failed actress who took one stab at playwriting while at Vassar. Hellman reached "center stage" very quickly, reminded Stwertka, so that Mary may have felt the critic's pangs of jealousy, of being an outsider looking in. And with Hellman's four successful memoirs, Lillian had made her mark, much more recently, in a genre closer to Mary's literary turf. Author Eileen Simpson noted that a number of writers had been wounded by "hatchet woman" McCarthy and had "felt that Mary deserves this . . . ." As in many feuds and/or lawsuits, ethics and principles were the garments which clothed the naked motives of rivalrous personal and professional differences.

Norman Mailer still contends that McCarthy's biggest error was an ethical one: hitting another writer when she was down. "A much-damaged warrior," he called the broken-down if iron-willed Lillian in 1980, when she was suffering from emphysema and glaucoma and "could not raise a pistol since she can no longer see." In turn, Mary would die after a series of infirmities—breast cancer, heart problems, emphysema, water on the brain, and an arthritic condition of the spine—that preceded the lung cancer which killed her at seventy-seven, six weeks after it was diagnosed.

After Hellman's anti-McCarthy (Joseph, that is) memoir *Scoundrel Time* was published in 1976 to nearly unanimous praise, reading the *letter*—in which she contemptuously responded to HUAC—became the highlight of Eric Bentley's off-Broadway play *Are You Now or Have You Ever Been*. Actresses like Liza Minnelli, Tammy Grimes, Colleen Dewhurst, and Peggy Cass asked to re-enact the scene where Hellman retorted, "I cannot and will not cut my conscience to fit this year's fashions." Each woman played it for about a week, and Dewhurst explained:

"Ms. Hellman is as she herself put it, 'An Unfinished Woman.' She is the last to claim she is without flaws. But her courage and fighting spirit, particularly in the times that have tried people's souls, have stood out as rare and laudable . . . . Lillian Hellman has been not just a describer . . . but a doer, an actor." Even if her actions fell short of her claims.

Tallulah!

Tallulah Bankhead was the first person to say in print that Lillian Hellman had deliberately lied. However, the accusation in the stage star's 1952 memoirs, concerning a benefit for Spanish Loyalists, was written off as a flamboyant actress' theatrics, possibly motivated by publicity-seeking. Not until the 1980s would Bankhead be vindicated. The lifelong feud began about a year into the triumphant run of Hellman's play *The Little Foxes*, acclaimed by many as Tallulah's greatest stage performance.

Tallulah Bankhead

In 1939 Russia invaded its tiny neighbor Finland. Hellman and Bankhead were both staunchly anti-Nazi and shared many of the same causes. But in late 1939, after Tallulah and the cast of *Little Foxes* informed the press they would be doing a benefit performance to aid Finland, they were stunned to learn that Hellman and producer Herman Shumlin declined to give permission. Hellman declared that it wasn't America's fight and she didn't want to encourage war-like sentiments. Tallulah told reporters, "I've adopted Spanish Loyalist orphans and sent money to China, causes for which both Mr.

Shumlin and Miss Hellman were strenuous proponents . . . . Why should [they] suddenly become so insular?"

Insiders knew that Hellman was hiding her real motive: a fanatical devotion to Soviet Russia. She countered her star by proclaiming, "I don't believe in that fine, lovable little Republic of Finland that everyone gets so weepy about. I've been there and it looks like a pro-Nazi little Republic to me." It was a slap in the face of freedom-loving Finland, which was as anti-Hitler as its Scandinavian neighbors. The comment marked Hellman's moral low point, and at the time, only her collaborator Shumlin knew that Lillian almost certainly had never been to Finland, though she would continue to paint it in fascistic colors.

She and Bankhead became mortal enemies. Tallulah didn't like being crossed when she knew she was in the right. Lillian didn't like being questioned and was used to getting her way minus the glare of publicity which a Broadway superstar brought to bear. By quashing Bankhead's benefit for Finland, Hellman made more than a handful of enemies. Up until then, the extent of her adherence to Marxism had not been widely known. The feud, conducted in the press, made her hardline views famous—and reviled.

Just as the incident was dying down, Hellman made things worse. Feeling a need for further vindication, she lied that the real reason she'd turned down Tallulah's benefit was that when the Spanish government had fallen to Franco, she and Shumlin had requested her to do a benefit for the Loyalists who were fleeing to neighboring France. Tallulah and company, she said, had refused! The star was outraged by the lie, but in any controversy pitting an outspoken, theatrical actress against a male producer and a serious, plain, and grim female playwright, the actress was usually dismissed.

In her autobiography, Tallulah wrote, "The charge that I had refused to play a benefit for Loyalist Spain was a brazen invention. Neither Shumlin nor Miss Hellman ever asked me to do any such thing. Nor did anyone else." After *The Little Foxes*, the two women never spoke again. They continued to speak ill of each other, and Hellman was able to create a more scathing portrait of Bankhead than vice versa, both via inclination and the fact that she wrote about Tallulah posthumously. Lillian also took special delight in over-praising the screen version of *The Little Foxes*, particularly Bette Davis's performance, in order to goad Tallulah.

Had Bette Davis been of a mind to, she and Tallulah Bankhead could have had one of the most legendary of feuds. It was Davis who played several of Bankhead's most cherished stage roles on screen, thus reaching a worldwide audience instead of a localized one (Tallulah's fame was launched on the London stage

in the 1920s, though she hailed from a prominent family in Alabama).

"*I* created those roles, and that cow came along and copied me and got all the acclaim," raged Tallulah. In the 1930s she'd gone to Hollywood and made several films but didn't achieve screen stardom. Actor Fredric March once said in her presence that acting in a play was like "leaving footprints in the sand." "Oh, *don't*!" she pleaded, dismayed by the reminder that stage stars are remembered relatively briefly.

She particularly resented that with one screen performance, Davis could almost wipe away the memory of her hundreds of performances in any number of her stage triumphs. "Tallulah had hopes of a big movie comeback by recreating her role as Regina," wrote columnist Sheilah Graham. "Several old hands believed that if Tallulah brought her performance to film, the Academy Award would be hers, and she'd be assured of a movie career, even if mostly in character parts," for she was six years older than Bette.

"That thief! That hussy!" shrieked Bankhead when she heard that the thirty-two-year-old Davis would be playing the middle-aged Regina Giddens in Samuel Goldwyn's prestigious film version. Bette was widely praised in the role and received an Oscar nomination. It was small comfort to Tallulah that *her* Regina was considered the definitive interpretation; by 1968 when she died at sixty-five, few people recalled her career peak as Regina, but most everyone had seen or heard of the classic 1941 movie. "Half her acting was in her [chalky] makeup," groused Tallulah, who like Regina was a Southern belle and disdained New Englander Davis's performance.

"She plays everything the same!" she often told friends, and when Bette got her final Oscar nomination for *What Ever Happened to Baby Jane?* (1962), she crowed, "That bitch . . . she's found her dream role! She doesn't have to act, or pretend to, and she can look the same way she does first thing in the morning!"

Bankhead's only widely known film was the 1943 *Lifeboat*, directed by Alfred Hitchcock. Davis never worked with Hitchcock, but to Tallulah's chagrin, *Lifeboat* was an ensemble piece, not a vehicle as she was used to on stage. Hitchcock admitted, "She's too strong for most moviegoers," though acknowledging that she and Davis had much in common.

Tallulah's Bette-phobia was rekindled with *All About Eve* (1950). The screen classic was said to be based on Bankhead's own experience with an ambitious understudy in a play. Margo Channing was perceived by many to be a thinly veiled caricature of Tallulah—an aging, neurotic stage star fooled by a talented younger woman (if so, the movie left out the star's bisexuality and the lesbian undercurrent between her and her beautiful young admirer). *Eve* gave Bette's career a new lease on life—and yet another Oscar nomination. Davis assured the press that she was nothing like the temperamental, self-destructive Margo.

Said Tallulah, "Don't think I don't know who's been spreading gossip about me and my temperament out there in Hollywood, where that film was made—*All About Me*. And after all the nice things I've said about that hag. When I get hold of her I'll tear out every hair of her mustache!"

For the rest of her life, Tallulah always saw red when she heard the name of Bette Davis. She allowed that though few people ever forgot her who'd seen her on the stage, in time her "footprints in the sand" would be washed from memory (she lives on indelibly in several book biographies and countless anecdotes). Today Tallulah is mostly remembered—other than in *Lifeboat*—for her guest appearances on TV, especially *Batman* and *I Love Lucy*. Ironically, she got the latter role as the celebrity next door after Bette Davis turned it down.

DUELING DIVAS:
Bette Davis vs. Joan Crawford

"She is a movie star. I am an actress."—Bette Davis, on Joan Crawford

"She may have more Oscars . . . she's also made herself into something of a joke."—Crawford, on Davis

Most people believe the legendary feud between Bette Davis and Joan Crawford began during their 1962 comeback cult film *What Ever Happened to Baby Jane?* Or after it was released and earned Academy Award nominations for Davis and third-billed Victor Buono but not Crawford. Actually, the feud began in the 1930s.

As the posthumous cults of Crawford and Davis have grown, so has the stature of their feud, to the extent that documentaries and biographies of either diva rarely neglect mentioning their seething rivalry and *Baby Jane* teaming. One joint bio was titled *Bette Davis and Joan Crawford—The Divine Feud.* Davis especially wouldn't have approved of the topic, for though she admitted she loathed Crawford, she always insisted there was no feud; a feud implies mutual involvement, and caring. But Bette would have approved and insisted on the first billing, as she did in her sole costarring effort with Joan.

Yet it was Crawford, nee Lucille LeSueur in 1904, who became a movie star first, hitting Hollywood in 1925 and rising to silent screen stardom a few years later. She consolidated her status by marrying into tinseltown's closest approximation of a royal family: Mary Pickford and Douglas Fairbanks Sr. Joan's first and younger husband was the son of Doug Sr. and stepson of Mary.

Bette, four years Joan's junior, didn't land in Hollywood until 1931. Though she'd had stage training—something Crawford didn't, as Davis pointed out more than once—she had a harder climb. Joan, who got her screen name via a fan magazine contest, made it on her face and figure, shapely legs, and peppy dancing. And she made it at MGM, one of the two leading movie studios, with Paramount. Crawford stayed at Metro over a dozen years, the most popular of its female triumvirate of Garbo, Norma Shearer, and herself. The others had more prestige and bigger incomes, but Joan was beloved of female middle-America, and in 1941 her two MGM rivals permanently retired.

By contrast, Davis had to battle an industry which valued its actresses according to their classical looks or lack thereof. At Warner Bros., known for its low budgets and realistic pictures, the bigwigs had Bette's hair dyed blonde and decided to rename her (she was born Ruth Elizabeth Davis; her

Bette Davis and Joan Crawford with Jack Warner

mother Ruthie nicknamed her Bette). How did she feel about being called *Bettina Dawes*? She retorted, "I will *not* go through life known as Between the Drawers."

Unlike the initially likeable Crawford, Davis finally made it by playing a "bitch." Her breakthrough was the 1934 film of W. Somerset Maugham's *Of Human Bondage*, starring Leslie Howard. The part of Mildred the waitress who dies of syphilis had been rejected by several actresses, who felt they had to retain audience sympathy to remain stars. Bette saw Mildred as a make-or-break chance for the status that had eluded her through almost two dozen movies. It worked, and the bitchy die was cast, though for a long time Davis alternated between "good" and "bad" characters. But as the movie ads put it, "No one's as good as Bette when she's bad!"

Crawford's bitchiness took longer to seep out. Maturity and her new look of broad shoulders, larger mouth, and caterpillar eyebrows brought out her toughness. Not until MGM dismissed her and she settled at Warner Bros. in the forties did her own gallery of hard-hitting dames take shape. It was at Warners, where Bette still reigned supreme, that their professional competition began in earnest. Yet their personal rivalry began in 1935 with *Dangerous*, the film that won Bette her first Oscar. Her leading man was Franchot Tone, an attractive actor from a wealthy, socially prominent family. Insiders said they had an affair. Bette later termed it "unrequited love."

Soon after *Dangerous* finished shooting, Joan Crawford married Tone. Davis was surprised and disappointed, though she knew the twosome had been photographed at nightclubs, premieres, etc. But so had Joan and dance buddy Cesar Romero, who was gay. Many wondered what the ex-hoofer and the cultured actor educated on the East Coast had in common. Others whispered that Crawford had again married *up*. According to biographer Shaun Considine, she explained, "Doug introduced me to great plays, and Franchot told me what they *mean*."

Bette felt that Joan was using Franchot. Ironically, he influenced Crawford to trade in her habitual roles as America's sweetheart for more demanding and

Davis-like parts. She didn't take much convincing, for Joan wanted an Oscar of her own. But in 1938 when Bette Davis won her second Academy Award for *Jezebel*, Crawford's movies were not successful, so she was named to a list of stars who were considered "box office poison."

Bette and Joan's paths didn't directly cross until Crawford was demoted to Bette's studio, where Davis was known as "the fifth Warner brother." By the early forties she was Hollywood's most popular and honored actress. Warner's best scripts reached her first, then were passed on to Crawford, Barbara Stanwyck, Ida Lupino, Alexis Smith, and so on. Bette declined the housewifely, mothering title role of *Mildred Pierce*, which thus became Joan's big comeback hit movie in 1945 and garnered her an Academy Award. Bette was again surprised and chagrined. For by the mid 1940s her star was slipping, and in the late forties she was dismissed by Warners, which did retain Crawford, by now doing the sort of heavy and/or bitchy roles Bette had excelled in.

Director George Cukor was quoted in *The Divine Feud*: "It seemed to me that each one coveted what the other possessed. Joan envied Bette's incredible talent, and Bette envied Joan's seductive glamour." But Crawford no longer had to be quite as jealous of Davis, and at Warners, Joan first voiced her hope of costarring with Bette. In 1944 they both participated in Jack Warner's patriotic production *Hollywood Canteen*, which boasted all the studio's stars, from Bette and—separately—Joan to Roy Rogers and Trigger. Davis was the president and co-founder of the Hollywood Canteen, created for American servicemen en route to the Pacific during World War II.

Unlike Crawford, who off screen concentrated on her marriages and social life, Bette relished power and contributory activity. She was also the first female president of the Academy of Motion Picture Arts & Sciences, until she found the position was that of a figurehead, not a doer. Where Davis was a staunch Democrat, Crawford was deliberately apolitical: at MGM, Louis B. Mayer had exhorted employees to vote Republican or else keep quiet about their affiliation.

It was Bette's nature never to admit rivalry with other actresses. But in the late forties, Crawford did grab some meaty roles which Davis desired. The April 1946 issue of *Motion Picture* magazine stated, "There's a new First Lady out on the Warner lot these days, and she's really getting the red carpet treatment. Name? Joan Crawford. Since her comeback all she has to do is ask and her wishes are granted. She walked off with the lead in *Humoresque*, right under Bette Davis's nose. Bette really wanted that part!"

The next month's issue confirmed, "The hottest feud to hit these parts since they thought up Technicolor [in 1935] is the one between Joan Crawford and Bette Davis at Warner Brothers. Since Joan's Oscar victory for *Mildred Pierce*, she's been getting pretty much of anything she wants at the studio. All of which leaves Davis sizzling." Bette later often proclaimed that she seldom gave Crawford a second thought during their Warner years. This writer, author of *Bette Davis Speaks*, once asked her about Joan's appearance in *Hollywood Canteen*. "Was *she* in that?"

Post-Warners, it was Bette's turn for a great comeback, in the 1950 classic *All About Eve*, which earned a record number of Oscar nominations. Davis fully expected a third Academy Award. For decades, she was the most nominated of stars, and hoped to be the first to win three awards. However, the Oscar went to newcomer Judy Holliday, partly because the competition included another legendary performance, Gloria Swanson—in *her* post-silent-movies comeback—as Norma Desmond in *Sunset Boulevard.*

Her *All About Eve* boost proved short-lived, as was the publicity from Bette's marriage to her younger costar, Gary Merrill (she and Joan each had four husbands; three of Bette's were non-actors, three of Crawford's were actors). Significantly, Davis's looks went downhill fast before her mid-forties. She did not concern herself with the time-consuming self-discipline, strenuous dieting, and meticulous attention to hair and wardrobe that took up so much of Joan Crawford's schedule (she supposedly had a special outfit for answering her fan mail). Bette's changing looks consigned her to movies other than love stories, roles devoid of sex appeal or

★ She Said...She Said

"Joan Crawford—I wouldn't sit on her toilet!"—Bette Davis

"Bette will play anything, so long as she thinks someone is watching . . . I'm a little more selective than that."—Joan Crawford

"Joan Crawford—Hollywood's first case of syphilis."—Bette Davis

"Working with Bette Davis was one of the greatest challenges I've ever had. I meant that kindly. Bette is of a different temperament than I. She has to yell every morning. I just sat and knitted. I knitted a scarf from Hollywood to Malibu."—Joan Crawford

"Why am I so good at playing bitches? I think it's because I'm not a bitch. Maybe that's why Miss Crawford always plays ladies."—Bette Davis

"I don't hate Bette Davis even though the press wants me to. I resent her—I don't see how she built a career out of a set of mannerisms instead of real acting ability. Take away the pop eyes, the cigarette, and those funny clipped words and what have you got? She's phony, but I guess the public likes that."—Joan Crawford

"She actually had the nerve to tell everyone we're the same age! I suppose just because we're playing sisters [in *Baby Jane*] . . . . She was in silent pictures before I even *heard* of Hollywood!"—Bette Davis

glamour. Joan Crawford continued playing glamourous, desirable women—eventually unbelievably—through the late 1960s. Unlike Joan, Bette had long since taken on non-glamourous roles. She'd played middle-aged women before she was one, and in 1939 and the late fifties she played Elizabeth I with an un-Hollywood-like realism.

Bette's risk-taking extended to the small screen, which Hollywood at first saw as its arch-enemy. In the early fifties she made her TV bow on Jimmy Durante's show. Crawford reminded the press, "Anyone who appears on TV is a traitor." Over the decades Bette made umpteen guest-starring appearances and pilots. None of the pilots became a series—she envied Stanwyck's 1960s success in *The Big Valley*—until *Hotel*, by which time Davis had to decline the *Hotel* series due to health problems.

In 1952 Davis lucked out with a movie about a washed-up actress titled *The Star*. It was penned by a disgruntled married couple, Dale Eunson and Katherine Albert, who were soon to be former friends of Joan Crawford. The title character, Margaret Elliott, was to some degree a nasty takeoff on Joan, though it was never stated at the time. In 1983 Bette admitted in *Playboy*, "Oh, yes, that was Crawford. I wasn't imitating her . . . . It was just that whole approach of hers to the business as regards the importance of glamour and all the offstage things. I *adored* the script."

Why the couple turned on their friend of twenty-five years is unclear, but during filming of *The Star*, Crawford got her revenge. Her goddaughter was the couple's daughter Joan, seventeen and in love with a car salesman named Kirby. Joan's parents felt she was too young to marry and worried that matrimony would end her promising screen career as Joan Evans (a stage name). They asked Crawford to speak to her namesake and talk her out of marriage. So Crawford invited the girl and her beau to her Brentwood home, and at midnight telephoned her ex-friends with the news:

"Dear Katherine and Dale, I want you to be the first to know. Joan and Kirby were married at my house tonight." Next morning on the set, Bette was reading about the wedding in the paper when the writers arrived. Eunson explained, "She set the whole thing up behind our backs. She called the judge and the press. She didn't invite us to our own daughter's wedding. We were both very angry and heartbroken." Bette warmly sympathized and urged the pair to visit Crawford "and scratch her eyes out."

(Joan Evans did give up her career, which meant one less rival named Joan ...)

The Star yielded another Best Actress Oscar nomination for Davis, who was proud she was never nominated in the supporting category. (Ingrid Bergman's third award was for Best Supporting Actress.) Critics said *The Star* was a more realistic portrait of an older actress than *Sunset Boulevard*. It was courageous of Bette to depict a blowsy has-been enduring an assortment of trials and humiliations. As the kudos poured in, Bette became convinced she would win a third Oscar, partly in consolation for not having won for *All About Eve* (her *Dangerous* Oscar had been widely considered a deferred award for her prior year's breakthrough performance in *Of Human Bondage*).

Meanwhile, Crawford privately fumed over *The Star*. According to Davis biographer Lawrence J. Quirk, she apprised Hedda Hopper, "That bitch is getting her revenge on me." Unlike the general public, Crawford was aware of each parallel in the movie: like Joan, "Margaret" had *an* Oscar. She'd been deemed "box office poison." Her "dewy" looks were intrinsic to her career. She'd had costars named "Clark" and "Garfield" (the script didn't fully name them as Clark Gable or John Garfield). She had a brother-in-law whom she'd gotten a job but who got himself fired (as with Joan's *brother*). She was a "simon-pure movie star . . . twenty-four hours a day" rather than "a dedicated actress." She used the expression "Bless you!" to her director and producer. And when Margaret submitted to the indignity of a screen test for a "sullen, middle-aged" role in a projected comeback film, she insecurely played the character as a kittenish young flirt and thus lost the role. (The improbable "happy ending" had the unemployed ex-star abandoning Hollywood for a younger man and his boat.)

Crawford claimed not to have seen *The Star*. Years later she admitted, "Of course I had heard she was supposed to be playing me, but I didn't believe it. Did you see the picture? It couldn't possibly be me. Bette looked so old, and so dreadfully overweight."

Nineteen-fifty-two was also a good year for Joan. Having been terminated by Warner Bros., she made her first independent picture. In *Sudden Fear* she played yet another self-made woman who is another Crawford victim "suffering in mink." Today a cult movie, *Sudden Fear* brought Joan an unexpected Academy Award nomination—her last—which meant she was competing with Bette Davis. Crawford enthused to the press, "I am *honored* to be in the same company as Julie Harris and Shirley Booth," ignoring Bette and Susan Hayward, who was sometimes known as "a bargain basement Bette Davis." It so happened the 1953 awards ceremony would be the first to air on television. Davis was slated as a co-host but had to cancel due to health problems. Crawford refused even to be a presenter on TV but told columnist Dorothy Kilgallen she would be in the audience, and if she won a second Oscar, "I'll be thrilled to accept."

The winner was Shirley Booth in *Come Back, Little Sheba*, a realistic role Bette had craved but which Booth brilliantly originated on Broadway. Due to a shortage of film work, Davis returned to the stage, unconsoled by her stormy final marriage, which disintegrated by decade's end. Joan Crawford's private life and image took a new turn in 1955 when she met Alfred Steele, president of Pepsi Cola. Unlike her previous husbands, Steele was older and not attractive. But their romance and then marriage made headlines, and when Steele died prematurely, Joan remained on the board of Pepsi and amended her image from aging movie star to busy, successful businesswoman (Davis dubbed her "the widow Steele").

As the sixties loomed, Davis and Crawford were both relegated to supporting roles on the big screen—until *What Ever Happened to Baby Jane?* Joan discovered and sent the novel to Robert Aldrich, who'd directed her in *Autumn Leaves* (1955), wherein she was victimized by younger man Cliff Robertson. (For *Sudden Fear*,

Crawford had requested Marlon Brando, who ignored her warm offers until she icily asked for a yes or a no. He boorishly replied that he wasn't interested "in doing any mother-and-son pictures at the present time." So Jack Palance played her murderous younger husband.)

Crawford warmly informed Davis that she'd "finally" found a project for them to costar in. Bette replied she had no idea Joan wanted to team with her. Davis asked Aldrich two questions. Would she be playing Jane? Of course. She realized Blanche was a relatively colorless part and no challenge for her. Joan was more comfortable with Blanche, the lady-like and sympathetic victim of sister Jane, an ex child star. Davis also asked Aldrich if he'd slept with Crawford? She felt that if he had, he would favor Joan camera-wise. Aldrich said no, but later gave differing answers to that question, stating that: a) he didn't have an affair with Crawford, b) he did, or c) he started to but backed out so as not to give her any leverage while working together.

Bette said yes, and asked for top billing—though Joan made sure their names appeared in tandem—and more money. A stellar salary was an important symbol of past glory and continuing clout. When Lucille Ball and Desi Arnaz invited her to costar on their hour-long TV show (she was Lucy's favorite actress), Davis held out for too much money, so Desilu hired Tallulah Bankhead to play their celebrity neighbor. Robert Aldrich informed Bette she was asking for more money than he could pay. Eventually she settled for $60,000 and 10 percent of the net profits. Joan had already accepted $30,000 and 15 percent of the profits. Joan's deal wound up the better one, after *Baby Jane* proved to be a hit.

Acquiring financing was difficult. Four studios declined, and Bette and Joan's former boss Jack Warner was quoted, "I wouldn't give you one dime for those two washed-up old bitches." In the press, the last word was changed to "broads." Finally, he agreed to distribute the film, only he wouldn't allow it to be made on his lot. It was shot on Melrose Avenue at the Producers Studio, a lot usually reserved for B westerns.

That spring of 1962, Crawford, no longer anti-television, got herself booked on the Academy Awards to present the Oscar for Best Actor. She took center-stage by installing a wet bar backstage, with plenty of Pepsi, and a generous buffet outside her dressing room. She made sure she was photographed with as many winners as possible. In the early nineties on *The Tonight Show*, Best Supporting Actress winner Rita Moreno (*West Side Story*) described her close encounter with Crawford, who grabbed "me to her bony bosom." Instead of allowing Moreno to make her way to the press room and answer reporters' questions, Joan maneuvered her into her dressing room so they could be photographed together.

"A week after, she sent me a thank-you note. It said, 'Dear Rita, It was so thoughtful of you on your night of triumph to take the time to stop by my dressing room. Love, Joan.' I thought, 'To take the time?' She would have torn my arm from its socket if I tried to break away from her."

The press eagerly awaited a Davis-Crawford feud during *Baby Jane*'s filming, which was scheduled for only six weeks due to a tight budget. But nothing happened, despite or because of the media's intense scrutiny. Bette told Mike Connolly of the *Hollywood Reporter* during the second week, "There is *no* feud. We wouldn't have one. A man and a woman, yes, and I can give you a list, but never two women—they'd be too clever for that." Friction did occur when Joan installed a Pepsi vending machine on the set. Whenever she posed for photographers she usually had a Pepsi bottle in hand. Bette reacted by bringing her own supply of Coca-Cola for photographic purposes.

The somewhat obsessive Crawford liked to toss out the Coke in director Aldrich's paper cup and replace it with *her* brand. Until one day when they were going over the script and he remarked, "Furthermore, Joan, I'd appreciate it if you'd stop filling my goddamn paper cup with Pepsi." On the set, Crawford extolled the varied uses of Pepsi. "It helps indigestion and irregularity, and it's good for tired

Crawford vs. . .

"I saw Shelley Winters in *A Place in the Sun* [1951]. She gave a very moving performance, which surprised me, because Shelley is not a sensitive girl socially."

"They are a disgrace to our business . . . all the same [hair color], and no respect for feminine modesty . . . . Underneath it all, the public likes to think actresses are also ladies."—Crawford, on fifties blondes like Marilyn, Mamie, and Mansfield

"I think it's sad that today's actresses feel they have to resort to advertising to make extra money [as Joan did in the 1920s. . .]. Esther Williams is selling swimwear and Marilyn Monroe sells everything under the sun. I don't mean that unkindly, but in my day, actresses had more class than that."—Crawford, in the 1950s

"On *Johnny Guitar* [1954] we had an actress [Mercedes McCambridge] who hadn't worked in ten years, an excellent actress but a rabble-rouser . . . . Her delight was to create friction. 'Did you hear what *he* said about *you*?' she'd tell me. 'And in front of a group of people!' I couldn't believe it . . . . She would finish a scene, walk to the phone on the set, and call one of the columnists to report my 'incivilities.' I was as civil as I knew how to be."

"I have just come from the Actors Studio where I saw Marilyn Monroe. She had no girdle on, her ass was hanging out. She is a disgrace to the industry." —Crawford, in 1955

"Miss [Elizabeth] Taylor is a spoiled, indulgent child, a blemish on public decency."—Crawford, in 1962

feet." She demonstrated the latter by removing her slippers and rolling a Pepsi bottle under each foot twenty times. She purred, "It relaxes the tootsies and keeps your ankles thin." Bette's reaction? "You hang around that woman long enough, and you'll pick up all *kinds* of useless shit."

Crawford was annoyed that Davis's daughter B. D. had a role in the picture, as the neighbor's teenage daughter. She tried to balance this by bringing her "twin" daughters (who weren't) onto the set for photographs. The girls wore gloves and matching outfits and were named Cindy and Cathy; Crawford gave each of her adopted children a name beginning with C, including Christopher and Christina.

Things soured between the divas when Joan asked B. D. please not to speak to her daughters. She explained, "They have been carefully brought up and shielded from the wicked side of the world, and you obviously have not. I don't want your influence to corrupt them." (B. D. married an older man at sixteen, to Bette's disappointment.)

When B. D. repeated the words to her mother, she reportedly exploded, "How dare she pull that crap with me! I'll kill her! That bitch is loaded half the time." In later years, she often referred to Crawford's habit of spiking her Pepsi with vodka (by the mid-fifties, she was known for drinking "white water," or straight vodka, out of an ever-present flask). On the other hand, Joan's drunken rages—since widely chronicled—never occurred during working hours. For example, she dumped costar Mercedes McCambridge's clothes out a hotel window while on location in Arizona making the cult film *Johnny Guitar* (1954).

Warner Bros. issued a press release: "*And Still No Feud . . . .* With one more week to go on the filming of *What Ever Happened to Baby Jane?* the film is on schedule and there is still no feud between the stars. Bette feeds her lines off-camera to Joan for her close-ups." Everyone involved confirmed that there was never a blow-up between the two. Each star was aware that much was riding on the outcome of *Baby Jane.* If together they could deliver a hit, it would extend their individually faltering careers. Any hint of "feminine temperament" or cost-escalating ego could only hurt them both.

Producer-director Aldrich later disclosed, "Crawford and Davis were perfect pros on the set . . . until 6 P.M. Then I'd get a call from Joan asking, 'Did you see what that bitch did to me today?' A couple of minutes later Bette would call and ask, 'What did that bitch call you about?' First one and then the other. I could count on it every night."

It was during promotion of their hit movie that the friction escalated. The more earthy and humorous Davis made the TV talk show rounds and on Jack Paar recalled how Jack Warner had termed the two leading ladies "old broads." She shortly received a message from Crawford asking that she not refer to her again in public as a "broad." Brooks Atkinson wrote in the *New York Times*, "If Bette Davis and Joan Crawford come to blows during the promotion of their film, it is now possible to make book on the probable winner. Bette Davis. Each of these movie queens has a good right cross and left hook, and both are formidable in-fighters.

But Bette Davis is the more aggressive. She can take out an opponent with one punch."

The film generated massive publicity, though often it was condescending and dwelt on the fact that two actresses in their fifties didn't look the way they did twenty years before. Bette confessed that she cried when she first saw how awful she looked in character. Critics praised her for going so far, but many older fans felt she'd gone too far. Crawford was later quoted: "Sure, she stole some of my big scenes, but the funny thing is, when I see the movie again, she stole them because she looked like a parody of herself, and I still looked like something of a star."

Warner pushed both actresses for Oscar nominations. But come the nominations, Crawford, who'd spent hours learning how to work her wheelchair, was bitterly disappointed. Many critics felt Blanche could have been played by any actress, while Bette's tour de force performance as Baby Jane Hudson was unique, riveting, and unforgettable—"like watching a traffic accident," said one.

Crawford and Davis in *What Ever Happened to Baby Jane?*

Bette told columnist Army Archerd, "Yes, I want that Oscar. I *have* to be the first to win three."

At the ceremonies, Joan showed up with escort Cesar Romero. She signed numerous autographs for her fans, even getting down on her knees to do so. Asked by reporters who she'd voted for, she grinned, "The winner!" Indoors, she played the gracious hostess, having set up a wet bar in the main dressing room. The Pepsi coolers were filled with scotch, bourbon, vodka, gin, and champagne, "plus four kinds of cheese and all the fixings." Bette arrived with B. D. and son Michael and Olivia de Havilland, who flew in from Paris. Olivia, Bette's friend and costar from their Warners heyday, advised the press, "Bette deserves to win. She's the greatest and the industry owes her this."

But Joan Crawford hadn't been idle. She may or may not have actively campaigned against Bette, as Davis forever after believed—and stated, after Joan's death—but she did contact the other Best Actress nominees and offered to accept their Oscars for them should they win and not be able to attend. Geraldine Page didn't wish to attend the Los Angeles function, and Anne Bancroft would be in New York performing in a play.

When the names of the five nominees were read, Bette handed her purse to Olivia and made ready to take the stage. "The winner . . . Anne Bancroft for *The Miracle Worker*."

From the wings, Joan Crawford swept past Davis and de Havilland and strode out onto the stage to accept the Academy Award on Ms. Bancroft's behalf.

The book *Inside Oscar* quoted Bette, "*I* should have won. There wasn't a doubt in the world that I wouldn't. And Joan—to deliberately upstage me like that—her behavior was despicable." Crawford: "Disloyalty never entered my mind. If Geraldine Page had won, I'd have been glad for her. I'm working for an industry, not an individual."

Time described it as "the triumph of the evening," illustrating Joan posing backstage with the winners, beaming. Columnist Sidney Skolsky wrote, "She kissed Gregory Peck, she kissed Patty Duke, she kissed Ed Begley. She would have kissed the doorman and the limo drivers too, if it meant she could get another photograph taken."

Hedda Hopper's column the next day stated, "I was rooting for Bette. But when it comes to giving or stealing a show, nobody can top Joan Crawford."

In 1963 *Baby Jane* was launched in Europe. To publicize it, its leading ladies would attend the Cannes Film Festival. Davis informed Robert Aldrich that she would go only on condition that Joan Crawford not be there. So Joan, the less outspoken interviewee and less honored actress, was disinvited. She informed journalists that she didn't care to attend the crowded film festival. But Aldrich's files at the American Film Institute reveal that she threatened him and Davis with legal action over her not being included and over Bette's remarks to the press that Joan was still hanging on to Anne Bancroft's Oscar.

Aldrich's and Davis's attorneys urged Bette to make no further public comments about her costar. At the Carlton Hotel in Cannes, Bette therefore answered the press that she had no idea why Joan wasn't there. "Certainly she was *invited.* But Joan is a busy, busy woman. And I know we will all miss her *terribly!*"

Bette then had her attorneys ask Aldrich if they could examine his bookkeeping regarding Davis's share of the *Baby Jane* profits. The books were duly checked, but she was still unhappy and incredulous that Crawford was earning more from their picture. Bette, who was already supporting her mother and sister, went all out paying for B. D.'s lavish wedding, and confessed she needed more work. She went to Italy and did a supporting role in an "art" film that was barely released in the United States. Joan meanwhile took a supporting role in an American movie starring Robert Stack and Polly Bergen. Then Aldrich, whose post-*Jane* project flopped, approached Bette and Joan about reuniting in a picture titled *What Ever Happened to Cousin Charlotte?*

Bette was wary and said the title would have to go. She also had no burning desire to work with Crawford again, and when Joan requested first billing this time, she yelled, "In a pig's eye! I will *not* have my name come second to Joan Crawford, not now, not ever."

Aldrich kept offering her more money, finally raising her salary to $200,000, the same as his directing and producing fee. "That makes us partners on this picture," he naively remarked. Bette pounced: "*Partners,* all the way down the line. I will *hold* you to that." She unofficially agreed to take second billing on the retitled *Hush, Hush, Sweet Charlotte.*

Twentieth Century-Fox would finance and distribute the film, and production was to commence in spring 1964. But Crawford asked for a postponement due to her travel schedule on behalf of Pepsi Cola. Davis was livid that this meant shooting would take place during the hot and humid Southern summer. On location in Louisiana, Crawford complained about the heat and inferior amenities, and kept her distance from Bette, whose role was again bigger and flashier, though Crawford got the designer wardrobe. Joan also distanced herself from the crew, still playing the grand lady. Sheilah Graham wrote, "Bette lets her hair down but Joan surrounds herself with the aura of a great of yesterday. Times have changed, and she doesn't seem to realize that."

Bette, who did lunch with the cast and crew, stayed on the set as much as possible, keeping a sharp eye on things. Joan usually remained in her air-conditioned trailer when not needed. Bette would sit and confer with the director, and managed to block Joan's attempts to augment her dialogue. She even falsely insinuated that she and Aldrich were more than friends, which made the already anxious Joan more distraught than ever. After location filming was completed, Crawford flew back to Los Angeles separately from Davis and the rest of the company. Upon arrival, she instructed her driver to take her not to her L.A. apartment but directly to Cedars Sinai Hospital.

For the next several weeks, the costar was in and out of the hospital, on and off the set, working only a few hours at a time, complaining of fatigue or illness, and getting more attention than ever. It was later theorized that she thought she could stall her way into a bigger role via her costly delays, which eventually shut down production indefinitely. Not long before, Marilyn Monroe's tardiness and delays had resulted in a shut-down on her latest project. Marilyn was fired by Fox and died of an apparent drug overdose weeks later. The difference was that Marilyn was a thirty-six-year-old box office star and her film's sole leading lady. And even she didn't get away with it.

When it became clear that Bette wouldn't back down and Aldrich wouldn't fatten Joan's role, she may have decided to drag Bette down with her. If the movie, which was already mostly filmed, were cancelled, the studio would be reimbursed by the insurance company. However, Bette would be deprived of the movie, of dominating Crawford on screen a second time, of the inevitable great reviews, and of perhaps yet another Academy Award nomination. Not to mention the potential profits from a possible hit film. Joan assured columnist Mike Connolly, "I feel terrible. This is the first time I ever held up a picture."

Crawford's "mystery illness" attracted extensive publicity, and Joan posed for photos from her hospital bed wearing a $110,000 sapphire necklace that set off her Dior hospital gown. "With her meals catered from Chasen's," reported Edith Gwynn, "Joan Crawford is the most glamourous and popular star at the Cedars celebrity hospital. The doctors and nurses line up each day for the privilege of taking care of her." Everyone speculated on what was wrong with her; even her doctors weren't in agreement. Nobody dared print that perhaps Joan was sick of Bette Davis's giant shadow.

Bette was enjoined against publicizing her belief that Crawford was faking, lest the insurance company not pay off. After Joan still failed to make a miraculous recovery, Fox's Richard Zanuck, Aldrich, and Davis had a meeting and decided to replace her; Zanuck okayed the added costs. Bette had costar approval and vetoed Katharine Hepburn. She also said no to the proposal of Vivien Leigh, who was nonetheless secretly contacted in London. She notified the Fox executive who called, "No, thank you. I can just about stand looking at Joan Crawford's face at six o'clock in the morning, but not Bette Davis."

Bette proposed her good friend Olivia de Havilland, who initially said no. Bette insisted that Aldrich travel to Switzerland and coax her. He dangled several perks before her and assured her the role of Cousin Miriam wasn't a bitch, just a cool, two-faced sophisticate. Olivia finally accepted, so long as she could take her two children to Hollywood, all expenses paid. Bette was elated at the news. Aldrich asked her to keep it secret until he returned to California in two days, when he would legally inform Joan Crawford and her attorney by letter.

But Bette couldn't suppress such news, and her press agent leaked the story to the media. "I heard the news of my replacement over the radio, lying in my hospital bed," announced Joan. "I wept for thirty-nine hours."

The next day she cried in front of the assembled press: "I still believe in this business, but there should be some gentleness. I think it takes a lot of guts to make pictures, and I'm going to make a lot more of them. But I am going to make them with decent, gentle people."

When shooting resumed, Bette and Olivia were seen toasting a new beginning (and perhaps good riddance to Joan) by smilingly brandishing their bottles of Coca-Cola. Crawford recovered and went on to do the campy film *Straitjacket*, as a schizophrenic accused of being a serial hatchet murderer (the real culprit was her daughter; from *Mildred Pierce* on, Joan frequently suffered at the hands of wretched celluloid daughters). *Charlotte* wrapped up without further incident and became a respectable if not huge hit. Bette and Olivia promoted it jointly—as she and Joan would never have done—usually without friction.

At a Chicago press luncheon, the topic turned to the late Errol Flynn, a Warner Bros. star who had died in 1959. Bette declaimed, "I was almost *hysterical*," when she'd heard the news of his premature death. Olivia, who'd been in love with him, chided Bette, saying Davis and Flynn had never been on friendly terms (Bette declined Scarlett O'Hara in *Gone With the Wind* because the offer stipulated that Flynn play Rhett Butler). Davis whispered to de Havilland, "Shut *up*, dear."

"How would you like to make this tour with Joan Crawford?" hissed Olivia.

"And how would *you* like to make it with Joan Fontaine?" Bette shot back, as reporters jotted down their loud whisperings.

In a better mood, Bette advised Olivia after a press screening of their film,

Davis vs. . . .

"[Marilyn Monroe] is the original good time that was had by all."

"Before I ever worked with Faye Dunaway, I admired her cheekbones. After all, she was a fashion model, wasn't she? Now I can only admire her cheek. And she *acts* like a fashion model!"

"Miriam Hopkins? She was a swine! . . . Unprofessional, born to upstage, not to act."

"Faye Dunaway is the most unprofessional actress I ever worked with, and that includes Miriam Hopkins, even!"

"Miss [Susan] Hayward was very unkind to me on the set of *Where Love Has Gone* [1964]."

"I always admired Katharine Hepburn's cheekbones. More than her films. She always wanted to be liked. Too much so. But I'd have killed for those cheekbones!"

"Although [Constance Bennett] was very highly paid at one time, she represented the sort of actress for whom I had contempt—the type that cared more about makeup than motivation. Her face was her talent, and when it dropped, so did her career, right out of sight!"

"Ann Sothern [*The Whales of August,* 1987] is a lovely person, a fine actress. She has been underrated, but she has lost her sense of self-discipline—she no longer believes in eating on an empty stomach!"

"[Lillian Gish in *The Whales of August*] ought to know about close-ups. Jesus, she was around when they invented them! The bitch has been around forever, you know!"

"I watched Barbara Stanwyck in *The Thorn Birds.* Augh! It was painful! *I* should have played that part! She was supposed to be a passionate older woman in love with this beautiful young priest. She and Richard Chamberlain were completely miscast . . . . Stanwyck had no fire or passion, not for a man in or out of the cloth!"

"There are no heroes today. Name *one.* Michael Jackson?"

"Nowadays, the women are sexually aggressive, to an extreme, like Madonna, and the men are sexually passive or not at all, like Michael Jackson. Worst of all, the biggest stars in Hollywood now aren't even actors; they're singers . . . . What ever happened to class?"

"You were very good in it, Olivia. When you weren't in a scene with me, you managed to keep the audience's attention."

Davis hoped for another Oscar nomination and did several TV talk shows with that goal in mind. But although *Charlotte* received seven nominations, Bette was not among them (Agnes Moorehead was up for Best Supporting Actress). Joan Crawford was well pleased and booked herself on the awards show to present Best Director. She gushed to journalists that she was "thrilled to death to meet Patti Page," who was to sing the nominated title song from *Charlotte* (Bette, despite her minimal singing voice, was chagrined not to have been asked to warble the tune on the Oscar telecast).

Crawford's final two movies were made in England: the 1967 *Berserk!* in which she was lusted after by all the men in the circus she owned (and her daughter was the villain), and *Trog* (1970), wherein she had no sex life but was an anthropologist making contact with a living prehistoric troglodyte. In 1971 she published *My Way of Life*, a guidebook that preached discipline for the kiddies, urged women to "Entertain, decorate, be sexy for your husband," and warned, "Sit on hard chairs—soft ones spread the hips."

Bette publicly derided the book. Joan told *Life* magazine the same year, "I'm the quiet one and Bette's explosive. I have discipline. She doesn't."

"My head is high as to my discipline as an actress," Bette blasted back. "I can provide witnesses."

Joan sniffed, "She has a cult . . . . I have *fans*. There's a big difference."

The sniping would continue on and off, but in the seventies the semi-retired Crawford started to become a recluse and saw less and less of her longtime friends and relatives, including the two older children she would disinherit. She did live to see a Davis renaissance, for although the early seventies were difficult for Bette—including an expensive aborted Broadway comeback—Davis persevered, taking the best of the roles offered to her on TV and in films. Her cult or fan base continued to grow, and her lengthy career came in for increasing praise and honors; Crawford's was longer but didn't number as many classics or standout performances.

In January 1977, Bette traveled to Washington, D.C., to attend the inauguration of President Jimmy Carter. Crawford was hurt when, during the same month, it was announced that Davis would become the first actress to be honored by the American Film Institute with its Life Achievement Award. Joan persuaded one of their mutual directors, Vincent Sherman (with whom she'd had an affair), not to attend the presentation, which was broadcast on TV in March. Joan claimed not to have watched it, and died two months later.

In 1975 Crawford had given up alcohol, astounding all who knew her. She also began to lose weight, reportedly concerned with "hanging flesh" on her jawline. She had undergone two facelifts, and certain intimates declared that the reason she seldom left her New York apartment was that she no longer felt she looked good enough. Joan's final days and her death were shrouded in mystery. The week she died, she gave away her beloved little dog, and it was rumored she'd lost so

All About Bette

"I was never so scared in my life. And I was in the war!"—Sir John Mills, on working with Davis

"The least couth actresses I've ever worked with? . . . Bette Davis and Jodie Foster." —Helen Hayes

"I did my first movie with Bette Davis. And you know what she said to me? Oh, it just haunts me. I wonder if it's true, maybe she's right. She said, 'You can't have a relationship and a career. You can't have both.'"—Rosanna Arquette

"Bette Davis says, 'My name goes above the title. I am a star.' Yes, she is a star, and a great one. But is it worth playing all those demented old ladies to maintain that status?"—Myrna Loy

"She should have played my grandmother, not my mother. Then the picture [Where Love Has Gone] might have been more interesting!"—Susan Hayward

"The fans are so young! Their parents could hardly have been born when Bette started out."—costar Olivia de Havilland, at the New York premiere of Hush, Hush, Sweet Charlotte (1964)

"I saw Bette Davis in a hotel in Madrid once and went up to her and said, 'Miss Davis, I'm Ava Gardner and I'm a great fan of yours.' And she behaved exactly as I wanted her to behave. 'Of course you are, my dear,' she said, 'of course you are.' And then she swept on."

"That face! Have you ever seen such a tragic face? Poor woman. How she must be suffering! I don't think it's right to judge a person like that. We must bear and forbear."—Lillian Gish

"[Bette Davis] started by snapping at me the first day. I said, 'Good morning,' and she looked right through me. Later, when the cast gathered for introductions, our eyes met, and I waved. 'What's that mean?' she snapped. 'I was saying good morning,' I answered. 'You already did that!' she snapped back."—Helen Hayes

"While Bette Davis has indeed always been one of my idols, she did make mincemeat out of poor Lillian [Gish] when they made The Whales of August, a lovely picture. Lillian swears she'll never act again. So first she drove me from the screen, now she's driven Lillian. She's making a clean sweep of everyone our age!"—Helen Hayes

All About Joan

"If Bette has an emotional scene, she tackles it completely consciously, and when you say 'Cut' she might ask, 'Do you think that was a little too much this or a little too much that?' But when Crawford plays an emotional scene, you have to wait twenty minutes until she comes out of it after you have said 'Cut,' because she is still crying or laughing or whatever; she's still going."—director Curtis Bernhardt

"She had perfect posture, but it was rather intimidating. She looked as if she'd swallowed a yardstick."—Glenn Ford

"She's like that old joke about Philadelphia. First prize, four years with Joan. Second prize, eight."—ex-husband Franchot Tone

"Much as I dislike the lady, she is a star."—Humphrey Bogart

"No comment. I saw her once at her very worst. I do not condone sadism."
—Estelle Winwood

"When I was growing up, my mother often would say I reminded her of Norma Shearer [who had small eyes], and she'd get a strange look on her face. Only later did I realize she was pathologically jealous of Shearer."—Christina Crawford

"People automatically think that if you're a star, your social calendar must

be filled weeks in advance. Not so. I remember years ago when I was going through a depression, I phoned Joan Crawford and said to her, 'Joan, you've been waiting for the phone to ring too, haven't you?' And she said, 'Yes.' So I said, 'Let's go and have a meal.' She was delighted to do so. And that was the great and glamourous Joan Crawford."—Rod Steiger

"Apparently Joan Crawford can't forget an innocent remark I made at my first Hollywood party. Back in 1947, I was a teenager looking forward to meeting movie stars, and Joan Crawford was my favorite. At the party I said, 'I'm glad to meet you, Miss Crawford. You've always been a great favorite of mine, and my mother's too.' I didn't mean to say she was older than Methuselah, but there was such an embarrassing silence I wanted to die. Since then, she's been needling me in print and at parties."—Arlene Dahl

"Joan Crawford had wanted Claire Trevor for my part in *Johnny Guitar.* Everything was all right until [filming] on location in Arizona. I had a four-page monologue, and because of my stage and radio background, I knew all the lines. We shot it in one take, and the crew applauded. Joan was in her trailer and heard the applause—and that started it. It made Joan mad, and *she* was the star of the picture . . . ."—Mercedes McCambridge

"Poor old rotten-egg Joan. I kept my mouth shut about her for nearly a quarter of a century, but she was a mean, tipsy, powerful, rotten-egg lady. I'm still not going to tell what she did to me. Other people have written some of it, but they don't know it all, and they never will because I am a very nice person and I don't like to talk about the dead even if they were rotten eggs."—Mercedes McCambridge

much weight she looked like a skeleton. Did she know she had cancer? One insider said she died of a heart attack. Another stated death from cancer. Debbie Reynolds disagreed:

"I never bought that story." Reynolds wasn't the only friend who believed it was suicide. "There were too many coincidental events leading up to it. I just feel Joan found some way to exit this life before she looked too bad, before she had to suffer the ravages of decay any more." A male friend remembered that when he'd recently invited Joan to the opening of the New York Film Festival she'd half-jokingly answered that it would take thirty days to "varnish" her face so she could look like Joan Crawford.

Bette Davis was on a sound stage making her first Disney movie when she heard of Joan's passing. Peggy Shannon, Joan's longtime personal hairdresser, was also at Disney. "Joan's secretary, Florence, called me from New York . . . . I thought it so strange. Joan was gone, and here I was working on Bette." Davis made no public comment. The *Village Voice*'s Arthur Bell explained, "I called Bette's press agent to get a quote for my column. But I was told she wasn't talking to anyone. That was understandable. What could she say? 'The bitch is dead; long live the bitch'?"

Joan Crawford's memorial service in Hollywood was the biggest in years. "We read telegrams from every director and star she ever worked with," said George Cukor. "But there wasn't a word from Bette Davis."

Bette's first semi-public pronouncement on her late rival took place about a year later at the Academy Awards ceremonies. She was preparing to go on stage following a filmed tribute to those stars who had died the year before. In the dressing room with her, watching the presentation on a TV monitor, were Barbara Stanwyck, Greer Garson, and Olivia de Havilland. As Bette primped, she heard a vocal ovation in the auditorium. Looking up, she saw the screen filled with the glowing face of Joan Crawford in her prime. After a moment's pause, Bette declared, "Poor Joan. Gone, but not forgotten. Bless you!" then left the room to make her entrance.

In late 1978 the Crawford image was forever altered by publication of *Mommie Dearest.* Joan's lady-like and ever-glamourous facade was divorced from reality by the revelations of child abuse. Ironically but not surprisingly, she'd once won the title of Mother of the Year, via Hollywood influence. A few celebrity friends confirmed the tales, as did Christina's brother Christopher, who despite his bitter feelings has never authored his own book. In the December 1944 issue of

Motion Picture, Joan had answered the question: Do you ever spank your children?

"Yes, Ma'am, with a capital S. I spank them almost daily. Spare the rod and you have brats."

In the book *Hollywood Greats*, Joan's lawyer boyfriend Greg Bautzer recounted a story about Sunday dinner at the Crawfords. Christopher, who was left-handed, used the "wrong" hand to cut his meat, whereupon Joan "immediately leaned across the table, knocked the food out of his hand, and hit him across the face." In 1967 Crawford apprised the *New York Post*, "Christopher is twenty-five now and is in Vietnam. He's in Saigon, that's all I know. He's been running ever since he was five. This is the one place he can't run from. It will make a man of him."

Bette Davis gloated over the revelations but was her typically over-confident self when she told the press she was too good a mother ever to have a book written about *her*. The film of *Mommie Dearest* starred Faye Dunaway, about whom Bette and Joan had opposite opinions. Davis had played her mother in a telefilm and ever after decried Dunaway's "unprofessionalism," specifically, keeping Bette and 1,500 extras standing around in 110-degree heat on location, then showing up late and allegedly "stoned," according to hairdresser Peggy Shannon, who called Dunaway "the biggest disaster in my years in the business . . . . I had to run like hell, because she was going to belt me."

Bette asseverated, "Compared to Miss Dunaway, Joan Crawford was a real pro." Crawford, seldom generous to actresses in print, said that of the newer crop of actresses, only Faye Dunaway "has the talent and the class and the courage to become a real star." Davis's favorite was double-Oscar-winner Glenda Jackson, who also played Elizabeth I brilliantly and more than once (she later gave up acting to become a Member of Parliament).

Post-*Mommie Dearest*, and as *What Ever Happened to Baby Jane?* became the mother of all cult movies, Bette was increasingly asked (and irked) to comment on her late costar. *Why*, she wondered, did people insist on linking them together? They had "nothing in common," she often repeated, always asserting that there had been *no* feud, and that it was Crawford who was jealous of her and had spitefully sabotaged her *Baby Jane* Oscar. But in 1978, when Bette published her first memoirs since the early 1960s, she devoted a page and a half to settling the score with her estranged daughter, B. D., author of *My Mother's Keeper*, and a *chapter* to her experiences opposite the gone but not forgotten Joan Crawford, her fellow Diva Dearest.

Through the 1980s Bette kept as busy as she could, mostly in quality TV-movies. She won a Best Actress Emmy for *Strangers*, a mother-daughter story. Therein, according to several friends and biographers, lay the key difference between Bette and Joan:

Both girls were abandoned by their fathers and had lifelong difficulty trusting men or maintaining long relationships with them. But Ruth Elizabeth Davis had a supportive and stable mother, while Lucille LeSueur had a mother who reportedly abused her and who definitely favored her son (Bette and Joan each had one sibling, but Bette was the confident elder of two girls). Anna LeSueur was quite fond of men and liquor and often found it hard to make ends meet. Early on, she put Lucille out to work, later sending her to a working boarding school. She gave her daughter minimal affection and played no part in her show business aspirations.

Conversely, Ruth Favor Davis was an independent and capable woman who put her children first and complimented her more ambitious daughter often . . . . When Bette accepted her AFI Life Achievement Award, she gave her biggest and most heartfelt debt of thanks to her late mother, without whom, she said, there would have been no Bette Davis, actress and star. In that order.

BIBLIOGRAPHY

Adler, Bill. *The Letterman Wit*. New York: Carroll & Graf, 1994.

Andersen, Christopher. *Madonna, Unauthorized*. New York: Simon & Schuster, 1991.

————. *Michael Jackson, Unauthorized*. New York: Simon & Schuster, 1994.

Anderson, Loni, and Larkin Warren. *My Life in High Heels*. New York: William Morrow & Co., 1994.

Arnaz, Desi. *A Book*. New York: William Morrow & Co., 1976.

Beaton, Cecil. *Cecil Beaton's Fair Lady*. New York: Holt, Rinehart & Winston, 1964.

Bernhard, Sandra. *Confessions of a Pretty Lady*. New York: Harper & Row, 1988.

Bojarski, Richard. *The Films of Boris Karloff*. Secaucus, New Jersey: Citadel Press, 1974.

Bono, Sonny. *And the Beat Goes On*. New York: Pocket Books, 1991.

Bowie, Angela, and Patrick Carr. *Backstage Passes*. New York: G. P. Putnam's Sons, 1993.

Brightman, Carol. *Writing Dangerously—Mary McCarthy and Her World*. New York: Clarkson Potter, 1992.

Brown, Peter H. *Such Devoted Sisters—Those Fabulous Gabors*. New York: St. Martin's Press, 1985.

Campbell, Lisa D. *Michael Jackson*. Boston: Branden Publishing, 1994.

Carter, Bill. *The Late Shift*. New York: Hyperion, 1994.

Castelluccio, Frank, and Alvin Walker. *The Other Side of Ethel Mertz: The Life Story of Vivian Vance*. Manchester, Connecticut: Knowledge, Ideas & Trends, 1998.

Clarens, Carlos. *George Cukor*. London: Secker & Warburg, 1976.

Clarke, Gerald. *Capote*. New York: Simon & Schuster, 1988.

Clinch, Minty. *Clint Eastwood*. London: Hodder & Stoughton, 1994.

Cohen, Shari. *Coping With Sibling Rivalry*. New York: Rosen Publishing Group, 1989.

Cohen-Sandler, Roni, and Michelle Silver. *I'm Not Mad, I Just Hate You!—A New Understanding of Mother-Daughter Conflict*. New York: Viking, 1999.

Collins, Joan. *Past Imperfect*. London: W. H. Allen, 1978.

————. *Second Act*. New York: St. Martin's Press, 1996.

Considine, Shaun. *Bette Davis and Joan Crawford—The Divine Feud*. New York: E. P. Dutton, 1989.

Davies, Hunter. *The Beatles*. New York: W. W. Norton, 1996.

Dick, Bernard F. *The Apostate Angel—A Critical Study of Gore Vidal*. New York: Random House, 1974.

Edwards, Henry, and Tony Zanetta. *Stardust—The David Bowie Story*. New York: McGraw-Hill Book Co., 1986.

Edwards, Larry. *Bela Lugosi, Master of the Macabre*. Bradenton, Florida: McGuinn & McGuire Publishing, 1997.

Eells, George, and Stanley Musgrove. *Mae West*. New York: William Morrow & Co., 1988.

Feibleman, Peter. *Lilly—Reminiscences of Lillian Hellman*. New York: William Morrow & Co., 1988.

Fontaine, Joan. *No Bed of Roses.* New York: William Morrow & Co., 1978.

Freedland, Michael. *The Warner Brothers.* New York: St. Martin's Press, 1983.

Gabor, Eva. *Orchids and Salami.* Garden City, New York: Doubleday & Co., 1954.

Gabor, Jolie, and Cindy Adams. *Jolie Gabor.* New York: Mason Charter, 1975.

Gabor, Zsa Zsa, and Wendy Leigh. *One Lifetime Is Not Enough.* New York: Delacorte Press, 1991.

Galatopoulos, Stelios. *Callas: La Divina.* London: Dent, 1966.

Gelderman, Carol. *Mary McCarthy, A Life.* New York: St. Martin's Press, 1988.

Giuliano, Geoffrey. *Two of Us—John Lennon and Paul McCartney.* New York: Penguin Studio, 1999.

Grey, Ian. *Sex, Stupidity and Greed—Inside the American Movie Industry.* New York: Juno Books, 1997.

Grobel, Lawrence. *Conversations With Capote.* New York: New American Library, 1985.

Hadleigh, Boze. *Bette Davis Speaks.* New York: Barricade Books, 1996.

_____. *Conversations With My Elders.* New York: St. Martin's Press, 1986.

_____. *Hollywood and Whine.* Secaucus, New Jersey: Birch Lane Press, 1998.

_____. *Hollywood Babble On.* New York: Perigee Books, 1995.

_____. *Hollywood Gays.* New York: Barricade Books, 1996.

_____. *Hollywood Lesbians.* New York: Barricade Books, 1994.

_____. *Sing Out!* New York: Barricade Books, 1998.

Harris, Warren G. *Lucy & Desi.* New York: Simon & Schuster, 1991.

Harrison, Rex. *Rex.* New York: William Morrow & Co., 1975.

Heilveil, Ira. *When Families Feud.* New York: Perigee Books, 1998.

Higham, Charles. *Sisters—The Story of Olivia de Havilland and Joan Fontaine.* New York: Coward-McCann, 1984.

Jackson, La Toya. *La Toya: Growing Up in the Jackson Family.* New York: Dutton, 1991.

Joyce, Aileen. *Julia—The Untold Story of America's Pretty Woman.* New York: Pinnacle Books, 1993.

Kienan, Robert F. *Gore Vidal.* New York: Frederick Ungar Publishing, 1982.

King, Norman. *Madonna, the Book.* New York: William Morrow & Co., 1991.

Knight, Gladys. *Between Each Line of Pain and Glory.* New York: Hyperion, 1997.

Kozinn, Allan. *The Beatles.* London: Phaidon, 1995.

Leider, Emily Wortis. *Becoming Mae West.* New York: Farrar Straus Giroux, 1997.

Leman, Kevin. *Growing Up Firstborn.* New York: Delacorte Press, 1989.

Leonard, Maurice. *Mae West, Empress of Sex.* London: HarperCollins, 1991.

Levy, Emanuel. *George Cukor, Master of Elegance.* New York: William Morrow & Co., 1994.

Locke, Sondra. *The Good, the Bad, and the Very Ugly—a Hollywood Journey.* New York: William Morrow & Co., 1997.

McGilligan, Patrick. *George Cukor, A Double Life.* New York: St. Martin's Press, 1991.

Nance, William L. *The Worlds of Truman Capote.* New York: Stein & Day, 1970.

Norman, Barry. *Hollywood Greats.* New York: Franklin Watts, 1980.

O'Mahony, John. *Elton John.* Zaragoza, Spain: Edelvives, 1995.

Pitrone, Jean Maddern. *Take It from the Big Mouth—The Life of Martha Raye.* Lexington, Kentucky: University Press of Kentucky, 1999.

Plimpton, George. *Truman Capote*. New York: Doubleday, 1997.

Quirk, Lawrence J. *Fasten Your Seat Belts: The Passionate Life of Bette Davis*. New York: William Morrow & Co., 1990.

Reynolds, Burt. *My Life*. New York: Hyperion, 1994.

Rhodes, Gary Don. *Lugosi*. Jefferson, North Carolina: McFarland & Co., 1997.

Rosenfield, Paul. *The Club Rules*. New York: Warner Books, 1992.

Rosenzweig, Ilene. *The I Hate Madonna Handbook*. New York: St Martin's Press, 1994.

Ross, Diana. *Secrets of a Sparrow*. New York: Villard Books, 1993.

Rovin, Jeff. *TV Babylon*. New York: New American Library, 1984.

Sanders, Coyne, and Tom Gilbert. *Desilu*. New York: William Morrow & Co., 1993.

Saxton, Martha. *Jayne Mansfield and the American Fifties*. Boston: Houghton Mifflin Co., 1975.

Scott, Michael. *Maria Meneghini Callas*. Boston: Northeastern University Press, 1992.

Sexton, Adam, ed. *Desperately Seeking Madonna*. New York: Dell Publishing, 1993.

Spada, James. *Shirley and Warren*. New York: Collier Books, 1985.

St. Michael, Mick. *Elton John*. New York: Smithmark, 1994.

Stallings, Penny. *Forbidden Channels—The Truth They Hide from TV Guide*. New York: HarperPerennial, 1991.

Strait, Raymond. *The Tragic Secret Life of Jayne Mansfield*. London: Robert Hale, 1976.

_____. *Call Her Miss Ross*. New York: Birch Lane Press, 1989.

Taraborelli, Randy J. *Cher*. New York: St Martin's Press, 1986.

Twerski, Abraham J. *I Didn't Ask To Be in This Family*. New York: Henry Holt, 1992.

Underwood, Peter. *Karloff*. New York: Drake Publishers, 1972.

Van Gelder, Peter. *That's Hollywood*. New York: HarperPerennial, 1990.

Vickers, Hugo. *Cecil Beaton: A Biography*. Boston: Little, Brown & Co., 1985.

Vidal, Gore. *Myra Breckinridge*. New York: Penguin Books, 1997.

Walker, Alexander, ed. *No Bells on Sunday—The Rachel Roberts Journals*. New York: Harper & Row, 1984.

Walker, Jay. *The Leno Wit*. New York: William Morrow & Co., 1997.

Ward, Burt. *Boy Wonder: My Life in Tights*. Los Angeles: Logical Figments Books, 1995.

West, Adam. *Back to the Batcave*. New York: Berkley Books, 1994.

Wiley, Mason. *Inside Oscar*. New York: Ballantine Books, 1986.

Wilson, Mary, and Patricia Romanowski and Ahrgus Juilliard. *Dreamgirl—My Life As a Supreme*. New York: St. Martin's Press, 1986.

_____, and Patricia Romanowski. *Supreme Faith*. New York: HarperCollins, 1990.

Wright, William. *Lillian Hellman*. New York: Simon & Schuster, 1986.

INDEX

Page numbers in italics indicate photographs.